GW00728154

PC Printers
Pocket Book

PC Printers
Pocket Book

Stephen Morris

NEWNES

Newnes
An imprint of Butterworth-Heinemann Ltd
Linacre House, Jordan Hill, Oxford OX2 8DP

 PART OF REED INTERNATIONAL BOOKS

OXFORD LONDON BOSTON
MUNICH NEW DELHI SINGAPORE SYDNEY
TOKYO TORONTO WELLINGTON

First published 1992

© Stephen Morris 1992

All rights reserved. No part of this publication may be
reproduced in any material form (including photocopying or
storing in any medium by electronic means and whether or not
transiently or incidentally to some other use of this publication)
without the written permission of the copyright holder except in
accordance with the provisions of the Copyright, Designs and
Patents Act 1988 or under the terms of a licence issued by the
Copyright Licensing Agency Ltd, 90 Tottenham Court Road,
London, England WCP 9HE. Applications for the copyright
holder's written permission to reproduce any part of this publication should be addressed to the publishers

British Library Cataloguing in Publication Data
Morris, Stephen
  PC printers pocket book.
  I. Title
  004.7

  ISBN 0 7506 0197 3

Produced by Butford Technical Publishing
Butford Farm, Bodenham, Hereford
Printed and bound in Great Britain

Contents

Preface

The weakest link in any computer system is undoubtedly the connection between the computer and the printer. Although there is an increasing level of compatibility between computers, the same cannot be said of printers. As a result users spend a great deal of time in the frustrating business of trying to get their printer to work.

For any printer to produce text satisfactorily, the program being run on the computer must send the data to the printer in the correct format. This format varies from one printer to another.

There are four main emulations currently being used for most printers. These are the Epson (FX-80 and LQ-850), IBM Proprinter, Hewlett Packard LaserJet and Diablo 630. The codes used by these emulations are described in detail in this book.

Unfortunately it is not possible to include the codes for those printers that do not stick rigidly to these four formats. Clearly, with many hundreds of different printers available, all of these cannot be covered in detail. However, the disk associated with this book includes a detailed database, which contains a mass of information that would not fit in the book. In addition, there are a number of sample programs. Information on how to obtain the disk is given at the back of the book.

The situation for laser printers is eased to a certain extent by the adoption of Postscript, a universal printer language that provides all the features needed to create any form of text or graphics. This provides compatibility over a wide range of printers, but requires careful programming.

The aim of this book is to provide the tools that users and programmers need to communicate with their printers. The book covers the theory of printer communications and describes the internal workings of the PC as it relates to the printer.

The codes for the common printer emulations are grouped according to the facilities they offer. There is also an introduction to such topics as user-defined character generation, graphics printing and colour.

There is extensive coverage of Postscript, showing how it may be used to send any form of output to a laser printer and the core PostScript operators are described in full, providing a useful reference for PostScript programmers.

I hope that this book will be beneficial to programmers and users alike, whether you want to produce a program that will work on a range of different printers or just want to find out how to print in italic. Above all, this book should help you to make the efficient use of your printer.

Acknowledgments

I would like to thank the following companies, who were very helpful in providing the information needed to compile this book:

Advanced Matrix Technology Inc
AEG Olympia (UK) Ltd
Agfa
AM Varityper
Amstrad plc
Apple Computers (UK) Ltd
Apricot Computers plc
ASD
AST Europe Ltd
Brother Office Equipment
Bull HN Information Systems
C Itoh Electronics Co Ltd
CalComp Ltd
Canon
Citizen Europe Ltd
Colorgraph
Compuprint Ltd
Daewoo UK Ltd
Data Dynamics
Dataproducts Ltd
Datatrade Ltd
DEC Direct
Decision Systems International
Dell Computer Corporation
Digital Equipment Co Ltd
Epson (UK) Ltd
Erskine Printing Systems
Everex Systems (UK) Ltd
Facit Ltd
Ferrotec
Fujitsu Europe Ltd
GADC
General Parametrics UK
Genicom International Ltd
Gestetner Data Systems
Headway Computer Products
Hermes Precisa Ltd
Hewlett-Packard Ltd
Hitachi Europe Ltd
Husky Computers
IBM (United Kingdom) Ltd
Integrex Ltd
Intelligent Interfaces
International Computer Systems
ISG Data Sales Ltd
Kirsta Products Ltd
Kodak Ltd

Kyocera Electronics (UK) Ltd
LaserMaster
Longs Computer Products Ltd
Mannesmann Tally Ltd
Memorex Telex (UK) Ltd
Micro Peripherals Ltd
Minolta (UK) Ltd
Mitsubishi Electric (UK) Ltd
Murrays
NEC (UK) Ltd
Newbury Data Recording Ltd
NewGen Systems Corp
OCE Graphics
OKI Systems
Olivetti Office Ltd
Olympia Business Machines
Philips Kommunications Ind.
Pragma Ltd
Pre Press Solutions
Printer Marketing company Ltd
Printronix Ltd
Printware Inc
QMS (UK) Ltd
Qume (UK) Ltd
Rank Xerox (UK) Ltd
Ricoh UK Ltd
Samsung Electronics (UK) Ltd
Sanyo Ltd
Seikosha (UK) Ltd
Sharp Electronics (UK) Ltd
Siemens Nixdorf
Silver Reed (UK) Ltd
Sintrom Electronics
Smith Corona
Star Micronics UK Ltd
Tandon plc
Tandy Corporation
Taxan (UK) Ltd
Technitron Data Ltd
Tektronix UK Ltd
Texas Instruments Ltd
Toshiba Information Systems (UK) Ltd
Triumph Adler (UK) Ltd
Unisys Ltd
Walters International Ltd
Wang (UK) Ltd
Wenger Printers Ltd
Zygal Dynamics plc

Special thanks are also due to Fay Wentworth, for many long hours spent on research, and Emily Morris, for her efforts in preparing the final manuscript.

1 PC Printers

There are many hundreds of PC printers currently available, from over fifty competing manufacturers. These printers vary from simple dot matrix printers, able to produce fast, draft output, to highly sophisticated laser printers, capable of near-typeset quality. This chapter examines the principles on which these printers operate.

Printer types

Printers are categorised according to the method used to produce the final output. There are half a dozen basic methods in common use, although there are many variations upon these. These main categories are described below.

Dot matrix printers

The dot matrix is the most common type of printer currently in use. The print head consists of a vertical column of wires which are fired at the print ribbon. The ribbon passes between the head and paper and when the wires strike the ribbon they force it onto the paper, creating a dot.

Each wire is seated on a magnet in a coil. When a current is passed through the coil, the magnetic field repels the magnet, forcing the wire out. The wire hits the ribbon against the paper. When the current is switched off, a spring pulls the magnet back into position.

The majority of dot matrix printers have either nine or 24 wires in the head, covering a vertical distance of ⅙th of an inch. Some printers have 48 wires. The vertical distance between dots is given in Figure 1.1.

The horizontal distance from one dot to the next is determined by movement of the print head.

There are several standards for dot matrix printers, Epson being the most commonly used. Other popular emulations include IBM Proprinter.

Wires	Vertical distance between dots	Dots per inch (vertically)
9	1/54 inch	54
24	1/144 inch	144
48	1/288 inch	288

Figure 1.1

Inkjet printers

Inkjet printers work by spraying tiny dots of ink on the paper rather than firing wires at a ribbon. The effect is identical to that of dot matrix printers. These printers also work by moving a print head backwards and forwards along the paper. Although they tend to be slower than dot matrix printers, they are considerably quieter. The main disadvantage is that, for the ink to dry quickly on the paper and remain fixed, special paper will produce a better result than normal copier paper.

The most successful inkjet printers have been produced by Hewlett Packard.

Thermal printers

The operation of thermal printers is similar to that of dot matrix printers but the tips of the wires are heated. These printers require special heat sensitive paper. When the hot wires touch the paper they leave a black mark. This type of printer is not particularly popular, mainly because the paper used is expensive and has a poor quality feel. In addition, any paper left in direct sunlight will turn completely black!

The IBM QuietWriter is a variation on this theme, using a thermal transfer process. In this case, normal paper is used but a special ribbon is required. The wires are heated in the usual way but when they push the ribbon against the paper they melt a small spot of ink which then sticks to the paper. However, these printers have never been particularly successful, since the ribbons are very expensive.

Although you can use ordinary paper with the QuietWriter, printed paper should not be left in direct sunlight, since the print on the paper will melt!

Daisywheel printers

Daisywheel printers are close to the typewriters from which all PC printers have evolved. The principle here is that the characters exist as solid blocks on the end of spokes radiating from the centre of a wheel. At each character position, the print wheel is spun and, when the correct character is at the top, a hammer hits this against the ribbon, forcing it onto the paper.

With the arrival of laser printers, the popularity of daisywheels is diminishing. Their advantage over dot matrix printers is the quality of output, which is comparable to the best electric typewriters. The disadvantages are that they are extremely noisy and incapable of any real graphics. Changing fonts on a daisywheel printer is a matter not of programming the internal software but of physically exchanging printwheels.

The main standard adopted for daisywheel printers is that set by Diablo, an emulation used by many other manufacturers (even though Diablo printers are no longer manufactured). Brother emulations are also catered for in some cases.

Laser printers

Laser printers produce a far more accurate result that any other type of printer and, with prices rapidly falling, are becoming the most commonly used form of output device. A laser beam is turned on and off in a pattern corresponding to the dots of the required image. The beam, emitting from a fibre optic cable, hits a mirror and is reflected onto a photosensitive drum. The angle of the mirror determines the point at which the beam hits the drum. The drum becomes charged at the point where it is hit by the beam.

As the drum rotates, it passes through a hopper of toner, which consists of tiny magnetic particles. These are attracted to the charged areas of the photosensitive drum. As it comes out of the hopper, the toner on the drum has the image that is required. This then passes over the paper. In the middle of the drum there is a *corona* wire. This wire is also highly charged, with an opposite charge to that of the drum. The result is that the toner is forced off the drum onto the paper.

The final stage is to pass the paper through *fusion rollers*. One of these rollers is heated, the heat melting the toner onto the paper and fusing it in place.

LED printers

A variation of the laser printer is the LED (light emitting diode) printer. The principle is similar except for the initial phase. There is no rotating mirror. Instead, there is a line of 2,400 lasers, giving a width of eight inches (at 300dpi). Each of the 2,400 LEDs is either turned on or off, producing a row of dots. The light from this array passes through a lens system to charge the drum in the usual way. From this point on, the principle is the same as for laser printers.

The advantage of LED printers is that there is one less moving part (the mirror assembly), so there is less to go wrong. In addition, printing speed should be improved.

LCS printers

The LCS (liquid crystal shutter) printer is almost identical to the LED printer, except that there is a single long light source that passes through an array of liquid crystal shutters before hitting the lens and travelling on to the drum. Each of the 2,400 shutters in the array can be switched to either allow the light to pass through or to block its passage. From then on, the operation is identical to that described above.

Plotters

Although plotters work along similar lines to a printer, they are not covered in this book. Drawings are produced using an object-based language, which is different to that found on most printers.

The sort of information that is printed is usually different. In addition, plotters tend to use the serial rather than parallel port. The programming considerations needed to drive a plotter are therefore very different to those for a printer.

Print head movement

Daisywheel, dot matrix and inkjet printers have a print head that moves from side to side as it prints. In some cases, the head can only print in a single direction (from left to right) and the head is moved back to the left-hand side after each line has been completed. A considerable amount of time is used in this additional head movement.

Many printers allow *bi-directional* printing, in which the print head moves first from left to right and then prints the next line from right to left. This is possible because the printer stores the complete line of text in memory. Therefore it is able to work out where the second line ends, the point at which it should start printing.

In addition, some bi-directional printers perform *optimisation* on the print head movement. After printing each line, such printers calculate the shorter of the distances to the start and end of the next line before actually moving the print head. This again reduces the amount of time wasted in non-productive print head movement.

The print head is physically moved either using a belt and pulley system or with a screw system. In the screw system, the head is mounted on a screw, the turning of which forces the print head to the left or right. With the belt and pulley systems, particularly, bi-directional printing may result in untidy printouts if the belt is not sufficiently tight.

In some cases, it is better to turn bi-directional printing off, especially for graphics printing or diagrams using the box-drawing characters, where the slight variations in start position at the beginning and end of alternate lines results in the joins in vertical lines being jagged.

The position of the print head is held internally by the printer and is either calculated by keeping track of cumulative head movement or measured by means of sensors. The use of sensors results in more accurate printing, since the mechanical movement of the head may not match precisely the instructions given by the software.

Commands for controlling print head movement are given in Chapter 4.

Feed mechanisms

Paper can be fed into matrix printers through two basic types of mechanism:

- *Tractor feed* printers have a mechanism that draws standard continuous stationery through the printer, the holes at the side of the paper fitting over the tractor sprockets.

- *Friction feed* printers draw the paper through by pressing the paper against a rubber-coated platen; as the platen rotates the paper is forced through.

For friction-fed printers, you can sometimes attach a cut sheet feeder. This is a device which sits on top of the printer, automatically inserting a new page into the feed mechanism when the previous page has been ejected.

Most page printers use a paper tray from which sheets of paper are collected as needed and are fed into the feed mechanism.

Interfaces

The link between the PC and the printer is referred to as the *interface*. There are several different interfaces in common use.

Parallel interface

Most modern printers have a standard *parallel* interface. This has a number of data wires that are used to transmit entire bits of data along eight wires simultaneously, giving fast transmission speeds and reliable data transfer.

The parallel interface is often referred to as a *Centronics* interface, after the company which first popularised it. However, it should be noted that it was Epson who took the original Centronics standard and transformed it into the parallel standard that is now followed by virtually all printer manufacturers.

Parallel interfaces are generally slower than their serial counterparts but, since there is only one standard of method of data transfer, are much easier to set up. Parallel cables are restricted to a maximum of 8ft.

Serial interface

The *serial* interface connects one of the PC's serial ports to a serial port on the printer. This interface transmits the data along a single wire as a stream of bits. There are two main types of serial interface: the RS-232C and RS-422.

RS-232 interfaces support a maximum distance of 50ft with standard cable. This distance increases to 300ft or more with shielded cable. RS-232 ports generally support speeds of 50Kbps or 110Kbps (kilobits per second).

The RS-422 interface (sometimes referred to as X27) supports speeds of up 240Kbps. Cables for RS-422 can be significantly longer than those for RS-232. Most printers with an RS-422 port can be configured to accept RS-232 data; however, the reverse is not generally true. The RS-422 port is sometimes referred to as Local Talk, especially in the Apple environment.

Video interface

The *video* interface has been designed to transfer graphics data directly from a video board to a printer. Transfer rates are very high (at up to 2Mbps) but this interface has not yet gained wide acceptance.

HPIB

The Hewlett-Packard Interface Bus (HPIB) is a bi-directional parallel interface. This interface, also known as IEEE 488 (after the number allotted it by the IEEE Standards Organisation) or GPIB (the

General Purpose Interface Bus – the name applied by the Standards Organisation), is currently only suitable for transfer between Hewlett-Packard PCs and their own printers. Therefore, it is not widely used.

SCSI

The Small Computers Systems Interface (SCSI), pronounced 'Scoo-Zee', is also a two-way parallel interface. It is currently used for connecting PCs to a variety of external devices, such as scanners and tape back-up drives. However, it is not yet widely used for printer connections.

Background printing

Many applications allow you to set up a series of files in a *queue*, which are to be printed while some other activity is going on. This is termed *background printing*. When background printing is in progress, you can continue with other work *in the foreground*, setting up new documents, creating new spreadsheets, etc. When nothing is happening in the foreground, the computer uses this opportunity to send part of the current document to the printer.

With some programs, such as WordStar, only one document can print in the background at a time. In other cases, such as WordPerfect, you can create a *queue* of documents which the program will work through in the sequence specified.

In other cases, there are *print spoolers*. These work in a similar way to print queues, except that the documents to be printed are usually added to a binary file on disk, which is directed to the printer when time is available.

The main problem is that printing in the background will inevitably cause some slowing of the foreground process. This is particularly the case when any sort of printer error occurs. When anything is sent to the printer, the foreground process cannot continue until an acknowledgment is received from the printer. If the printer is not responding (for example, because it is off-line), the computer waits until the process 'times out', during which nothing can happen in the foreground (this may be anything up to one minute).

Buffer boxes

Another alternative to speed up printing is to introduce a *buffer box* between the PC and the printer. All output is sent to the buffer box and stored in RAM there. The buffer box deals directly with the printer, sending new output as and when required. The result is that the data can be sent from the PC much more quickly, leaving the computer free to carry on with its normal activities (assuming the buffer is large enough to take the entire output). The RAM in buffer boxes can vary from as little as 2K to several megabytes.

Paper characteristics

The *weight* of a paper gives you the physical weight, measured in terms of grammes per square metre (gsm).

The paper thickness is termed the *calliper* and is measured in millimetres.

The smoothness of the paper is measured according to the *Sheffield scale*. Laser printers generally accept paper in the range 100-300.

The *wax pick* indicates the strength of the surface of the paper, providing an indication of how much dust will flake off the surface during printing.

The acidity of the paper is measured in terms of the pH value. This is important for laser printers, which heat up the paper, for which the pH value should be at least 5.5.

Power supply

All printers use a DC (direct current) power supply. They include a transformer which converts the mains AC (alternating current) supply into DC. In the PC world, printers are powered separately to the computer and require their own mains connection.

Printer Self-test

All printers perform an internal diagnostic check when switched on. This is termed the *Power-On Self-Test* (POST). This may be a simple test (such as checking that there is paper loaded) or an extensive examination of the system, checking the memory and so on.

If an error is found, the printer may produce a series of beeps, it may display a message on its front panel display (if it has one) or, most frequently, it will just refuse to come on-line and will do nothing.

Command:	Interface self-test	
Printers:	LaserJet	
Syntax:	ESC z	(ASCII)
	1B 7A	(hex)
	27 122	(dec)
Parameters:	None	
Effect:	Prints all data in the buffer and then carries out an interface self-test. If no errors are found, normal printing resumes.	

Test page for page printers

Most laser printers produce a test page when they are first switched on. This shows you that the printer is working satisfactorily and, in most cases gives you a printout of the number of pages so far printed using this machine. Although this can be useful, it is also wasteful of toner. Some printers provide an option – either via a front panel switch or through software control codes – to turn off the printing of the start-up page.

User-generated tests

In addition, it is usually possible for the user to perform a test on the printer when it is powered up. Such tests are normally effected by holding down one or more of the front panel buttons while the printer is being switched on. The usual result for dot matrix printers is to produce a complete print of the internal character sets in a 'barber pole' pattern, with the character set being shifted one place to the left on successive lines (see Figure 1.2). Another common alternative is to print details of the printer's capabilities, in terms of its fonts and typestyles.

Page printers can usually be encouraged to reproduce their test page at any time after they have been switched on.

```
)123456789:;<=>?@ABCDEFGHIJKLMNOPQRSTUVWXYZ[\]^_
123456789:;<=>?@ABCDEFGHIJKLMNOPQRSTUVWXYZ[\]^_`
23456789:;<=>?@ABCDEFGHIJKLMNOPQRSTUVWXYZ[\]^_`a
3456789:;<=>?@ABCDEFGHIJKLMNOPQRSTUVWXYZ[\]^_`ab
456789:;<=>?@ABCDEFGHIJKLMNOPQRSTUVWXYZ[\]^_`abc
56789:;<=>?@ABCDEFGHIJKLMNOPQRSTUVWXYZ[\]^_`abcd
6789:;<=>?@ABCDEFGHIJKLMNOPQRSTUVWXYZ[\]^_`abcde
789:;<=>?@ABCDEFGHIJKLMNOPQRSTUVWXYZ[\]^_`abcdef
89:;<=>?@ABCDEFGHIJKLMNOPQRSTUVWXYZ[\]^_`abcdefg
9:;<=>?@ABCDEFGHIJKLMNOPQRSTUVWXYZ[\]^_`abcdefgh
```

Figure 1.2

Printer initialisation

After self-testing is complete, the printer checks the dip switch settings and configures itself accordingly. For example, the dip switches can be used to switch between italics and graphics printing and to choose the character set.

The dip switches should always be set before the computer is switched on.

The default settings (whether built-in or determined by dip switches) can be overridden either by the front panel buttons or by sending command codes from the computer. These have equal priority: either can override the other. Therefore, the user can change the settings produced by the application software, by turning the printer off-line and making front-panel selections after printing has begun; the software can send command codes that will override the user's front panel settings.

At any time, a program can reset the printer to its defaults by *re-initialising* the printer.

Command:	Initialise the printer	
Printers:	ESC/P 81	
Syntax:	ESC @	(ASCII)
	1B 40	(hex)
	27 64	(dec)
Parameters:	None	
Effect:	Resets the printer to its default settings, including top-of-form, margins, line spacing, horizontal and vertical tabs, justification, font, character size and print direction. The print buffer is cleared of any existing text or commands and all typestyles are cancelled.	

Command:	Reset	
Printers:	LaserJet	
Syntax:	ESC E	(ASCII)
	1B 45	(hex)
	27 69	(dec)
Parameters:	None	
Effect:	Prints all data waiting in the buffer and then resets all printer features to their default values. Normal printing then continues.	

Command:	Remote reset	
Printers:	Diablo	
Syntax:	ESC CR P *or* ESC SUB I	(ASCII)
	1B 0D 50 1B 1A 49	(hex)
	27 13 80 27 26 73	(dec)
Parameters:	None	
Effect:	Cancels all software settings, restoring all values to their power-on defaults.	

Some printers (such as Citizen) also allow you to change the power-on defaults by selecting option on the front panel. After these changes, the printer will be configured to the new set of defaults each time it is switched on or initialised.

On-line and off-line

All printers have an on-line switch, which turns the printer either on-line or off-line. When the printer is *on-line* it is able to receive instructions, text and graphics data from the computer and can print the data. When the printer is *off-line*, it sends a message to the computer to say that it is not ready to receive data; if the printer is trying to send data, it will eventually time-out and an error message will be reported to the user. The terms 'on-line' and 'off-line' are often referred to as 'selected' and 'deselected'.

Command:	Deselect printer	
Printers:	ESC/P ext, IBM Proprinter	
Syntax:	DC3	(ASCII)
	13	(hex)
	19	(dec)
Parameters:	None	
Effect:	Switches the printer off-line. Turn back on-line with DC1; pressing the on-line button is ineffective. This command may be disabled on some printers by dip switch settings.	

Command:	Deselect printer	
Printers:	IBM Proprinter	
Syntax:	ESC Q *n*	(ASCII)
	1B 51 *n*	(hex)
	27 81 *n*	(dec)
Parameters:	*n* = # (23h, dec 35) (Proprinter XL24)	
	$ (24h, dec 36) (Proprinter X24)	
Effect:	Switches the printer off-line. Turn back on-line with DC1; pressing the on-line button is ineffective.	

Command:	Stop printing	
Printers:	IBM Proprinter	
Syntax:	ESC j	(ASCII)
	1B 6A	(hex)
	27 106	(dec)
Parameters:	None	

Effect:	Turns the printer off-line, sends a 'Busy' signal to the computer and sounds the beeper. Before going off-line, all data in the buffer is printed; no further data is accepted. To start the printer again, the user must press the on-line button.

Command:	Select printer
Printers:	ESC/P ext, IBM Proprinter
Syntax:	DC1 (ASCII)
	11 (hex)
	17 (dec)
Parameters:	None
Effect:	Switches the printer on-line after it has been deselected by DC3. The command is ineffective if the printer has been deselected using the on-line button.

2 Programming the Printer

Printers are capable of many different variations in the way their output is produced. You can change the character sets and fonts used, the style of print, the size and spacing of characters and many other features. This is achieved from within a program by sending instructions to the printer. The principles of programming a printer are outlined in this chapter.

The computer language

All communication within the computer system – main PC unit, keyboard, monitor and printer – is carried out using a standard computer language: *binary*. For example, data is transmitted from one part of the system to another as a series of pulses. When a key is pressed on the keyboard, a unique sequence of pulses is sent to the PC. Each pulse may take either a high or low voltage. Similar systems are used for storing data, by setting the polarity of tiny magnets. Every display on the VDU is set by lighting or not lighting individual pixels, whether or not they are lit being determined by whether an electron beam is switched on or off. Finally, all printer output (apart from daisywheels) is made up of dots or the absence of dots.

Thus, any data can be represented as a sequence of ones and zeros, representing the presence and absence of pulses, whether or not the electron beam is switched on, whether or not a dot is printed and so on. This same system is used for storing, printing and transferring data in all parts of the system.

Number formats

The system of ones and zeros described above is known as *binary*. Any numeric value can be represented as a string of binary digits. Binary works in the same way as the decimal system but in this case each digit can have only two values (0 or 1) rather than the ten (0-9) available in the decimal system.

In the decimal system the right-most digit represents units, the next digit to the left represents tens, the next is hundreds and so on. With the binary system the right-most digit is the unit, the next represents 2, the next is 4, then 8 and so on. An example of the conversion from a decimal number into binary is given in Figure 2.1.

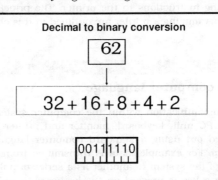

Decimal to binary conversion

$$62$$

$$32 + 16 + 8 + 4 + 2$$

$$0011\,1110$$

Figure 2.1

Each element of the binary string is termed a *bit* (binary digit). Clearly, the complexity involved in even the simplest number makes binary impossible to handle in most circumstances. Therefore, for convenience, each set of eight bits is grouped together into a *byte* (see Figure 2.2). (Within the computer, there are other amalgamations, such as *words* of 16 bits; however, all PC printers work purely in terms of 8-bit bytes.)

A byte can represent 256 (2 to the power of 8) different combinations of zeros and ones, giving numbers in the range 0 to 255. This is a wholly inconvenient number in the decimal system, so a new number format has been developed and has become the preferred system for programming. This is the *hexadecimal* system. This system uses base 16 with each digit representing a value from 0 to 1 (compared with the 0-9 used in decimal). Because we do not have sufficient characters to represent

Bit numbering

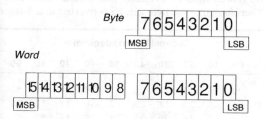

Figure 2.2

the sixteen digits, the values from 10 to 15 are represented by the letters A-F.

Figure 2.3 shows how any four-digit binary number may be converted to hexadecimal and its equivalent decimal value. The advantage of hexadecimal is that it produces fairly compact numbers that, with practice, can be easily recognised. In addition, the conversion from binary to

Decimal	Binary	Hexadecimal
0	0000	0
1	0001	1
2	0010	2
3	0011	3
4	0100	4
5	0101	5
6	0110	6
7	0111	7
8	1000	8
9	1001	9
10	1010	A
11	1011	B
12	1100	C
13	1101	D
14	1110	E
15	1111	F

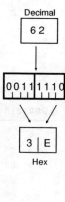

Figure 2.3

hexadecimal is very simple. Since we are working in units of 16, every four bits in a binary number can be represented by precisely one hexadecimal digit. Therefore an 8-bit byte can be converted to a 2-digit

Decimal to Hexadecimal

	00	10	20	30	40	50	60	70	80	90
0	00	0A	14	1E	28	32	3C	46	50	5A
1	01	0B	15	1F	29	33	3D	47	51	5B
2	02	0C	16	20	2A	34	3E	48	52	5C
3	03	0D	17	21	2B	35	3F	49	53	5D
4	04	0E	18	22	2C	36	40	4A	54	5E
5	05	0F	19	23	2D	37	41	4B	55	5F
6	06	10	1A	24	2E	38	42	4C	56	60
7	07	11	1B	25	2F	39	43	4D	57	61
8	08	12	1C	26	30	3A	44	4E	58	62
9	09	13	1D	27	31	3B	45	4F	59	63

	100	110	120	130	140	150	160	170	180	190
0	64	6E	78	82	8C	96	A0	AA	B4	BE
1	65	6F	79	83	8D	97	A1	AB	B5	BF
2	66	70	7A	84	8E	98	A2	AC	B6	C0
3	67	71	7B	85	8F	99	A3	AD	B7	C1
4	68	72	7C	86	90	9A	A4	AE	B8	C2
5	69	73	7D	87	91	9B	A5	AF	B9	C3
6	6A	74	7E	88	92	9C	A6	B0	BA	C4
7	6B	75	7F	89	93	9D	A7	B1	BB	C5
8	6C	76	80	8A	94	9E	A8	B2	BC	C6
9	6D	77	81	8B	95	9F	A9	B3	BD	C7

	200	210	220	230	240	250
0	C8	D2	DC	E6	F0	FA
1	C9	D3	DD	E7	F1	FB
2	CA	D4	DE	E8	F2	FC
3	CB	D5	DF	E9	F3	FD
4	CC	D6	E0	EA	F4	FE
5	CD	D7	E1	EB	F5	FF
6	CE	D8	E2	EC	F6	
7	CF	D9	E3	ED	F7	
8	D0	DA	E4	EE	F8	
9	D1	DB	E5	EF	F9	

Decimal	Hex	Decimal	Hex	Decimal	Hex
100	0168	1000	04EC	10000	2814
200	01CC	2000	08D4	20000	4F24
300	0230	3000	0CBC	30000	7634
400	0294	4000	10A4	40000	9D44
500	02F8	5000	148C	50000	C454
600	035C	6000	1874	60000	EB64
700	03C0	7000	1C5C		
800	0424	8000	2044		
900	0488	9000	242C		

Hexadecimal to Decimal

	00	10	20	30	40	50	60	70
0	0	16	32	48	64	80	96	112
1	1	17	33	49	65	81	97	113
2	2	18	34	50	66	82	98	114
3	3	19	35	51	67	83	99	115
4	4	20	36	52	68	84	100	116
5	5	21	37	53	69	85	101	117
6	6	22	38	54	70	86	102	118
7	7	23	39	55	71	87	103	119
8	8	24	40	56	72	88	104	120
9	9	25	41	57	73	89	105	121
A	10	26	42	58	74	90	106	122
B	11	27	43	59	75	91	107	123
C	12	28	44	60	76	92	108	124
D	13	29	45	61	77	93	109	125
E	14	30	46	62	78	94	110	126
F	15	31	47	63	79	95	111	127

	80	90	A0	B0	C0	D0	E0	F0
	128	144	160	176	192	208	224	240
	129	145	161	177	193	209	225	241
	130	146	162	178	194	210	226	242
	131	147	163	179	195	211	227	243
	132	148	164	180	196	212	228	244
	133	149	165	181	197	213	229	245
	134	150	166	182	198	214	230	246
	135	151	167	183	199	215	231	247
	136	152	168	184	200	216	232	248

	80	90	A0	B0	C0	D0	E0	F0
9	137	153	169	185	201	217	233	249
A	138	154	170	186	202	218	234	250
B	139	155	171	187	203	219	235	251
C	140	156	172	188	204	220	236	252
D	141	157	173	189	205	221	237	253
E	142	158	174	190	206	222	238	254
F	143	159	175	191	207	223	239	255

Hex	Decimal	Hex	Decimal
100	256	1000	4096
200	512	2000	8192
300	768	3000	12288
400	1024	4000	16384
500	1280	5000	20480
600	1536	6000	24576
700	1792	7000	28672
800	2048	8000	32768
900	2304	9000	36864
A00	2560	A000	40960
B00	2816	B000	45056
C00	3072	C000	49152
D00	3328	D000	53248
E00	3584	E000	57344
F00	3840	F000	61440
		10000	65536

Figure 2.4

```
D2H:        ;Program to convert decimal to hex

            ;Value to be converted is included
            ;as command line parameter
            ;(e.g. D2H 12345)

            ;Limitations: No checking for validity
            ;of parameter. Maximum 65536.

            ;Calls PARSE (2.19), NEXTPARM (2.19),
            ;DISWRD (8.10), DEC2HEX

            jmp d2hstart
```

```
declen        db ?              ;Number of digits in
                                ;decimal parameter

d2hstart:
    call parse                  ;Parse the command
                                ;line
    mov al,[paramlen]           ;Get no. digits and
                                ;save in DECLEN
    mov [declen],al
    call nextparm               ;Read decimal into
                                ;PARAMETER
    cld
    xor cx,cx
    mov cl,05h
    mov al,00h
    lea di,decin
    rep stosb                   ;Fill DECIN with
                                ;nulls
    lea si,parameter
    lea di,decin
    mov cl,[declen]             ;Transfer contents
                                ;of PARAMETER
    rep movsb                   ;to DECIN
    call dec2hex                ;Decimal-to-hex
                                ;conversion
    call diswrd                 ;Display result
    int 20h

;-------------------------------------------------

DEC2HEX:      ;Convert decimal value to hex

    ;Entry values: DECIN holds decimal
    ;                value
    ;Exit values:  AX=hex value
    ;              AX,BX,CX,DX,SI changed

    jmp decstart

decin       db '     ',00
    ;Decimal value to be converted, as
    ;ASCII string, terminated by null
    ;character.  Maximum value 65535.
    ;Routine does not check that number
    ;is valid.

decstart:
    xor ax,ax                   ;Set AX=0 (AX will
                                ;hold hex value)
    xor bx,bx                   ;Clear BX
    mov bl,0Ah                  ;Move 10 into BX
    xor si,si                   ;Clear SI (pointer
                                ;to next decimal
```

```
                                  ;digit)

startcon:
      xor  cx,cx             ;Clear CX
      mov  cl,decin[si]      ;Get next decimal
                             ;digit
      cmp  cl,00h            ;Check against 0
      jz   endcon           ;If 0, conversion is
                             ;complete
      mul  bx               ;Otherwise, multiply
                             ;value in AX by 10
      sub  cl,30h           ;Otherwise, subtract
                             ;30h to convert ASCII
                             ;number to actual val
      add  ax,cx            ;Add new digit
      inc  si               ;Increase SI, point
                             ;to next digit
      jmp  startcon         ;Jump to start of
                             ;loop
endcon:
      ret
```

Figure 2.5

hexadecimal number. There is no such precise conversion to the decimal system.

Figure 2.4 gives tables for converting between decimal and hexadecimal; Figure 2.5 lists an assembler program to convert from decimal to hex.

Notations

To avoid confusion, a special notation is needed to denote hexadecimal values. As a general rule, the convention is that decimal numbers are written in the normal manner and an extra character is appended to hexadecimal values. The convention in this book is that all hexadecimal numbers are followed by the letter 'h'. In addition, any hexadecimal values representing bytes are always padded with leading zeros so that they are two digits long. Thus a byte can represent values in the range 00h to FFh.

Other books and manuals use a variety of systems. For example, 4Fh may be written as 4FH $4F, &4F, &H4F or 0x4F. The decimal 79 may appear as 079, 79D or (79)D. Before trying to get programming information out of any printer manual, you should always check to see what sys tem is in use so that you do not confuse decimal and hexadecimal values.

Binary Coded Decimal

One way of overcoming the problem of converting from binary to decimal is to use an intermediate form known as *Binary Coded Decimal* (BCD). This system, like hexadecimal, works with groups of four bits. In this case, however, the four bits represent the decimal numbers from 0 to 9, as shown in Figure 2.6. Because only ten digits are to be converted, the binary codes from 1010 to 1111 are not used. This means that any decimal value from 0 to 99 can be represented by an 8-bit byte. Similarly, any byte can be translated back into decimal (bearing in mind that 156 of the binary combinations have no meaning).

A later adaptation of the BCD system, the *Binary Coded Decimal Interchange Code* (BCDIC) is a 6-bit code that includes 64 characters, including a large range of letters and other symbols. This character set is used in some paper tape machines.

In a later evolutionary step, the *Extended BCDIC* (EBCDIC) code was developed. This is an 8-bit character set that is widely used on mainframe computers and their printers but has little relevance to PC printers.

Binary Coded Decimal	
Decimal	BCD
0	0000
1	0001
2	0010
3	0011
4	0100
5	0101
6	0110
7	0111
8	1000
9	1001

Figure 2.6

Baudot code

Another character set that might be encountered is the *Baudot* code. This is a 5-bit code that defines two sets of 32 characters. One of these codes is used to switch between the two sets of characters. Although used on some earlier printers, you are unlikely to come across implementations now.

ASCII

The number systems described above are fine for representing numeric values but we also need a system for representing letters, symbols and other characters. The system that has been adopted throughout the computer world is that of ASCII (pronounced 'ASS-KEY'). This is the American Standard Code for Information Interchange. The standard ASCII system is used to represent most of the characters we need within the computer. The codes from 65 (41h) onwards are used to represent capital letters. For example, the letter J is represented by ASCII code 74 (4Ah). Similarly, codes from 97 (61h) onwards represent lower case letters; therefore, lower case j is represented by 106 (6Ah).

When you press the J key on the keyboard, the code that is sent to the PC is translated to this ASCII code and stored as 6Ah in memory. When the character is displayed, the display software translates the code 6Ah into the pattern of dots required to produce the lower case j on the screen. Similarly, when printing the letter j, the code 6Ah is sent to the printer and there converted into the pattern of dots needed to produce the character.

If you hold down one of the Shift keys, the PC interprets the letter as an upper case character; for example, Shift-J produces ASCII code 4Ah.

When storing numbers as characters, rather than for their numeric value, the ASCII codes from 30h are used. The various other characters between 20h and 7Eh are filled out with punctuation marks, mathematical symbols and various other common characters.

ASCII character set

Dec	Hex	Char	Dec	Hex	Char	Dec	Hex	Char	Dec	Hex	Char
0	00	NUL	32	20	Space	64	40	@	96	60	`
1	01	SOH	33	21	!	65	41	A	97	61	a
2	02	STX	34	22	"	66	42	B	98	62	b
3	03	ETX	35	23	#	67	43	C	99	63	c
4	04	EOT	36	24	$	68	44	D	100	64	d
5	05	ENQ	37	25	%	69	45	E	101	65	e
6	06	ACK	38	26	&	70	46	F	102	66	f
7	07	BEL	39	27	'	71	47	G	103	67	g
8	08	BS	40	28	(	72	48	H	104	68	h
9	09	HT	41	29	)	73	49	I	105	69	i
10	0A	LF	42	2A	*	74	4A	J	106	6A	j
11	0B	VT	43	2B	+	75	4B	K	107	6B	k
12	0C	FF	44	2C	,	76	4C	L	108	6C	l
13	0D	CR	45	2D	-	77	4D	M	109	6D	m
14	0E	SO	46	2E	.	78	4E	N	110	6E	n
15	0F	SI	47	2F	/	79	4F	O	111	6F	o
16	10	DLE	48	30	0	80	50	P	112	70	p
17	11	DC1	49	31	1	81	51	Q	113	71	q
18	12	DC2	50	32	2	82	52	R	114	72	r
19	13	DC3	51	33	3	83	53	S	115	73	s
20	14	DC4	52	34	4	84	54	T	116	74	t
21	15	NAK	53	35	5	85	55	U	117	75	u
22	16	SYN	54	36	6	86	56	V	118	76	v
23	17	ETB	55	37	7	87	57	W	119	77	w
24	18	CAN	56	38	8	88	58	X	120	78	x
25	19	EM	57	39	9	89	59	Y	121	79	y
26	1A	SUB	58	3A	:	90	5A	Z	122	7A	z
27	1B	ESC	59	3B	;	91	5B	[	123	7B	{
28	1C	FS	60	3C	<	92	5C	\	124	7C	|
29	1D	GS	61	3D	=	93	5D	]	125	7D	}
30	1E	RS	62	3E	>	94	5E	^	126	7E	~
31	1F	US	63	3F	?	95	5F	_	127	7F	△

Figure 2.7

The standard ASCII character set is shown in Figure 2.7.

Control codes

The first 32 ASCII codes, from 00h to 1Fh, are used for *control codes*. These codes represent a set of standard computer operations. Although they are based on the most commonly-used operations in the mainframe computer world, their use in the PC world has become distorted and many of them are now redundant.

Commonly used for printing purposes are: 0Ah (line feed, LF), 0Ch (form feed, FF) and 0Dh (carriage return, CR). Some others also have a recognisable effect. For example, 07h (bell, BEL) is often used to activate the computer beeper and 08h (tab, HT) moves the print head to the next tab position. In some cases, the effect of these control codes varies. For example, 0Fh (shift in, SI) may be used to produce condensed typed (that is, 'shifted in') or it may just select a different font.

Each of these control codes has a special use and, since there is no character to go with it, has a two- or three-letter abbreviation to represent it.

You should also note that these control codes can be produced on the keyboard by holding down the control key and pressing one of the character keys. For example, pressing Ctrl-I generates ASCII code 09h and most software duplicates the effect of the Tab key. Figure 2.8 shows the 32 ASCII control codes, with their abbreviations, meanings and corresponding control sequences.

The DEL code (ASCII 7Fh) is also treated as a control code rather than a character.

The standard ASCII is a 7-bit character set. This has the advantage that, if you do not want to use the extended characters, the eighth bit can be used for error checking during serial communications.

ASCII control codes

Dec	Hex	Abbrev	Meaning
0	00	NUL	Null character
1	01	SOH	Start of header
2	02	STX	Start text
3	03	ETX	End text
4	04	EOT	End of transmission
5	05	ENQ	Enquiry
6	06	ACK	Acknowledge
7	07	BEL	Bell
8	08	BS	Backspace
9	09	HT	Horizontal tab
10	0A	LF	Line feed
11	0B	VT	Vertical tab
12	0C	FF	Form feed
13	0D	CR	Carriage return
14	0E	SO	Shift out
15	0F	SI	Shift in
16	10	DLE	Data line escape
17	11	DC1	Device control 1
18	12	DC2	Device control 2
19	13	DC3	Device control 3
20	14	DC4	Device control 4
21	15	NAK	Negative acknowledge
22	16	SYN	Synchronisation idle
23	17	ETB	End transmission block
24	18	CAN	Cancel
25	19	EM	End of medium
26	1A	SUB	Substitute
27	1B	ESC	Escape
28	1C	FS	File separator
29	1D	GS	Group separator
30	1E	RS	Record separator
31	1F	US	Unit separator

Figure 2.8

Conventions

The following conventions are used in this book:

- When the contents of memory are referred to, hexadecimal values are used.

- When numeric quantities are described, the usual convention is to use decimal (e.g. a 24-pin printer; page length of 66 lines).

- When describing screen displays or text to be printed, ASCII characters are used.

- Control codes and command sequences are also given in ASCII, consisting of the control code abbreviations for the first 32 ASCII codes and the standard letters and symbols for the remainder.

The most important rule is that different representations should not be mixed within a single expression. For example, the code to turn bold type on in an Epson printer is given as ESC E. This means the escape code followed by ASCII code E. This two-character code starts bold printing; it does not print the letter E. This escape sequence could be converted to either decimal (27, 69) or hexadecimal (1Ah, 45h).

Compatibility and emulations

Over the years, a number of 'standards' have evolved. These are sets of command codes that are used in a range of printers and are copied by other manufacturers. For example, Brother and Star dot matrix printers support many of the codes used by the Epson range and are said to be *Epson-compatible*. Other regularly-quoted standards are provided by IBM, Hewlett-Packard and Diablo.

Many printers allow you to choose between the codes that are to be used. Such printers offer one or more *emulations*. That is, if you select the Epson emulation for a Panasonic, that printer becomes

Epson-compatible; alternatively, choosing the Laser-Jet emulation converts the printer to an HP-compatible.

Unfortunately, the codes offered as 'standards' vary from one printer to another, even within the original printer range. For instance, the Epson range has five levels of standard codes (see below), so there will be variations between models in the range. In addition, printers that are supposedly compatible with another model generally have some variations in their code set. The result is that the most common codes can be expected to work (e.g. turning bold type on and off) but the more exotic commands should be carefully checked for each printer.

Selecting an emulation

Inevitably, the method by which any particular emulation is selected varies from one printer to another. For example, the following command selects the emulation for Citizen printers.

Command:	Select emulation (Citizen)	
Printers:	Citizen	
Syntax:	ESC ~ 5 *n*	(ASCII)
	1B 7E 35 *n*	(hex)
	27 126 53 *n*	(dec)
Parameters:	*n* = 0 Epson	
	1 IBM	
	2 NEC	
Effect:	Selects emulation mode, affecting character sets and some escape sequences. Horizontal and vertical tab settings are cleared.	

Epson emulations

Each Epson printer uses one of five sets of control codes, labelled ESC/P 80 to ESC/P 84. ESC/P 84 contains the full set of standard Epson-compatible codes. Each of the other code levels is a subset of the one above; ESC/P 83 contains some but not all of those in ESC/P 84, for example. In addition, there are some extra commands in an 'extension' set, which are available to some printers.

Epson printers are defined as being compatible with one of these levels (with exceptions and additions in each case). However, other manufacturers tend to emulate either the Epson FX-80 or the Epson LQ-850.

Figure 2.9 lists the Epson commands. In each case it gives the level at which the command was introduced and indicates whether or not it is supported by the FX-80 and LQ-850 printers.

IBM emulations

The IBM Proprinter is emulated by many printers. The command set is largely a subset of the Epson commands, with a few additions. Some commands work in a slightly different way. Figure 2.10 lists the IBM Proprinter commands and indicates those that are the same as or similar to the Epson commands.

LaserJet emulations

Many printers emulate the Hewlett Packard Laser-Jet series. Their PCL commands are listed in Figure 2.11. These commands consist of several characters each, so require more care when programming. In particular, note that many of the commands use lower-case letter l; the page orientation command also uses capital O. The numbers 1 and 0 are used only as values for the parameters.

Diablo emulations

The Diablo 630 command set, originally designed for daisywheels, is still available on many printers. These commands are very simple, mostly with no parameters required at all. The commands are listed in Figure 2.12.

Epson Commands

Command	Level	FX	LQ	Meaning
BEL	ESC/P 81	*	*	Sound beeper
BS	ESC/P 80	*	*	Back space
HT	ESC/P 80	*	*	Tab horizontally
LF	ESC/P 80	*	*	Line feed
VT	ESC/P 81	*	*	Tab vertically
FF	ESC/P 80	*	*	Form feed
CR	ESC/P 80	*	*	Carriage return
SO	ESC/P 80	*	*	Select double-width printing (one line)
SI	ESC/P 80	*	*	Select condensed printing
DC1	ESC/P ext	*	*	Select printer
DC2	ESC/P 80	*	*	Cancel condensed printing
DC3	ESC/P ext	*	*	Deselect printer
DC4	ESC/P 80	*	*	Cancel double-width printing (one line)
CAN	ESC/P ext	*	*	Cancel line
ESC SO	ESC/P 80	*	*	Select double-width printing (one line)
ESC SI	ESC/P 80	*	*	Select condensed printing
ESC EM	ESC/P 82		*	Cut sheet feeder control
ESC SP	ESC/P 82	*	*	Set inter-character space
ESC !	ESC/P 81	*	*	Master select for typestyle and pitch
ESC #	ESC/P ext	*	*	Cancel eighth bit control
ESC $	ESC/P 82		*	Set absolute dot position
ESC %	ESC/P 82	*	*	Select/deselect RAM based characters for printing
ESC &	ESC/P 82		*	Define user defined characters
ESC (-	ESC/P ext		*	Define and apply a style of scoring
ESC *	ESC/P 81	*	*	General bit image command
ESC +	ESC/P ext		*	Set n/360 inch line spacing
ESC -	ESC/P 80	*	*	Turn underlining on/off
ESC /	ESC/P ext	*	*	Select vertical tab channel
ESC 0	ESC/P 80	*	*	Select ⅛ inch line spacing
ESC 1	ESC/P ext	*		Select 7/72 inch line spacing
ESC 2	ESC/P 80	*	*	Select ⅙ inch line spacing
ESC 3	ESC/P 81	*	*	Set n/180 inch line spacing (24-pin printers)
ESC 4	ESC/P 82	*	*	Select italic typestyle
ESC 5	ESC/P 83	*	*	Cancel italic typestyle
ESC 6	ESC/P 84		*	Expand the range of printable characters

ESC 7	ESC/P 84		*	Cancel expanded range of printable characters
ESC 8	ESC/P ext	*		Disable paper out sensor
ESC 9	ESC/P ext	*		Enable paper out sensor
ESC :	ESC/P 82	*	*	Copy ROM based character set to character RAM
ESC <	ESC/P ext	*	*	Uni-directional printing for one line
ESC =	ESC/P ext	*	*	Clear eighth bit of incoming data
ESC >	ESC/P ext	*	*	Set eighth bit of incoming data
ESC ?	ESC/P ext		*	Re-assign bit image commands
ESC @	ESC/P 81	*	*	Initialize the printer
ESC A	ESC/P 80	*	*	Set n/60 inch line spacing (24-pin printers)
ESC B	ESC/P 81	*	*	Set vertical tab stops
ESC C	ESC/P 80	*	*	Set page length in lines
ESC C NUL	ESC/P 80	*	*	Set page length in inches
ESC D	ESC/P 81	*	*	Set horizontal tab stops
ESC E	ESC/P 80	*	*	Select emphasized printing
ESC F	ESC/P 80	*	*	Cancel emphasized printing
ESC G	ESC/P 80	*	*	Select double-strike printing
ESC H	ESC/P 80	*	*	Cancel double-strike printing
ESC I	ESC/P ext	*	*	Set/cancel redundant control codes to print as RAM based characters
ESC J	ESC/P 81	*	*	Perform n/180 inch line feed (24/28-pin printers)
ESC J	ESC/P 81	*	*	Perform n/216 inch line feed (9-pin printers)
ESC K	ESC/P 80	*	*	Select 8-bit single-density bit image printing
ESC L	ESC/P 80	*	*	Select 8-bit double-density bit image printing
ESC M	ESC/P 81	*	*	Select 12-pitch characters
ESC N	ESC/P 81	*	*	Set margin for skip-over perforation
ESC O	ESC/P 81	*	*	Cancel skip-over perforation
ESC P	ESC/P 81	*	*	Select 10-pitch characters
ESC Q	ESC/P 81	*	*	Set right margin
ESC R	ESC/P 81	*	*	Select international character set
ESC S	ESC/P 81	*	*	Select superscript/subscript mode

		FX	LQ	
ESC T	ESC/P 81	*	*	Cancel superscript/subscript mode
ESC U	ESC/P 80	*	*	Turn uni-directional printing on/off
ESC W	ESC/P 80	*	*	Turn double-width printing on/off
ESC Y	ESC/P 81	*	*	Select 8-bit double-speed density bit-image printing
ESC Z	ESC/P 81	*	*	Select 8-bit quadruple-density bit-image printing
ESC \	ESC/P 80	*		Set relative dot position
ESC ^	ESC/P ext	*		Select 9-pin graphics mode
ESC a	ESC/P 83		*	Select justification mode
ESC b	ESC/P ext	*	*	Set vertical tabs in channels
ESC e	ESC/P ext			Set vertical/horizontal tab spacing
ESC f	ESC/P ext			Perform horizontal/vertical skip
ESC g	ESC/P ext		*	Select 15-pitch characters
ESC i	ESC/P ext	*		Turn incremental print mode on/off
ESC j	ESC/P ext	*		Perform n/216 inch line feed (9-pin printers)
ESC k	ESC/P 83			Select font family
ESC l	ESC/P 81	*		Set left margin
ESC m	ESC/P ext			Select special graphics characters
ESC p	ESC/P 83	*		Proportional characters on/off
ESC q	ESC/P ext		*	Select/cancel outline/shadow printing
ESC r	ESC/P ext			Select printing colour
ESC s	ESC/P ext	*		Turn half speed mode on/off
ESC t	ESC/P 84			Select character table
ESC w	ESC/P 84			Turn double height printing on/off
ESC x	ESO/P 82			Select draft quality or NLQ/LQ fonts
DEL	ESC/P ext	*	*	Delete character

FX: If FX column contains *, command is supported by FX-80
LQ: If LQ column contains *, command is supported by LQ-850

Figure 2.9

IBM Proprinter Commands

Command	Epson	Meaning
BEL	*	Beeper
BS	*	Backspace
HT	*	Horizontal tab
LF	*	Line feed
VT	*	Vertical tab
FF	*	Form feed
CR	*	Carriage return
SO	*	Double-width printing by line
SI	*	Condensed printing
DC1	*	Select printer
DC2	*	10-characters-per-inch print
DC3	*	Deselect printer
DC4	*	Cancel double-width printing by line
CAN	*	Cancel data
ESC *		Select graphic mode (AGM)
ESC -	*	Continuous underscore
ESC 0	*	1/8-inch line spacing
ESC 1	*	7/72-inch line spacing
ESC 2	*	Start text line spacing
ESC 3	*	Graphics line spacing
ESC 4		Set top of form
ESC 5		Automatic line feed
ESC 6		Select character set 2
ESC 7		Select character set 1
ESC :		Select 12 cpi text
ESC =		Character font image download
ESC A	*	Set text line spacing
ESC B	*	Set vertical tabs
ESC C	*	Set form length in lines or inches
ESC D	*	Set horizontal tabs
ESC E	*	Emphasized printing
ESC F	*	Cancel emphasized printing
ESC G	*	Double-strike printing
ESC H	*	Cancel double-strike printing
ESC I		Select print mode
ESC J	*	Graphics variable line spacing
ESC K	*	Normal-density bit-image graphics
ESC L	*	Dual-density bit-image graphics (half-speed)
ESC N	*	Set automatic perforation skip
ESC O	*	Cancel automatic perforation skip
ESC P		Proportional space mode
ESC Q		Deselect printer
ESC R		Set all tabs to power on settings
ESC S	*	Subscript or superscript printing

ESC T	*	Cancel subscript or superscript
ESC U	*	Print in one direction
ESC W	*	Continuous double-wide printing
ESC X		Set horizontal margins
ESC Y	*	Dual-density bit-image graphics (normal speed)
ESC Z	*	High-density bit-image graphics
ESC [@		Combined height and width
ESC [\		Set vertical tab units
ESC [g		High-resolution graphics
ESC \		Print continuously from all characters chart
ESC ^		Print single character from all characters chart
ESC _		Continuous overscore
ESC j		Stop printing
ESC d		Move print head right

NB. If **Epson** column contains *, command is equivalent to same Epson command.

Figure 2.10

HP LaserJet Commands

Command	Meaning
BS	Backspace
HT	Tab horizontally
LF	Line feed
FF	Form feed
CR	Carriage return
SO	Select secondary font
SI	Select primary font
ESC 9	Clear left/right margins
ESC E	Reset
ESC Y	Display functions mode start
ESC Z	Display functions mode end
ESC z	Interface self-test
ESC & a *n* C	Move horizontally (by columns)
ESC & a *n* H	Move horizontally (by decipoints)
ESC & a *n* L	Set left margin
ESC & a *n* M	Set right margin
ESC & a *n* R	Move vertically (by lines)
ESC & a *n* V	Move vertically (by decipoints)
ESC & d D	Automatic underlining start

ESC & d *n* D	Automatic underlining (general)
ESC & d @	Automatic underlining end
ESC & f *n* S	Push/pop position
ESC & f *n* X	Macro control
ESC & f *n* Y	Designate macro ID
ESC & k *n* G	Line termination
ESC & k *n* H	Set HMI
ESC & k *n* S	Set/cancel compressed pitch
ESC & l *n* C	Set VMI
ESC & l *n* D	Set lines per inch
ESC & l *n* E	Set top margin
ESC & l *n* F	Set text length
ESC & l *n* H	Paper input control
ESC & l *n* L	Perforation skip on/off
ESC & l *n* O	Set page orientation
ESC & l *n* P	Set page size (page length)
ESC & l *n* X	Set number of copies
ESC & p *n* X	Transparent print data
ESC & s *n* C	End-of-line wrap
ESC (s *n* B	Set stroke weight - primary font
ESC (s *n* H	Select character pitch - primary font
ESC (s *n* P	Select proportional/fixed space - primary font
ESC (s *n* S	Select character style - primary font
ESC (s *n* T	Select typeface - primary font
ESC (s *n* V	Set character height - primary font
ESC (s *n* W	Download character
ESC (*n* letter	Select symbol set - primary font
ESC (*n* @	Set primary font defaults
ESC) s *n* B	Set stroke weight - secondary font
ESC) s *n* H	Select character pitch - secondary font
ESC) s *n* P	Select proportional/fixed space - secondary font
ESC) s *n* S	Select character style - secondary font
ESC) s *n* T	Select typeface - secondary font
ESC) s *n* V	Set character height - secondary font
ESC) s *n* W	Create font descriptor
ESC) *n* letter	Select symbol set - secondary font
ESC) *n* X	Designate download font as secondary font
ESC (*n* X	Designate download font as primary font
ESC) *n* @	Set secondary font defaults
ESC * b *n* W	Transfer Raster graphics
ESC * c *n* A	Set horizontal rule/pattern size - (in dots)
ESC * c *n* B	Set vertical rule/pattern size - (in dots)
ESC * c *n* D	Specify font ID
ESC * c *n* E	Specify character code
ESC * c *n* F	Font and character control
ESC * c *n* G	Designate pattern ID
ESC * c *n* H	Set horizontal rule/pattern size - (in decipoints

ESC * c n P	Print rule/pattern
ESC * c n V	Set horizontal rule/pattern size - (in decipoints)
ESC * p n X	Move AP horizontally (by dots)
ESC * p n Y	Move AP vertically (by dots)
ESC * r B	End Raster graphics
ESC * r n A	Start Raster graphics
ESC * t n R	Select Raster graphics resolution
ESC =	Half line feed

Figure 2.11

Diablo Commands

Command	Meaning
BS	Backspace
CR	Carriage return
HT	Horizontal tab
LF	Line feed
VT	Vertical tab
FF	Form feed
ESC BS	Incremental backspace
ESC CR P	Remote reset
ESC HT	Absolute horizontal tab
ESC LF	Reverse line feed
ESC VT	Absolute vertical tab
ESC FF	Set page length
ESC DC1	Set inter-character spacing
ESC EM	Paper cassette selection
ESC C	Clear top/bottom margin
ESC D	Reverse – half-line feed
ESC E	Set underlining mode
ESC L	Set bottom margin
ESC M	Automatic justification mode
ESC O	Set bold printing mode
ESC P	Set proportional spacing
ESC Q	Cancel proportional spacing
ESC R	Cancel underlining mode
ESC S	Cancel HMI
ESC T	Set top margin
ESC U	Forward – Half-line feed
ESC W	Set shadow printing mode
ESC X	Cancel inter-character spacing
ESC Y	Special character 2
ESC Z	Special character 1
ESC &	Cancel bold/shadow printing mode

ESC -	Set vertical tab stop
ESC =	Automatic centering mode
ESC ?	Set automatic carriage return
ESC SUB I	Remote reset
ESC RS	Set VMI
ESC US	Set HMI
ESC I	Cancel automatic carriage return
ESC 0	Set right margin
ESC 1	Set horizontal tab stop
ESC 2	Clear all tab stop
ESC 3	Select graphics mode
ESC 4	Cancel graphics mode
ESC 5	Cancel backward printing
ESC 6	Set backward printing
ESC 7	Print suppression
ESC 8	Release horizontal tab stop
ESC 9	Set left margin

Figure 2.12

Printer configuration programs

An important part of any application is the printer configuration program. This may be either a separate program (such as the PRCHANGE program for WordStar) or an option in the main application. Such a program will list the printers that are supported by the application and invite the user to choose one. If you are only supporting the main features for a particular range of features, then just the basic printer name will do. For more sophisticated packages, using the more unusual features, the make and model are required.

Help should be given to the user to indicate the features that are being supported for any particular model, the features of the application that are only available for particular printer models and the action to be taken if the required printer is not included in the list. Most printers not included in such lists will be compatible with one of the 'standards'. If the needs of the application are modest (i.e. only simple codes are required), the program may need to list only the emulations that are supported.

Any printer configuration program should also include a set of defaults, so that the user can at least get a basic printout even if the printer being used does not appear to be compatible with any of those offered. Such a list of defaults should include a standard PostScript printer (where such printers are supported) and options to apply only the core matrix features, such as bold and underline.

For bold and underline, there should be three choices:

- Generate the features by overprinting the line (effective on most modem printers)

- Generate the features by backspacing and overprinting the character (where a CR and LF cannot be generated separately)

- Ignore even these core features (for older printers that do not allow backspacing)

This should ensure that no matter what printer is attached, any user can at least print the text of a document if nothing else.

On-screen printer commands

The way in which a document is finally printed may or may not be similar to that shown on the screen. The method of displaying printer information varies quite considerably. From the user's point of view, life is easier if the display on the screen is similar to that of the final output but from the programmer's point of view this can create problems. Broadly speaking, displays can be produced in two modes:

- *Text modes* use the computer's main character mode (display mode 0) to produce character-based displays, where each character takes up exactly the same amount of space as every other. Usually, there are 80 characters along each row with 25, 33, 50 or 60 rows on the screen.

- *Graphics modes* create their displays by turning individual pixels on a screen display on or off.

It can be seen that the display modes mimic the modes that are available on the printers.

Text modes

For text modes, only a single character set of 256 characters is available, so it is not possible to show features such as italics and underlining, let alone proportional text or different-sized fonts. Display text is held as a series of ASCII codes in memory; the conversion to pixel patterns is handled by the display software in ROM.

Most word-processing, database and spreadsheet packages use character modes for their displays and therefore a number of approaches have been taken to indicate to the user what the final display may look like:

- Different styles can be represented by displaying the characters in different colours.

- Special characters can be embedded within the text.

- Style and formatting instructions can be displayed on separate lines.

- The screen can be split, with one half showing just the text and the other giving formatting information.

- A special window can show the current format and font used by the character at the screen cursor position.

Some programs use more than one of these methods. For example, WordStar displays different type styles (bold, italics, etc.) in different colours within the text of its character-based display. Any font changes are indicated by a code appearing in angle brackets embedded in the text; formatting instructions appear on separate lines, preceded by a full stop in the first column. A display of how the text will eventually appear when printed can be generated by a special command (Ctrl-OP). The WordStar Ctrl-OP command temporarily changes from character to graphics mode, showing the final format.

Another market leader, WordPerfect, uses the split screen approach to show normal text in the top half of the screen, and printer and formatting codes in the bottom half.

Graphics modes

For graphics modes, each character is displayed on the screen by setting the relevant pixels. This means much more information must be stored in memory. The program needs to store a set of tables, giving the dot positions for each character in the set. There needs to be a table in memory for each font that may be used.

Ventura Publisher uses a graphics mode to display all text as it will eventually appear but also has a small box in the bottom left-hand corner that shows any special attributes that are embedded in the text at the cursor position. This helps to identify special codes (such as those to stretch or compress the text) that may not otherwise be obvious from the screen display.

It should be noted that even in graphics modes, the screen display is only an approximation of the final printed output. For example, on a VGA screen, each character position is represented by a grid of 14 x 9 pixels. In a standard 300 dpi laser printer, a similar character is printed on a block of 30 x 50 dots.

For each font that is to be printed, there must be a corresponding screen font in the computer memory; since this is only an approximation of the font in the printer, some fonts in particular will not print exactly as expected.

ASCII files

An ASCII file is a simple text file that contains only the 95 printable characters of the ASCII character set plus the three main printer instructions (CR, LF and FF). An ASCII file is terminated by the Ctrl-Z (1Ah, 26) character. Such a file can be directed to any printer that is in text mode and its contents should print without difficulty.

For example, if the file is called TEXT.DOC, it can be directed to the printer with the DOS command:

```
COPY TEXT.DOC PRN:
```

When this instruction is entered on the DOS command line, the file will be sent to the standard parallel port (usually, LPT1) and accepted by the printer, assuming it is on-line.

Most application programs can create ASCII files of this type. In doing so, they remove any special printer control codes and, where possible, replace them with ASCII equivalents. For example, tabs are often replaced by the required number of spaces. In many cases, bold type is produced by sending a line with a carriage return but no line feed, then repeating the emboldened sections of the line in the relevant positions. Underlining is produced in a similar way.

You can display an ASCII file on the screen with the DOS TYPE command, which interprets the CR and LF commands in the manner you would expect and shows any form feed as ^L. The TYPE command continues displaying text until it finds a Ctrl-Z character. To display a file a screenful at a time use the MORE filter. For example, the file TEXT.DOC can be displayed on the screen, a 'page' at a time, with the command:

```
TYPE TEXT.DOC | MORE
```

ASCII files are used when programming Post Script printers.

Extended ASCII files

There is no reason why you should not include other characters in an ASCII file, such as the extended ASCII characters or some of the control codes. The TYPE command will handle extended ASCII characters perfectly well but may produce unexpected results with the control characters. However, such a file can be sent to a printer if that printer can handle the characters and codes it contains.

Binary files

A file that can contain any of the possible characters and codes is called a *binary file*. Such a file can contain the full extended ASCII set, as well as any control codes or command sequences being sent to the printer. Since the Ctrl-Z character may appear in such a file as part of some other sequence of instructions, this character is not used to terminate the file. Instead, the end of the file is determined either by one or more NUL characters (00h) or by the file length as stored in the disk directory. The method adopted varies from one application program to another.

Many packages can be persuaded to produce binary files by redirecting printer output. The main distinction between these and ASCII files is that the control codes are not stripped out. By redirecting printer output to a binary file you can inspect the contents of a file to see what codes have been set. This is one method of detecting whether a printer error is being caused by the software or the printer.

The disk associated with this book also includes a program that allows you to display any file on the screen, in text, decimal and hex modes.

Not all programs can produce binary files in this way but there are many background utility programs that will redirect output from almost any application to a binary file. You should also remember that most printers have a hex dump mode which automatically prints the hex version of the text and codes received.

Remember that most printers have a hex dump mode, where control codes are listed to the printer as well as or instead of the text they produce.

Graphics mode binary files

Matching the contents of a binary file with the output produced in printer graphics mode is much more difficult. If a problem arises in graphics mode, the best way of tackling this is to split the output into short sections, so that only very small binary files are created and the instructions within them can be identified much more easily.

Keyboard keys

The first step in understanding the path taken by a character on its way to the printer is to look at the effect of pressing a key on the keyboard.

The majority of the keys on any PC keyboard represent the standard ASCII characters. When one of these keys is pressed, the resulting ASCII value is passed to the software program. There are a number of modifying keys: Shift, Ctrl and Alt, for example. These keys change the effect of pressing any of the character keys.

The Shift key is used, as on the typewriter, to produce capital letters and upper case symbols. Pressing the Shift key and then holding it while the character key is pressed sends a different ASCII code to the software to that produced by the character key on its own.

The Ctrl key is used in combination with the letter and other character keys in the same way as Shift. However, the character produced is ASCII *control code*. For instance, pressing Ctrl-B produces ASCII code 02. Each of the ASCII control codes can be generated by a Ctrl-character key combination (see Figure 2.8).

The Alt key also works like Shift and Ctrl but when used with the main part of the keyboard does not produce a printable character. Instead, produces a special code which can be extracted by the software and used to perform some action. The code consists of two bytes: a *null* byte (00h) to indicate that a special key combination has been selected, followed by another byte to indicate the keys that have been pressed. Alt keys are generally used as shortcuts to menu options. For example, pressing Alt-J is interpreted by some spreadsheet programs as an instruction to change the width of a column.

Alt also has a special use for producing the extended ASCII characters. If you press and hold the Alt key and then type an ASCII code on the numeric keypad (*not* the keys along the top of the keyboard the result is that the extended ASCII character is produced when the Alt key is released.

For example, holding down Alt and then pressing 1, 5 and 6 on the keypad produces ASCII code 156, which is interpreted as the £ sign on most UK computers.

If you press more than three keys while holding down the Alt key only the last three are used. If you type a number greater than 255, it is converted to a number in the range 0-255 (e.g. Alt-330 is the same as Alt-74).

The Alt key combination can be used to produce any ASCII characters. For instance Alt-74 will produce 'J'. Alt with the numbers 0-31 has the same effect as the control codes.

Control keys

The keyboard contains three particular keys that are used to produce control functions. Each of these produces one of the ASCII control codes which is then passed to the program for interpretation.

Key	ASCII code	Equivalent control char	Effect
Tab	08	Ctrl-I	Tab
Return/Enter	0D	Ctrl-M	Carriage return
Esc	1B	Ctrl-[	Escape

These codes are never passed directly to the printer. The way they are used by the program varies depending upon the application and the operation taking place. The Tab key may move to the next tab stop and result in a tab character being inserted in a piece of text; it may also be used to move from one box to another in a multiple-choice screen.

The Return/Enter key may be used to end a paragraph in a document and result in the CR LF sequence of codes being inserted in the file. This key is also used to complete the entry of filenames, confirm options to be taken and so on.

The Esc key is usually used to finish the entry of text, escape out of an option that is not required, interrupt a process and so on; most printer codes are preceded by an ESC character but this must be inserted specifically by the software.

Whether or not the other control and extended characters – the Ctrl key and Alt key combinations – are used for a special purpose or allowed to pass on through to the printer is a matter for the program to decide. You may check for these special keys and take action accordingly or you may just add them to the text being typed, store them in a file or send them directly to the printer. Be careful with the Ctrl-Z character, however; if sent to an ASCII file, this will insert an end-of-file marker.

Methods of issuing commands

There are three ways of issuing commands to a printer:

- By setting dip switches before power is on (user)

- Using the front panel buttons (user)

- By sending command sequences from the PC (programmer)

The dip switch settings take effect when the printer is switched on but may be overridden by either of the other methods. If the printer is re-initialised, any front-panel settings or PC commands are forgotten and the dip switch settings again take effect. Some printers allow the user to store front panel settings permanently, so that they become the defaults whenever the print is initialised (thus having the same effect as dip switches).

The front panel buttons and PC command sequences take equal precedence; the latest button press/command is always effective. Therefore the user may override commands issued from the PC by pressing the buttons after printing has begun; any front-panel settings may be overridden by commands arriving from the PC.

For HP-compatible printers, there are two PCL commands that allow you to disable and enable all command sequences.

Command:	Start display function
Printers:	LaserJet
Syntax:	ESC Y (ASCII)
	1B 59 (hex)
	27 89 (dec)
Parameters:	None
Effect:	Cancels all following control codes and escape sequences, printing them as spaces. Only the CR control code is allowed through, which is interpreted as a CR LF sequence. This continues until you give the ESC Z command.

Command:	End Display Function
Printers:	LaserJet
Syntax:	ESC Z (ASCII)
	1B 5A (hex)
	27 90 (dec)
Parameters:	None
Effect:	Cancels any previous ESC Y command, restoring all following control codes and escape key sequences to their normal actions. Note that the command itself is printed as a space and Z.

Command:	Transparent printer data
Printers:	LaserJet
Syntax:	ESC & p n X (ASCII)
	1B 26 70 n 58 (hex)
	27 38 112 n 68 (dec)
Parameters:	n = number of bytes
Effect:	Prints characters that would normally be control codes as symbols (if available). If no symbol is specified for a control character, a space is printed. This action continues for the specified number of bytes received at the printer. All control codes are

therefore disabled for this number of
bytes.

Parameters

Some printer commands have only one effect: for
example, FF to produce a form feed and ESC @ to
initialise an Epson printer. Many other commands
include *parameters*: values that determine the
previse effect of the command.

For instance, the Epson command to select a
character is ESC t and must be followed by a single
byte number; this parameter determines the
character set that is selected.

In this book, the command is referred to without
its parameters (e.g. ESC t). The parameters are rep
resented by symbols such as *n*, *n1* and *n2* (given in
italics). The *syntax* of the command includes both
the code sequence and the parameters, as in:

ESC t *n*

In the description of printer commands in this
book the 'Printers' category specifies the printers or
groups of printers which support the command.

Combining commands

For the Hewlett Packard PCL commands, two or
more commands can be combined to reduce the
number of bytes needed for the command se
quence. This can only be done if the first two
characters after the ESC code are identical. The last
character of the first command must be converted
to lower case: for the second command the ESC and
first two character may be omitted; if another ab
breviated command follows, the last character must
again be lower case.

For example, the following two commands set the
top margin to 6 lines and the text length to 6
lines:

```
ESC & l 6(dec) E
ESC & l 60(dec) F
```

They may be combined as follows:

```
ESC & l 6(dec) e 60(dec) F
```

On/off parameters

In many cases the parameter may take one of two values: 0 (off) or 1 (on). For example, the Epson ESC p command turns proportional spacing either on or off. For all such commands the printer will accept either the numeric codes 0 and 1 or the ASCII characters for 0 and 1. The permissible values are:

	ON	OFF
ASCII	NUL or 0	SOH or 1
Hex	00 or 30	01 or 31
Decimal	0 or 48	1 or 49

For instance, you can turn proportional spacing on with either ESC p SOH or ESC p 1.

When reading or entering commands in ASCII format, take care not to confuse the number 0 with capital letter O, or number 1 with lower-case letter l. If in doubt, check the hex or decimal values:

ASCII	0	O	1	l
Hex	30	4F	31	6C
Decimal	48	79	49	108

This is particularly important with the Hewlett Packard commands, where these values are widely used.

Sending codes directly

You can send control codes directly to the printer in a number of ways. The first method is to use the ECHO command from the DOS prompt. Anything following the ECHO command is normally printed to the screen, so this command is usually found in batch files. However, by using the DOS *redirection operator* (>) you can direct the output from this (or any other) command to either a file or another device. For example, the output can be directed to the standard printer port, PRN (parallel port 1, unless altered with a MODE command). The command takes the form:

```
ECHO Printer Test > PRN
```

In this case, the effect is to send the text 'Printer Test' to the printer; if the printer is active, the result should be printed immediately. Note that the text must not be enclosed in quotes.

Using the Alt-number pad method, you can send escape sequences and control codes. For example, to turn on bold type on an Epson-compatible (ESC E), the procedure is as follows:

1 At the DOS prompt, type ECHO, followed by a space.

2 Press and hold Alt; press 2 and 7; release the Alt key. This adds the ESC code (1Bh, decimal 27) to the command line.

3 Type E, followed by a space.

4 Complete the line with > PRN and press Return.

5 The ESC E command is sent to the printer. Any following ECHO > PRN commands, with straight text, should print in bold.

This method can be used with almost any control codes. The exceptions are:

NUL (00h, decimal 0)	No effect on command
ETX (03h, decimal 3)	Ignored by printer
ACK (06h, decimal 6)	Ignored by printer
BS (08h, decimal 8)	Deletes last character in command
HT (09h, decimal 9)	Moves cursor to right
LF (0Ah, decimal 10)	Completes command
CR (0Dh, decimal 13)	Completes command
SI (10h, decimal 16)	Ignored by printer
DC3 (13h, decimal 19)	Ignored by printer
DEL (7Fh, decimal 127)	Ignored by printer

However, if your printer is set up to duplicate the control codes in the Extended ASCII set, you can include any of these codes by adding 128 to their value; for example, use Alt-137 to send a tab character (HT).

Printing from a file

In a similar way, a sequence of control codes and text can be stored in a file, allowing you to send the same commands whenever they are required. For example, you can create a file containing just the Form Feed (FF) code, as follows:

1. At the DOS prompt, type COPY CON FF and press Return. This copies all following text from the keyboard (the 'CONsole') to a DOS file called FF.

2. Press and hold Alt; press 1 and 2 on the number pad; release the Alt key. Do not press Return. This stores control code FF (0Bh, decimal 12) in the file.

3. Close the file by pressing Ctrl-Z. (Press and hold the Ctrl key; press Z; release both keys.) This completes the file and stores it on disk.

4. The DOS prompt is redisplayed.

At any time, you can now force a form feed on the printer with the DOS command:

```
COPY FF PRN
```

This command 'copies' the file FF to the standard printer port (PRN). Such a command can be included in batch files to start a new page for output sent to the printer.

The method can be used to create a file of many commands and text items. Each time you press Return while creating the file, you can start a new one. When the file is sent to the printer, a carriage return is automatically sent with each line of text or commands.

You can include any control codes, except those mentioned above for the ECHO command. Also disallowed is the end-of-file Ctrl-Z (1Ah, decimal 26) control code, which closes the file.

Text editors

You can create control files, using the same Alt sequences, with a standard text editor. Text editors can also be used to edit these files (including any created by the COPY CON method).

A text editor is a program which stores text exactly as it is typed, using standard ASCII codes and with no formatting characters, apart from CR at the ends of lines.

Almost all PCs have the EDLIN text editor but there are many other, better text editors, which will create simple ASCII files. In addition, most word processors have a facility for creating and editing ASCII files: for example, the N (Non-document) command in WordStar. With EDLIN, you cannot include the NUL, HT, LF, CR or Ctrl-Z characters in the file.

Batch files

You can combine both methods, to include control codes directly in a batch file. For example, the following batch file prints a floppy disk directory listing on a new sheet of paper:

```
ECHO OFF
ECHO Load a floppy disk in drive A
ECHO Check printer is connected an on-line
PAUSE
ECHO ^L > PRN
DIR A: > PRN
ECHO Directory listing complete
```

This file can be created with either a text editor or the COPY CON method.

The first line switches off the echoing of the batch commands on the screen. If you are using DOS version 3.2 or later, you can use @ECHO OFF rather than ECHO OFF.

In the fifth line, ^L means that you should include the Ctrl-L character (FF), by typing Alt-12.

Data length

Data is sent to the printer as a series of bytes. The data may be sent as a string of bits (serial printers) or a whole byte may be sent (parallel printers). For most serial printers, bits 0-6 are used for the data (representing an ASCII character in the range 0-127) and bit 7 is used as a *parity bit* (for error checking).

For parallel printers, and serial printers where there is no parity checking, all eight bits are available for data, allowing characters with codes in the range 0-255. Interpretation of codes from 128 to 255 varies according to the character set selected. For example, on Epson printers you may choose between a graphics character set and an italic character set; a number of character sets may be available for different languages.

Setting and clearing bit 7

In some circumstances you need to ensure that the printer receives only standard ASCII codes (in the range 0-127) or the full extended ASCII set. There are two commands which set or clear the eighth bit of each incoming byte and a third command which cancels these other commands.

Command:	Set eighth bit	
Printers:	ESC/P ext	
Syntax:	ESC >	(ASCII)
	1B 3E	(hex)
	27 62	(dec)
Parameters:	None	
Effect:	Sets the eighth bit to 1 on all bytes as they arrive at the printer. This command only affects text data. The command can also be used when defining characters or for bit image printing, but must be sent before these other instructions. This command is cancelled by either ESC = or ESC #.	

Command:	Clear eighth bit
Printers:	ESC/P ext
Syntax:	ESC = (ASCII)
	1B 3D (hex)
	27 61 (dec)
Parameters:	None
Effect:	Clears the eighth bit (to 0) for all bytes arriving at the printer. The command operates in the same way as ESC >, above.

Command:	Cancel eighth bit control
Printers:	ESC/P ext
Syntax:	ESC # (ASCII)
	1B 23 (hex)
	27 35 (dec)
Parameters:	None
Effect:	Cancels the ESC > and ESC = commands, so that the eighth bit of incoming data is unchanged. The computer is now free to send the full extended ASCII set of characters.

Buffered input

When the printer receives data from the PC, it places this in an internal *buffer*. This is a part of the printer's memory set aside for storing data. Once there, it is able to extract the data and determine whether it is text to be printed or instructions relating to the format.

Having identified the instructions the printer will proceed to produce the output. However, different printers produce output at different times:

- At the end of each page
- At the end of each line
- After each character has been received

This will not usually cause a problem for programmers but users need to be aware of the situation.

Page printers

Most laser printers and other *page printers* wait until the entire page has been received before printing it. This can cause problems if you do not end the output with a form feed character, as the text and graphics will sit in the printer waiting for the next output to arrive. The user can force the page to be printed by putting the printer off-line and pressing the form feed key.

For page printers, the buffer must be large enough to hold the entire contents of one page. In some cases, it may be that there is insufficient space in the buffer to hold all the information required for the page. You may run out of memory in the following circumstances:

- There are a large number of font changes in the document.

- A particularly complex graphics picture is being produced.

- Large paper (e.g. legal size) is being used.

In the short term, you can overcome the problem by editing the document or picture, so that it has fewer font changes or less complex graphics. As a long-term solution, you can usually increase the size of the printer's memory by adding further RAM chips.

Line and character printers

Most other modern printers (referred to here as *line printers*) wait until a line of text has been completed before printing. In such cases, the final line will not be printed immediately if it was not followed by a CR or LF character. Such printers only print a line when they have received CR or LF (or both), or the print line is full. Some other characters – notably HT, VT and FF – who cause the line to be printed. Again, the user can force the last line to print by switching the printer off-line and pressing the form feed or line feed key.

Character printers print each character as it arrives or carry out the action required by a control character. No data is held in the buffer.

You can determine whether a printer prints after each character or at the end of the line with the following BASIC instruction:

```
LPRINT "START OF LINE";
```

Since this instruction is terminated with a semicolon, BASIC sends the text to the printer but does not send a CR LF sequence. For character printers, the text will print immediately (but the paper will not be advanced to the next line); for line printers, the text will not print until another LPRINT command is executed, such as:

```
LPRINT " AND END"
```

If there is too much text to fit on a single line for a line printer (or too much for one page on a page printer), the printer will either ignore the additional text or carry it over to the next line or page. Most printers automatically carry the additional text over.

Editing the buffer

Two commands allow you to change the contents of the print buffer for line printers, after text has been transmitted by the computer but before it is printed (i.e. before a CR, LF, HT, VT or FF command).

Command:	Delete character
Printers:	ESC/P ext
Syntax:	DEL (ASCII)
	7F (hex)
	127 (dec)
Parameters:	None
Effect:	Cancels the last character waiting to be printed in the buffer. The command has no effect on control codes but affects any preceding text character. The command is ignored if there are no text characters in the buffer or if it follows an HT, ESC \ or ESC $ command. A series of DEL commands will progressively delete a series of characters.

Command:	Cancel line
Printers:	ESC/P ext, IBM Proprinter
Syntax:	CAN (ASCII)
	18 (hex)
	24 (dec)
Parameters:	None
Effect:	Cancels all text characters currently waiting in the buffer. Control codes are not affected. The effect is the same as a string of DEL commands.

Printer speed

You can change the speed at which the printer operates, in order to improve the quality of the output (lower speeds result in more precise positioning of the print head and therefore clearer text). Sound levels are also reduced at slower speeds.

Command:	Select/cancel half-speed mode
Printers:	ESC/P ext
Syntax:	ESC s n (ASCII)
	1B 73 n (hex)
	27 115 n (dec)
Parameters:	n = 0 (cancel)
	1 (select)
Effect:	When n=1, printing proceeds at half the normal speed. Full speed is restored with a setting of n=0.

Preparing the output

As the data is received and stored in the buffer, the internal program within the printer starts to prepare the line or page to be output. In text modes, for each character in the buffer, the program finds the relevant pattern of dots from the character set table. It is then able to calculate the dots that are to be printed. The pattern of dots may be amended if the printer has received instructions to print in a different typestyle (e.g. bold) or size (e.g. condensed).

In graphics modes, the printer simply translates the data received into the appropriate, corresponding dots.

For instruction-based data (e.g. PostScript), the printer matches the instruction received against its internal programming language and, using the parameters supplied, calculates the lines that need to be drawn or the shape of the text to be printed, converting these into the dots that are required.

When the line or page is complete, another part of the printer program instructs the hardware to carry out the mechanical process of converting the dot image in memory into the printed image.

Paper out sensor

Most printers have a *paper out sensor*. This is a device that tells the printer when it is out of paper. The usual procedure is to have a small metal flap that activates a switch. A spring forces the flap open, indicating that there is no paper; when paper has been loaded, it holds the flap down.

When the sensor detects that there is no paper, it forces the printer to issue an error message to the computer (via pin 12 on parallel cables), printing stops and the printer beeps (where possible).

Inevitably, the sensor is lower than the print head on matrix printers so, when using single sheets, the sensor will be activated before the print head is at the bottom of the paper. If you need to print to the bottom of the sheet, the sensor must be disabled. This can be done through a command sequence.

Command:	Disable paper-out sensor	
Printers:	ESC/P ext	
Syntax:	ESC 8	(ASCII)
	1B 38	(hex)
	27 56	(dec)
Parameters:	None	
Effect:	Disables the paper-out sensor, so that the paper-out alarm is not	

activated when the end of the sheet passes the sensor; no error condition is reported to the PC. However, pin 12 of the parallel cable is still set and will cause an error in any software that monitors this pin. The command is cancelled by ESC 8.

Command:	Enable paper-out sensor	
Printers:	ESC/P ext	
Syntax:	ESC 9	(ASCII)
	1B 39	(hex)
	27 57	(dec)
Parameters:	None	
Effect:	Re-enables the paper-out sensor, after it has been disabled with ESC 8, restoring the default condition.	

Beeper

Most modern printers have a beeper, which is capable of generating a single tone. In many cases, the beeper sounds when the printer is switched on or initialised. The beeper may also be used to emit a continuous tone when the paper-out sensor is activated or when the ribbon runs out (for instance, on many daisywheel printers).

In addition, you may want to force the beeper to sound to alert the user to some conditions (for example, if a change of paper type or printwheel is required, or when printing is complete).

Command:	Sound beeper	
Printers:	ESC/P ext, IBM Proprinter	
Syntax:	BEL	(ASCII)
	07	(hex)
	7	(dec)
Parameters:	None	
Effect:	Sounds the beeper once.	

Transmission modes

Software can produce output to the printer using any of three modes:

- *Text mode.* In this case, data is sent in the form of the characters that are to be printed, with any instructions embedded as command sequences.

- *Graphics mode.* Here, the entire output is created as graphics, whether it is pictures or text. The software must send a stream of bytes that defines the dots that are to be printed to make up the pictures and text.

- *Instruction mode.* In this case, the software sends a series of instructions to the printer, which are interpreted by what effectively amounts to a programming language built into the printer. PostScript is an example of this.

The text-based mode is the easiest to program, since all you need worry about is embedding the necessary control codes within the text. For graphics mode, you need a table in memory from which you can convert each character into the necessary dots to send to the printer and, for any graphics, you need to calculate the dot positions. For instruction modes, you must effectively generate a small computer program to create the correct type of output.

Character mode

In some circumstances, it is useful to make a matrix printer behave like a typewriter, printing each character as it is received, rather than strong the characters in its buffer. Some Epson printers have a command that produces this effect:

Command:	Select/cancel character mode
Printers:	ESC/P ext
Syntax:	ESC i *n* (ASCII)
	1B 69 *n* (hex)
	27 105 *n* (dec)
Parameters:	*n* = 0 (cancel)
	1 (select)
Effect:	For line printers with no automatic sheet feeder, a value of *n*=1 selects character more (sometimes called *incremental print mode*). This mode continues until the command is repeated with *n*=0 or the printer is re-initialised.

Fundamental instructions

There are three main instructions that are understood by all PC matrix printers:

CR (Carriage Return)	Moves the print head to the beginning of the current line
LF (Line Feed)	Advances the paper by one line
FF (Form Feed)	Advances the paper to the top of the next sheet

These three instructions are represented by three ASCII codes that can be generated at the keyboard by equivalent control codes.

ASCII	Hex	Decimal	Control keys
CR	0D	13	Ctrl-M
LF	0A	10	Ctrl-J
FF	0C	12	Ctrl-L

The CR LF sequence can usually be generated on the keyboard by pressing the Return/Enter key.

The CR instruction on its own is important when a line of text is to be printed in bold or underlined, since this moves the print head back to the start of the line without advancing the paper, thus allowing a second pass across the same line. As an alternative, some printers use the backspace action to move the print head back one character, emboldening or underlining each character individually.

When an Epson-compatible printer receives an LF code (0Ah, dec 10) it usually performs a carriage return as well; IBM-compatibles advance the paper *without* moving the print head. IBM Proprinters can also be made to add to LF code every time a CR is received.

Command:	Automatic line feed	
Printers:	IBM Proprinter	
Syntax:	ESC 5 *n*	(ASCII)
	1B 35 *n*	(hex)
	27 53 *n*	(dec)
Parameters:	*n* = 0 (cancel)	
	1 (select)	
Effect:	When *n* = 1, a line feed is automatically added every time a CR code is received (overriding any dip switch or front panel settings). When *n* = 0, the LF must be inserted by the software.	

LaserJet-compatible printers allow you to determine how the printer responds to three line termination commands: LF, CR and FF.

Command:	Line termination	
Printers:	LaserJet	
Syntax:	ESC & k *n* G	(ASCII)
	1B 26 6B *n* 47	(hex)
	27 38 107 *n* 71	(dec)
Parameters:	*n* = 0...3	
Effect:	What action the printer takes when it receives one of the three line termination codes. The effect on each of these three codes is determined according to the parameter as follows:	

n	LF	CR	FF
0	LF	CR	FF
1	LF	CR LF	FF
2	CR LF	CR	CR FF
3	CR LF	CR LF	CR FF

Command:	End-of-line wrap
Printers:	LaserJet
Syntax:	ESC & s *n* C (ASCII)
	1B 26 73 *n* 43 (hex)
	27 38 115 *n* 67 (dec)
Parameters:	*n* = 0 (enable)
	= 1 (disable)
Effect:	Automatically inserts a CR LF sequence when an attempt is made to print beyond the right margin. Set *n* = 0 to enable this function or *n* = 1 to disable it. Usually, you will want to disable the function and create new lines from within the application.

The LF and FF instructions can also be generated manually from the front panel buttons on most printers.

Core instructions

There is a common core of printer instructions that is available on almost all printers. In addition, most printers provide a range of other facilities, some of which are available on many different machines, others that are unique to specific models. Making you software work with all of these facilities is an almost impossible task.

The number of facilities you need to account for depends upon the complexity of the application and the quality of output required. For example, for simple tabular results, the common core may be sufficient. For word processing and desktop publishing, as many as possible of the features should be used. WordPerfect 5.0, for instance, utilises the majority of the features available on most printers.

Using the more exotic features can provide problems for users, however. They may be able to incorporate the feature into the document being prepared but this does not mean that the printer will be able to handle it.

Sending data to the printer

All data is transferred to the printer via one of its parallel or serial ports. As a rule, this will be the first parallel port (called LPT1 or PRN) or the first serial port (COM1 or AUX). If you are programming the printer at machine-code level, using the BIOS interrupts, you can specify the port directly. Otherwise, if using the DOS interrupts or a high-level language, you can send data only to the *standard* parallel or serial port. By default, this is the first port in each case. To work with a different port you must redirect all standard output using the DOS MODE command.

BASIC

Most versions of BASIC allow you to write directly to the standard parallel port with the LPRINT command. For example, a line of text can be printed with an instruction in the form:

```
LPRINT "Printer test"
```

You can store the text in a variable prior to printing:

```
Text$ = "Printer test"
LPRINT Text$
```

The CR LF *sequence*

After each LPRINT command, BASIC automatically adds a CR LF (Carriage Return/Line Feed) pair of codes to take the print head to the left-hand margin and advance the paper one line. To leave the print head on the same line (so that the next printed text follows on directly), terminate the command with a comma or semi-colon.

Even then, BASIC will insert a CR LF sequence after each 80-character block. To prevent this (for example, when printing to wide-carriage printers or in condensed mode), issue the command:

```
WIDTH "LPT1:",255
```

This special case of the WIDTH command suppresses all line feeds. (Substitute the appropriate name in place of LPT1: for other than the first parallel port). Until the width is re-assigned with WIDTH "LPT1:",80 all lines must be terminated manually from within the program by adding the function CHR$(13) to the LPRINT command.

Note that in some versions of BASIC the command is entered as:

```
WIDTH LPRINT 255
```

Whenever BASIC encounters a lone CR (13, 0Dh) or LF (10, 0Ah), it automatically inserts the extra code to make up the CR LF pair. This is not always what you want. You can overcome this (for example, to advance the paper without returning the print head) with the same WIDTH command. The following program gives you full control of carriage returns and line feeds:

```
WIDTH "LPT1:", 255    'Make continuous lines
Text$ = "Printer test"
FOR I% = 1 to LEN(Text$)
  Letter$ = LEFT$(Text$,I%) 'Get next char
  IF Letter$ = LEFT$(Text$,I%) 'If not space:
    LPRINT Letter$; CHR$(10)
               'Print letter, advance paper
  ELSE                        'Otherwise:
    LPRINT CHR$(13)
               ' Move left but do not advance
  END IF
  NEXT I%
WIDTH "LPT1:",80      'Restore 80-char lines
```

The effect is as follows:

```
p
 r
  i
   n
    t
     e
t     r
 e
  s
   t
```

The above program is written in QuickBASIC 4.5. In other versions of BASIC you may need to insert line numbers at the start of each line or make other amendments (for example, if multi-line IF...END IF statements are not allowed).

A BASIC program can usually be listed on the printer with the LLIST command.

ASCII codes

The text can also be sent directly as ASCII codes, using the CHR$ function. For instance, the letter J (ASCII 74) is sent with the instruction:

```
LPRINT CHR$(74)
```

You *must* use CHR$ (either directly or in a variable) if sending control codes. For example, on an Epson-compatible printer, the following instructions would print some sample text in bold type:

```
BoldOn$ = CHR$(27) + "E"
BoldOff$ = CHR$(27) + "F"
LPRINT BoldOn$; "Printer test";BoldOff$
```

The effect is to send the Epson code to turn bold type on (ESC E), followed by the text itself and finally the code to turn bold type off (ESC F).

Non-standard ports

To direct text to other than the standard parallel port, you can treat the port as a file and 'write' the data to it. For example:

```
OPEN "LPT2:" AS #2
PRINT #2, "Printer text"
CLOSE #2
```

To omit automatic line feeds, you should include WIDTH #2,255 after the OPEN statement.

In some versions of BASIC this is the only way of printing directly. In other cases (e.g. BBC BASIC and Apple BASIC), you may need to write the text on the screen, having first switched on a *printer echo* function, so that all screen output is echoed to the printer.

Other languages

Other high-level languages have similar facilities for sending codes to the printer.

Word processors

Word-processing programs generally have their own printer drivers to send particular codes to the printer. However, for unsupported printers or unusual code sequences, there is usually a method of sending control codes from within a document.

Spreadsheets

Some spreadsheets allow you to change the format when printing data by selecting different styles, either for the entire print run or for ranges of cells. You can also put control codes directly into cells (in most spreadsheet programs). For instance, in Lotus 1-2-3 and most other spreadsheets you can use the CHR$ function to insert one or more codes within a cell. By adding the contents of cells to produce data in other cells, you can combine control codes and text.

Databases

Most databases and other programs with macro facilities have simple printing instructions, similar to those described for BASIC above. The use of CHR$ or an equivalent function allows you to include control codes.

Macros

Some printers allow you to download a macro to the printer, either when the application is first started or before printing a document. A macro is simply a series of instructions to the printer which may be called by other instructions within the document. Macros are sometimes termed *headers*.

For LaserJet-compatibles, the following commands are used to create and execute macros.

Command:	Designate Macro ID
Syntax:	Esc & f *n* Y
	1B 26 66 *n* 59
	27 38 102 *n* 89
Parameters:	*n* = 0...32767

Effect:	Assigns a number to a macro. This command must be issued before any other macro command.

Operator:	Macro Control
Syntax:	ESC & f *n* X
	1B 26 66 *n* 58
	27 38 102 *n* 88
To stack:	*n* = 0 Start definition of macro
	1 End definition of macro
	2 Execute macro
	3 Call macro
	4 Enable automatic macro overlay
	5 Disable automatic macro overlay
	6 Delete all macros
	7 Delete all temporary macros
	8 Delete specific macros
	9 Specify macro as temporary
	10 Specify macro as permanent
Effect:	These various functions allow you to create, execute and delete macros.

3 Page Layout

Most printers give you complete control on how you use the page: the margins at each of the four sides, the text length and width, and the way in which ends of pages are handled. This chapter describes the commands to set these features.

Paper size

Most printers can accomodate a variety of paper sizes, including the standard sizes available in both the USA and Europe. A minor complication arises from the fact that the USA paper sizes are specified in inches while the European sizes are in millimetres. Figure 3.1 lists the most commonly supported paper sizes, giving their dimensions in both inches and millimetres.

It should be noted that character spacing for matrix printers is almost always specified in terms of lines per inch or characters per inch. For page

Paper size

A4	210 x 297 mm
A5	149 x 210 mm
B5	176 x 250 mm
Letter	8.5 x 11 in
Half-letter	5.5 x 8.5 in
Legal	8.5 x 14 in
Executive	7.25 x 10.5 in
Double	11 x 17 in
Broad Sheet	18 x 25 in

Envelopes

C5	162 x 229 mm
DL	110 x 220 mm
Monarch	3.875 x 7.5 in
COM-10	4.125 x 9.5 in

Figure 3.1

printers, the dot density is given in terms of *dots per inch* (typically 300 dpi or 400 dpi).

Labels

While the number of standard paper sizes is limited, that for labels is almost unlimited. The labels are stuck on backing paper, which is usually of one of the standard page sizes, but the labels themselves can be arranged in many different ways. There may be between one and four labels across each sheet and up to twelve labels down the sheet. Therefore, any label-printing software should be written to work with a selection of label sizes. You must also take account of the fact that there will be a non-printable gap between each pair of neighbouring labels, both vertically and horizontally.

Note that you should always use special laser printer or photocopier labels for laser printers, since the heat process will cause ordinary labels to peel off and may cause damage to the printer. Dot matrix printers can also be damaged by peeling labels if these stick to the rollers, so you should make sure that the printer is adjusted to allow for the extra thickness.

Envelopes

Very few printers are capable of satisfactorily handling envelopes, mainly because of their size. Again, pre-gummed envelopes can cause problems and should be avoided.

An alternative is to print addresses for envelopes on labels or to design the printed document so that the address can show through on a window envelope.

Form feeds

The printer keeps track of the current vertical position of the print head on the page. When the page is full, the printer automatically executes a form feed command to eject the sheet and move on to the next sheet. This is true whether you are using single sheets (on a laser printer, daisywheel o matrix) or continuous stationery on a dot matrix printer. For most printers, there is usually a hardware setting – front panel button or dip switch – to determine the size of the page (A4, Legal, etc.) and the number of lines to be printed on the page.

The printer determines that the page is to be ejected when it processes an LF, VT or Epson ESC J command, the effect of which would be to move the print head below the last printing line. The printer's calculation usually allows for a certain amount of unused margin at the bottom of the sheet.

The printer is only able to assess the current position accurately if it is set to top of form when a new sheet is inserted. When the printer is switched on, it assumes that the paper is set at top of form; likewise, after a form feed.

Some printers include a front panel button that resets the top of form. If you manually adjust the paper position, after top of form has been set the printer will not be aware of the changes. However, most printers have a paper end detector so that they can tell when they are out of paper, even if this is earlier than expected.

The software application may also keep track of the position on the page and send a form feed at regular intervals. If the form feed arrives before the printer is expecting an end of page, the page is ejected and the printer resets its calculations for top of form. However, if the page length according to the software application is longer than that used by the printer, there will be a form feed both when the printer calculates the page end and when the software sends the form feed character. In such cases, the software settings must be adjusted so that they match those of the printer.

Most printers – apart from PostScript devices – require only a single control character to force a form feed.

Command:	Form feed	
Printers:	All	
Syntax:	FF	(ASCII)
	0C	(hex)
	12	(dec)

Parameters:	None
Effect:	Advances paper to next top-of-form, after printing any data in the buffer. The print head is reset at the left margin.

For page printers and printers with sheet feeders, the top of form is set automatically whenever a new sheet is loaded. Problems will only arise when the computer sends more lines than the printer is set up to receive. After filling one page, the printer performs a form feed and then prints the remainder of the text at the top of the next sheet. The second sheet is ejected when a form feed instruction is received from the computer.

Similar problems arise for continuous stationery, though here the result is large gaps in the text where the computer's form feed is executed.

IBM printers and their emulations allow you to redefine the top of form at any time.

Command:	Set top of form	
Printers:	IBM Proprinter	
Syntax:	ESC 4	(ASCII
	1B 34	(hex
	27 52	(dec
Parameters:	None	
Effect:	Sets the current paper position as the top of form. The effect is the same as switching the printer off and on, or initialising the printer, but no other settings are affected.	

The top of form is also rest when you change the page length (see ESC C below).

Multiple copies

For page printers, you can determine the number c copies to be printed for each page. For PostScrip printers, this consists of an instruction include within the PostScript instruction file (as describe in Chapter 10).

For other page printers, based on the LaserJe commands there is an instruction for this purpose

Command:	Print multiple copies	
Printers:	LaserJet	
Syntax:	ESC & l *n* X	(ASCII)
	1B 26 6C *n* 58	(hex)
	27 38 108 *n* 88	(dec)
Parameters:	*n* = 1...99	
Effect:	Prints the number of copies specified by the parameter for each page that is printed, until the command is used again to change the number or the printer is reset. The command can be given at any time before the page is printed. For a multiple-page document, each page is printed the given number of times in turn. The multiple copies are not collated.	

Cut-sheet feeders and paper trays

Many line printers permit one or more optional cut-sheet feeders to be attached, allowing you to print on single sheets rather than continuous stationery. Usually, the user must set dip switches to inform the printer that the sheet feeder has been fitted. Although sheet feeders tend to be found on daisywheel printers, they can also be fitted to many bubble jet and dot matrix printers. Some sheet feeders allow you to select from more than one stack of paper; these are referred to as *bins*.

When any sheet is ejected (following a FF command, or the LF, VT or Epson ESC J commands when near the bottom of the sheet), a new sheet is loaded automatically.

As an alternative, some printers may be fitted with an optional paper cutter, which can use a tractor feed unit either at the front or rear of the printer.

Those Epson-compatibles that allow the attachment of sheet feeders have a command for operating the feeder and taking account of its effects.

Command:	Cut-sheet feeder control	
Printers:	ESC/P 82	
Syntax:	ESC EM *n*	(ASCII)
	1B 19 *n*	(hex)
	27 25 *n*	(dec)
Parameters:	*n* = 0 (turns off cut-sheet feeder)	
	1 (selects bin 1 on double-bin printers)	
	2 (selects bin 2 on double-bin printers)	
	4 (turns on cut-sheet feeder)	
	B (selects rear feed for sheet cutter)	
	F (selects front feed for sheet cutter)	
	R (ejects sheet, does not load new sheet)	
Effect:	The mode that allows the automatic use of the cut-sheet feeder is selected with *n*=4 or cancelled with *n*=0. The default depends on dip switch settings. A value of *n*=0 is ignored if the paper-out has been activated. For printers with two bins, the required bin is selected with *n*=1 or *n*=2 (defaults to bin 1). The tractor feed unit for sheet cutters is selected with *n*=B or *n*=F. The *n*=R option ejects the current sheet without printing the text in the buffer and does not load a new sheet.	

Paper trays

Page printers are fitted with one or more paper trays, which automatically feed paper into the printer as required. For more than one tray, the tray is selected by front-panel settings or additional commands.

Command:	Paper input control	
Printers:	LaserJet	
Syntax:	ESC & l *n* H	(ASCII)
	1B 26 6C *n* 48	(hex)
	27 38 108 *n* 72	(dec)

Parameters:	n =	0 (Eject page)
		1 (Feed from upper paper tray)
		2 (Feed manually)
		3 (Feed envelopes)
		4 (Feed from lower paper tray)
Effect:		Determines the source for the next sheet of paper: this may indicate that the paper is to be fed manually, that it is an envelope or that it is to come from the paper tray. Where the paper feeder has two trays, you can select the upper or lower tray. When a value of n = 0 is given, the effect is merely to eject the current sheet and load a new one in the normal way.

Command:	Select printing cassettes	
Printers:	Diablo	
Syntax:	ESC EM n	(ASCII)
	1B 19 n	(hex)
	27 25 n	(dec)
Parameters:	n = E (envelopes)	
	1 (lower cassette)	
	2 (upper cassette)	
	R (reject page)	
Effect:	Selects the cassette from which paper is to be fed or forces a form feed. The effects may vary from one printer to another, depending on the cassettes and options that are available.	

Page length

The printer needs to know how much text is to be printed on each page. This is the *page length* or *form length* and is given in terms of inches or lines. When the specified length has been reached, the printer performs a form feed to take the print head to the top of form on the next sheet, regardless of whether or not a form feed instruction has been received from the computer. If the page length is set too long, the paper-end detector will be activated before the printer believes the page-end has been reached.

For single sheets there will usually be a non-printable region at the top and bottom of the sheet where it is physically impossible for the printer to print text. For daisywheel, dot matrix and other line printers, the top margin is needed to hold the paper on the platen, above the print head; the bottom margin is needed below the print head, to keep the paper in position and de-activate the paper-end detector. For page printers, there is a border all around the paper where nothing can be printed. Therefore, the maximum page length (identifying the printable area) will always be less than the physical paper size.

For continuous paper, the printer has no way of knowing where one sheet ends and the other begins. The page length must be set to equal the actual page length. If this is not the case, the top of form will be out of step with the paper and printing will begin at a different position on each page. For continuous paper, you can fill each page, with no top or bottom margins.

The page length will be set to a default when the printer is initialised. This may depend on dip switch settings and the user may also change the page length with front panel buttons. These are overridden by software commands.

Whatever type of paper, the page length can be set either as a fixed length (in inches) or in terms of the number of lines, where the print length will depend on the current line spacing. Epson and IBM share commands for this purpose.

Command:	Set page length (inches)
Printers:	ESC/P 80, IBM Proprinter
Syntax:	ESC C NUL *n* (ASCII)
	1B 43 00 *n* (hex)
	27 67 0 *n* (dec)
Parameters:	*n* = 1...22
Effect:	Sets page length in inches; current line becomes top-of-form. Perforation skip (ESC N) is cancelled.

Command:	Set page length (lines)
Printers:	ESC/P 80, IBM Proprinter
Syntax:	ESC C *n* (ASCII)
	1B 43 *n* (hex)
	27 67 0 *n* (dec)
Parameters:	*n* = 1...127
Effect:	Sets page length in lines; current line becomes top-of-form. Physical page length depends on current line spacing and must not exceed 22". Perforation skip (ESC N) is cancelled.

Command:	Set page length (lines)
Printers:	LaserJet
Syntax:	ESC & l *n* P (ASCII)
	1B 26 6C *n* 50 (hex)
	27 38 108 *n* 80 (dec)
Parameters:	*n* = number of lines
Effect:	Sets page length in lines. The maximum allowed depends on paper size and line spacing.

Command:	Set top margin
Printers:	Diablo
Syntax:	ESC T (ASCII)
	1B 54 (hex)
	27 84 (dec)
Parameters:	None
Effect:	Sets top margin at current print position.

Command:	Set bottom margin
Printers:	Diablo
Syntax:	ESC L (ASCII)
	1B 4C (hex)
	27 76 (dec)
Parameters:	None
Effect:	Sets bottom margin at current print position.

Command:	Clear top/bottom margin
Printers:	Diablo
Syntax:	ESC C (ASCII)
	1B 43 (hex)
	27 67 (dec)
Parameters:	None
Effect:	Clears the top and bottom margins, resetting them to their defaults.

Command:	Set page length
Printers:	Diablo
Syntax:	ESC FF *n* (ASCII)
	1B 0C *n* (hex)
	27 12 *n* (dec)
Parameters:	*n* = 1...126
Effect:	Sets the page length in terms of the number of lines per page. The current line becomes the top-of-form.

Perforation skip

For matrix printers, if page layout is under the control of the printer, then you need some way of ensuring that nothing is printed over the perforations between pages of continuous paper. This is done by setting a non-printing area at the bottom of each page: the *perforation skip*. The blank area is split equally between the bottom of one page and the top of the next, so that the perforations will be in the middle of this area (assuming the top of form is correctly set).

Command:	Set perforation skip
Printers:	ESC/P 81, IBM Proprinter
Syntax:	ESC N *n* (ASCII)
	1B 4E *n* (hex)
	27 78 *n* (dec)
Parameters:	*n* = 1 - 127 lines (Epson)
	0 - 255 lines (IBM)
Effect:	Sets non-printing margin to skip perforations. Physical length of the margin depends on current line spacing (but must not exceed 22"); subsequent changes to line spacing do not affect the margins. Margins

are also created for single-sheet printing. The command is cancelled by ESC C, ESC C NUL or ESC O.

Command:	Cancel perforation skip
Printers:	ESC/P 81, IBM Proprinter
Syntax:	ESC O
Parameters:	None
Effect:	Turns off perforation skip for ends of pages.

Remembering that the page length determines the physical distance from one top-of-form to the next, the perforation skip reduces the printable area. For example, for 11" paper with 6 lines per inch, a perforation skip of 5 lines will have the following effect:

Top margin	3 lines
Print length	61 lines
Bottom margin	2 lines
Page length	66 lines

In this case, before printing begins on the first page, the print head will move down 3 lines. The effect is the same on single sheets, even though there is no perforation.

For PCL printers, the margins are determined by the current settings.

Command:	Set perforation skip	
Printers:	LaserJet	
Syntax:	ESC & l n L	(ASCII)
	1B 26 6C n 4C	(hex)
	27 38 108 n 76	(dec)
Parameters:	n = 0 (cancel)	
	1 (set)	
Effect:	Turns the perforation skip on (n = 1) or off (n = 0). By default, perforation skip is off. When the perforation skip is on, a form feed is effected whenever the print position goes beyond the current text length and printing resumes on the next page,	

after allowing for the current top margin. When perforation skip is off, printing continues until the bottom of the physical page and starts at the top of the next physical page; as a result, text may be printed in the unprintable areas of the page.

Software-controlled margins

The perforation skip is fine if you are happy to giv the printer control over what is printed on eac page. The only command needed is FF, to start new page when essential (for example, at the star of a chapter).

If you need to include *headers* and *footers* (line of text to be printed at the top and bottom of eac page), or want the top and bottom margins to b different sizes, you must control the printing fror the software.

The way to do this is to create the top margin b sending the relevant number of LF commands, the count the lines as they are printed. When the co rect number have been sent to the printer, send form feed and repeat the process.

To include a header at the top of each page, yo must allow one or more lines for the text of th header and at least one blank line below it. Simil considerations are needed for the footer.

An example of how the printable length is calc lated is as follows:

Top margin	2
Header line(s)	1
Space below header	1
Printable length	56
Space above footer	1
Footer line(s)	1
Bottom margin	4

Page length	66

Page printer margins

For page printers, you need to be able to set the top and bottom margins to determine the space above and below the text. Hewlett-Packard PCL provides a command for each of these.

Command:	Set top margin	
Printers:	LaserJet	
Syntax:	ESC & l *n* E	(ASCII)
	1B 26 6C *n* 45	(hex)
	27 38 108 *n* 69	(dec)
Parameters:	*n* = margin size	
Effect:	Sets the margin at the top of each sheet in terms of the number of lines in the current line spacing. The text length is adjusted automatically. Changing the line spacing alters the top margin accordingly. If the top margin is less than the height of the unprintable region at the top of the page, the top lines of text will be lost. The default top margin is 0.5".	

Command:	Set text length	
Printers:	LaserJet	
Syntax:	ESC & l *n* F	(ASCII)
	1B 26 6C *n* 46	(hex)
	27 38 108 *n* 70	(dec)
Parameters:	*n* = number of lines	
Effect:	Sets the length of text for each page in terms of a number of lines in the given line spacing. Effectively, therefore, this command sets the bottom margin, which may be calculated from:	

bottom margin =
     page length - top margin - text length

The text length is automatically reset when the top margin changes, so this command should be used with the one above. The default text length is set such that the bottom margin is 0.5".

Orientation

The orientation can be determined on printers that use the LaserJet command set with a single command.

Command:	Set page orientation
Printers:	LaserJet
Syntax:	ESC & l *n* O (ASCII)
	1B 26 6C *n* 4F (hex)
	27 38 108 *n* 79 (dec)
Parameters:	*n* = 0 (portrait)
	1 (landscape)
Effect:	Select between portrait printing (*n* = 0) and landscape printing (*n* = 1). The default is portrait. This command should be used at the beginning of a page; you cannot combine both portrait and landscape on the same page (unless the paper is fed through the printer twice). If there is any data waiting to be printed when the command is received by the printer, this data is printed and then a form feed is automatically issued. All page formatting commands are reset to their defaults.

Print width

The maximum printable width depends upon the printer model but most printers follow certain standards. For most line printers, the maximum print width is either 8" or 13.6". At 10 cpi this allows either 80 or 136 characters respectively. The actual number of characters per line depends on the current character pitch and will vary from line to line for proportional spacing.

By default, most printers use the full carriage width. However, you can vary the print width by moving the left and right margins. This can be done in one of two ways:

- The margins can be set within the software, by sending spaces at the start of each line (for a left margin) and by sending a CR when the right margin is reached.

- The printer can be directed to print within specified margins.

If you are working with a printer that can determine its own margins, this is by far the easiest approach. The printer margins are adjusted with the following commands.

Command:	Set left margin
Printers:	ESC/P 81
Syntax:	ESC l *n* (ASCII)
	1B 6C *n* (hex)
	27 108 *n* (dec)
Parameters:	*n* = 0...255 characters
Effect:	Sets position for start of printing on each line, relative to default print head position. Margin depends on current character width; for proportional spacing, 10 cpi is assumed. Subsequent changes to character width do not affect the margin. The left margin must not be greater than 4.5" (standard carriage) or 8" (wide carriage). This command must be given at the start of a line (as any preceding text is lost). Any existing tab settings are cleared.

Command:	Set left margin
Printers:	LaserJet
Syntax:	ESC & a *n* L (ASCII)
	1B 26 61 *n* 4C (hex)
	27 38 97 *n* 76 (dec)
Parameters:	*n* = columns
Effect:	Sets the left margin in terms of the number of columns in the current character pitch. The value is measured from the edge of the printable area of the sheet and must be less than the setting for the right margin.

Command:	Set left margin
Printers:	Diablo
Syntax:	ESC 9 (ASCII)
	1B 39 (hex)
	27 57 (dec)
Parameters:	None
Effect:	Sets left margin at current print position.

Command:	Set right margin
Printers:	ESC/P 81
Syntax:	ESC Q n (ASCII)
	1B 51 n (hex)
	27 81 n (dec)
Parameters:	n = 1...255 characters
Effect:	Sets position at which text wraps around to next line. Margin depends on current character width; for proportional spacing, 10 cpi is assumed. Subsequent changes to character width do not affect the margin. Right margin is measured from the power-on left margin position (*not* from the maximum right-hand position). The right margin must be less than the maximum print width and at least two characters greater than the left margin. The command must be given at the start of a line (since any preceding text is lost). Any existing tab settings are cleared.

Command:	Set left and right margins
Printers:	IBM Proprinter
Syntax:	ESC X n1 n2 (ASCII)
	1B 58 n1 n2 (hex)
	27 88 n1 n2 (dec)
Parameters:	n1 = 0...255 characters (left margin)
	n2 = 0...255 characters (right margin)
Effect:	Sets the margins for all future lines. The margins are measured in terms of character positions; values of 0 indicate that the *current* margin should be used. If a parameter

exceeds the maximum paper width
(8" standard, 13.6" wide carriage), the
margin is set at the right-hand edge.
The margins take effect after the next
carriage return.

Command:	Set margin
Printers:	LaserJet
Syntax:	ESC & a *n* M (ASCII)
	1B 26 61 *n* 4D (hex)
	27 38 97 *n* 77 (dec)
Parameters:	*n* = columns
Effect:	Sets the right margin in terms of a number of columns in the current character pitch. The margin is measured from the start of the printable area on the left of the page and must be greater than the left margin and less than the total printable width. By default, the right margin is at the right-hand printable edge of the paper.

Command:	Clear left and right margins
Printers:	LaserJet
Syntax:	ESC 9 (ASCII)
	1B 39 (hex)
	27 57 (dec)
Parameters:	None
Effect:	Restores the left and right margins to their default settings, at the edges of the printable region of the page. The print head will only move to the default left margin when a CR command is issued.

Command:	Set right margin
Printers:	Diablo
Syntax:	ESC 0 (ASCII)
	1B 30 (hex)
	24 48 (dec)
Parameters:	None
Effect:	Sets right margin at current print position.

For example, if printing at 10 cpi on a standard width Epson printer, the following command sequence sets a left margin of 2" and a right margin of 1½" (giving a print width of 4½"):

```
ESC l DC4 ESC Q -      (ASCII)
1B 6C 14 1B 51 2D      (Hex)
27 108 20 27 81 45     (Dec)
```

In text mode, the printer automatically inserts a CR when the right margin is reached, whether this is the default margin or a specified margin. Any text held in its buffer is automatically wrapped around to the next line. The wrap-around occurs after a specific number of characters (or line length, for proportional text) so words may well be split at the line end.

This is suitable for dumps of files, ASCII files with single-line paragraphs and printouts whose appearance is not important. For most documents you will want to take complete control of the printing by setting your own line ends (with the CR command).

In graphics modes, there is no automatic wrap around. Any data that will not fit on the line is discarded.

Most fonts are *portrait* fonts, designed to be printed horizontally on the page, usually on paper that has a height greater than its width. On wide carriage printers, you can use the same fonts on *landscape* paper, which is rotated so that the width is greater than the height. On laser printers, and some dot matrix printers, there may be *landscape fonts*. These fonts are designed to be printed vertically rather than horizontally, allowing you to print on landscape paper. Since the paper tray in most laser printers only accepts paper in portrait mode, such fonts are essential if you want to print in landscape mode.

In some cases the landscape fonts are separate fonts, designed specifically for the purpose. In other cases, they are same font in which the dot pattern has been rotated through 90.

4 Print Position

In text modes the position of the print head can be set to any position on the paper, using a variety of commands.

Moving the print head to the left

Two basic commands apply to almost all printers: CR (backspace: to move the print head back to the beginning of the line) and BS (to move the head left one position).

Command:	Carriage return	
Printers:	All matrix printers	
Syntax:	CR	(ASCII)
	0D	(hex)
	13	(dec)
Parameters:	None	
Effect:	Moves the print head left to the start of the line, without advancing the paper, after printing any data in the buffer. This command allows overprinting of a line and can be repeated any number of times. To start a new line, follow the command with a line feed; most printers can be set up to automatically insert an LF after each CR.	

Command:	Backspace	
Printers:	All matrix printers	
Syntax:	BS	(ASCII)
	08	(hex)
	8	(dec)
Parameters:	None	
Effect:	Moves the print head left one position, after printing any data in the buffer. Therefore, the previous character can be overprinted. The command is ignored in the following circumstances: the text is justified, right-justified or proportional; the	

print head is already at the left
margin; the previous character is HT
or a dot position command. In bit
image printing, the print head is
moved back to the point at which bit
image mode was selected. See also
the DEL command.

It is important to note that both of these commands force all characters in the buffer to be printed before any further action is taken.

Command:	Incremental backspace	
Printers:	Diablo	
Syntax:	ESC BS	(ASCII)
	1B 08	(hex)
	27 8	(dec)
Parameters:	None	
Effect:	Moves the print head backwards by $1/120$".	

Moving the print head to the right

When any text is printed, the print head automatically moves to the right. You can advance the print head a specific distance by printing one or more spaces (20h, 32). You can also specify the distance to advance with the ESC f command (functionally equivalent to the BASIC PRINT SPACE$(n) command). The ESC f command can also be used to replace a sequence of LF characters.

Command:	Horizontal/vertical skip	
Printers:	ESC/P ext	
Syntax:	ESC f n1 n2	(ASCII)
	1B 66 n1 n2	(hex)
	27 102 n1 n2	(dec)
Parameters:	n1 = 0 (horizontal)	
	1 (vertical)	
	n2 = number of spaces/lines	
Effect:	When n1=0, n2 spaces are printed.	

When $n1$=1, $n2$ line feeds (in current line spacing) are generated.

Horizontal tabs

To line up columns of output, you can set *tab positions*. These are predefined points to which the print head will move when an HT (horizontal tab) command is received.

Command:	Horizontal tab	
Printers:	All matrix printers	
Syntax:	HT	(ASCII)
	09	(hex)
	9	(dec)
Parameters:	None	
Effect:	Moves print head to next horizontal tab position (by default, every eight characters). Tabs are changed with ESC D. If the print head is already beyond the last tab position, the printer executes a CR LF sequence. Tab stops outside the current margins are ignored. Tabs are only effective when printing unjustified text (monospaced or proportional). HT characters are often found in ASCII files.	

No scoring (underscore etc.) is done for the distance moved by the print head; the tabbed area is completely blank.

If you are controlling the printout directly from the printer, you may want to replace the HT characters by a calculated number of spaces.

When creating text files, the usual convention is to translate the Tab key to an HT character.

For graphics printing, the horizontal position can be changed with ESC $ and ESC \.

Tab positions

By default, there is a tab stop every eight characters. For example, a standard width printer, printing at 10 cpi, will have default tab stops at 0.8", 1.6", 2.4", ..., 7.2". These are not affected by later changes to character width but can be replaced by a new set of tabs. Some printers allow the setting of variable tabs with ESC D; in other cases, tab stops are set with ESC e and are equidistant.

Command:	Set horizontal tabs
Printers:	ESC/P 81, IBM Proprinters
Syntax:	ESC D *n1 n2* ... NUL (ASCII)
	1B 44 *n1 n2* ... 00 (hex)
	27 68 *n1 n2* ... 0 (dec)
Parameters:	*n1,n2* = 1...255 characters
Effect:	Sets horizontal tab position in terms of characters in the current pitch, relative to the current left margin. For proportional spacing, 10 cpi is assumed. Subsequent changes in pitch do not affect the tab positions. Up to 32 tabs can be set for Epsons, 28 for IBM. The parameters (*n1, n2*, etc.) must be in ascending order and terminated by a NUL character. The command must be at the start of a line; otherwise it is ignored. All tabs are cleared by an ESC D NUL command, or by a change to the margins (ESC l or ESC Q); subsequent HT commands have no effect. Re-initialisation of the printer restores the default tabs. On IBM-compatibles, ESC R resets horizontal and vertical tabs without re-initialising other settings.
Variations:	Epson MX, RX allow a maximum 28 tab stops.
	IBM tabs are set at specific *column* positions, so changing the pitch also changes the tabs.

Command:	Set horizontal/vertical tabs
Printers:	ESC/P ext
Syntax:	ESC e *n1 n2* (ASCII)
	1B 65 *n1 n2* (hex)
	27 101 *n1 n2* (dec)

Parameters:	$n1$ = 0 (horizontal tabs)
	1 (vertical tabs)
	$n2$ varies
Effect:	When $n1$ = 0, horizontal tab stops are set at regular intervals from the current left margin. The distance between tab stops is given by $n2$, in terms of characters. The maximum value for $n2$ is 21 (10 cpi), 25 (12 cpi) or 36 (condensed). The tabs are cancelled or replaced by any subsequent ESC D command. When $n1$=1, vertical tab stops are set at regular intervals from the current top-of-form. The distance between tab stops is given in $n2$, in terms of lines (in the current line spacing). This command is overridden by any later ESC B or ESC b 0 command.

Command:	Reset all tabs	
Printers:	IBM Proprinter	
Syntax:	ESC R	(ASCII)
	1B 52	(hex)
	27 82	(dec)
Parameters:	None	
Effect:	Cancels the effects of ESC D and ESC B. Resets all horizontal tabs to their power-on defaults and clears all vertical tabs.	

Incremental print head movement

On the IBM Proprinter and compatibles, you can move the print head to the right by any amount, in units of $1/120$".

Command:	Move print head right	
Printers:	IBM Proprinter	
Syntax:	ESC d *n1 n2*	(ASCII)
	1B 64 *n1 n2*	(hex)
	27 100 *n1 n2*	(dec)
Parameters:	$n1$ = Number of units to move	
	$n2$ = Number of 25-unit blocks to move	

Effect:	Moves the print head to the right by a number of units given by the formula $n1 + (n2 \times 256)$. The units are measured in terms of $1/120$". For example, to move right three inches, set $n1 = 104$ (decimal) and $n2 = 1$. The print head cannot be moved beyond the right margin. Any underscoring and overscoring remains in effect.

Command:	Set horizontal tab stop	
Printers:	Diablo	
Syntax:	ESC 1	(ASCII)
	1B 31	(hex)
	27 49	(dec)
Parameters:	None	
Effect:	Sets a horizontal tab stop at the current print position. Up to 63 tabs can be effective at any time. Release a tab with ESC 8 or cancel all tabs with ESC 2 .	

Command:	Release horizontal tab stop	
Printers:	Diablo	
Syntax:	ESC 8	(ASCII)
	1B 38	(hex)
	27 56	(dec)
Parameters:	None	
Effect:	Cancels the horizontal tab stop at the current print position. Cancel all tabs with ESC 2.	

Command:	Clear all tab stops	
Printers:	Diablo	
Syntax:	ESC 2	(ASCII)
	1B 32	(hex)
	27 50	(dec)
Parameters:	None	
Effect:	Cancels all horizontal and vertical tab stops. New tabs can be set with ESC 1 and ESC -. Individual horizontal tabs can be cancelled with ESC 8.	

Command:	Absolute horizontal tab	
Printers:	Diablo	
Syntax:	ESC HT n	(ASCII)
	1B 09 n	(hex)
	27 9 n	(dec)
Parameters:	n = 1...126	
Effect:	Moves the print head to column n, measured from the absolute left-hand edge of the page. This command is ignored when the HMI is set to 0.	

Command:	Set HMI	
Printers:	Diablo	
Syntax:	ESC US n	(ASCII)
	1B IF n	(hex)
	27 31 n	(dec)
Parameters:	n = 1...126	
Effect:	Sets the Horizontal Motion Index (HMI) to be (n-1) x 1/120". The HMI is the width allocated to each character in fixed-space fonts, or the width allocated to spaces in proportional fonts. The default is reset with ESC S.	

Command:	Cancel HMI	
Printers:	Diablo	
Syntax:	ESC S	(ASCII)
	1B 53	(hex)
	27 83	(dec)
Parameters:	None	
Effect:	Cancels the HMI set by ESC US, restoring the default setting from the front panel.	

One-directional printing

In some circumstances, it is useful to select a mode in which the print head moves in one direction only. This is particularly helpful when using the box-drawing characters or other graphics. Obviously, print speeds are also reduced. One-directional printing can be selected for either a single line or for all subsequent lines; printing is always from left to right.

Command:	Select one-directional printing (one line)
Printers:	ESC/P ext
Syntax:	ESC < (ASCII)
	1B 3C (hex)
	27 60 (dec)
Parameters:	None
Effect:	One-directional printing is selected for the current line only and is cancelled when the line is printed. See also ESC U.

Command:	Select/cancel one-directional printing (permanent)
Printers:	ESC/P 80, IBM Proprinter
Syntax:	ESC U *n* (ASCII)
	1B 55 *n* (hex)
	27 85 *n* (dec)
Parameters:	*n* = 0 (bi-directional)
	1 (one-directional)
Effect:	When *n*=1, one-directional printing is selected. This mode continues until the command is repeated with *n*=0 or the printer is re-initialised. For Epson-compatibility see also ESC <.

Command:	Set backward printing
Printers:	Diablo
Syntax:	ESC 6 (ASCII)
	1B 36 (hex)
	27 54 (dec)
Parameters:	None
Effect:	All characters are printed backwards, from right to left. This continues until the ESC 5 command is issued or a CR is received. With care, this command can be used to produce bi-directional printing.

Command:	Cancel backward printing
Printers:	Diablo
Syntax:	ESC 5 (ASCII
	1B 35 (hex
	27 53 (dec

Parameters:	None
Effect:	Cancels the reverse printing that was activated by ESC 6.

Moving the paper up and down

For line printers, the vertical position of the print head is determined not by physical movement of the print head but by moving the paper. To position the print head lower down the page the paper must move up, and vice versa.

Two basic commands apply to all matrix printers: LF (to advance the paper one line) and FF (to advance the top of the next page).

Command:	Line feed	
Printers:	All matrix printers	
Syntax:	LF	(ASCII)
	0A	(hex)
	10	(dec)
Parameters:	None	
Effect:	Advances the paper by one line (in current spacing), without moving print head, after printing any data in the buffer. Most printers can be set up to automatically add a CR to any lone LF.	

For multiple line feeds, you can use ESC f (described above). The FF command is covered earlier in this chapter.

The CR LF sequence

Some applications send a complete CR LF sequence at the end of each line while others send only the CR. Most printers can be configured to automatically add a line feed after each carriage return received. This can be done in a number of ways:

- Send a command sequence to turn on or off the automatic line feed.

- Set a dip switch or other external switch on the printer to automatically add a line feed.

- Clear pin 14 of the parallel cable.

If the software and printer are not configured correctly, the result will be either that a line continually overprints (an extra LF is needed for each CR) or the text is double-spaced when it should not be (both ends of the process are adding an LF).

Command:	Set automatic carriage return	
Printers:	Diablo	
Syntax:	ESC ?	(ASCII)
	1B 3F	(hex)
	27 63	(dec)
Parameters:	None	
Effect:	Automatically inserts a CR LF sequence when the print head moves beyond the print area. The command is cancelled by ESC !.	

Command:	Cancel automatic carriage return	
Printers:	Diablo	
Syntax:	ESC !	(ASCII)
	1B 21	(hex)
	27 33	(dec)
Parameters:	None	
Effect:	Cancels the automatic insertion of CR LF set by ESC ?.	

Variable line feeds

You can also advance the paper by a specific amount (rather than by a precise number of lines) using the Epson ESC J command. On some printers, you can move the print head back up the paper by performing a reverse feed (Epson ESC j). These commands do not affect the position of the print head; there is no carriage return added.

Command:	Variable line feed	
Printers:	ESC/P 81, IBM Proprinter	
Syntax:	ESC J *n*	(ASCII)
	1B 4A *n*	(hex)
	27 74 *n*	(dec)
Parameters:	*n* = 1...255 (fractions of inch)	
Effect:	The paper is advanced by a specified amount, in units of ½₁₆" for 9-pin Epson printers or ½₁₈₀" for all other Epson printers. The print head is not affected and the current line spacing is irrelevant.	

For IBM Proprinters in normal mode, the line feed is in units of ½₁₆" and *n* should be an exact multiple of 3; the units can be varied by the ESC [\ command. When in Alternate Graphics Mode, the effect is the same as for the Epsons.

Command:	Forward half-line feed	
Printers:	Diablo	
Syntax:	ESC U	(ASCII)
	1B 55	(hex)
	27 85	(dec)
Parameters:	None	
Effect:	Moves the print head down by half a line. This command is ignored when the VMI is set to 0.	

Command:	Variable reverse line feed	
Printers:	ESC/P ext	
Syntax:	ESC j *n*	(ASCII)
	1B 6A *n*	(hex)
	27 106 *n*	(dec)
Parameters:	*n* = 1...255 (½₁₆")	
Effect:	The paper is reverse fed in units of ½₁₆". The print head is not affected. Use of this command should be avoided. Accuracy suffers if the movement is more than ½₁₂" and the command may cause the paper to jam if it is near the top of bottom of the sheet. Never attempt to reverse feed when printing labels. The	

	command is ignored if a sheet feeder is in use.	

Command:	Reverse line feed	
Printers:	Diablo	
Syntax:	ESC LF	(ASCII)
	1B 0A	(hex)
	27 10	(dec)
Parameters:	None	
Effect:	Moves the print head back up the page one line.	

Command:	Reverse half-line feed	
Printers:	Diablo	
Syntax:	ESC D	(ASCII)
	1B 44	(hex)
	27 68	(dec)
Parameters:	None	
Effect:	Moves the print head back up the page by half a line. This command is ignored when VMI is 0.	

The variable line feed command is useful where precise positioning is important. Reverse line feed should only be needed if a line being printed requires some additional printing in the space immediately above.

Alternate Graphics Mode (AGM)
The IBM Proprinters X24 and XL24 have an *Alternate Graphics Mode* (AGM), selected by dip switches, in which a high-resolution 24-pin mode is put into effect. The result is that the ESC J, ESC 3 and ESC A commands, which affect line spacing, adopt the standard 1/180" units of the corresponding Epson commands.

Vertical tabs

You can set vertical tabs in a similar way to horizontal tabs. The vertical tab is a point to which the paper will be moved, positioning the print head at a specific distance from the top-of-form. Each time a vertical tab command is received, the paper advances to the next vertical tab stop.

Command:	Vertical tab
Printers:	ESC/P 81, IBM Proprinter, Diablo
Syntax:	VT (ASCII)
	0B (hex)
	11 (dec)
Parameters:	None
Effect:	Advances paper so that print head is at next vertical tab stop. By default, there are no vertical tab stops and the effect is the same as an LF command. Tab positions are set with the ESC B and ESC b commands. If the print head is below the last vertical tab stop (or the next tab is in an active perforation skip area), the paper advances to the next top-of-form. Most printers can be set up to add an LF to each CR; in such cases, an LF is automatically added to the VT.

Channels and tab positions
Unlike horizontal tabs, you can create up to eight sets of vertical tab stops. These are referred to as *channels* and are numbered 0 to 7.

If you are only using channel 0 (the default), the tabs can be set with the ESC B command. For some printers, the channel 0 tabs can also be set with ESC e, which also sets horizontal tabs and is described above. For more than one channel, use ESC b. The current channel (to which any subsequent VT commands apply) is set with ESC /.

Command:	Set vertical tabs (channel 0)
Printers:	ESC/P 81, IBM Proprinter
Syntax:	ESC B *n1 n2* ... NUL (ASCII)
	1B 42 *n1 n2* ... 00 (hex)
	27 66 *n1 b2* ... 0 (dec)
Parameters:	*n1, n2,* ... = 1...255 lines
Effect:	Sets vertical tab positions for default channel 0, in terms of lines (using the current line spacing), relative to the current top-of-form. Subsequent changes to line spacing do not affect existing vertical tabs. Up to 16 vertical tabs can be set for Epsons, 64 for IBM. The parameters (*n1, n2,* etc.) must be in ascending numerical order and terminated by a NUL character. Any tabs set by ESC b 0 are overridden by this command. All tabs are cleared by an ESC B NUL command or re-initialisation of the printer. On IBM-compatibles, the ESC R command clears all horizontal and vertical tabs.

Command:	Set vertical tabs (all channels)
Printers:	ESC/P ext
Syntax:	ESC b *n n1 n2* ... NUL (ASCII)
	1B 62 *n n1 n2* ... 00 (hex)
	27 98 *n n1 n2* ... 0 (dec)
Parameters:	*n* = 0...7 (channel)
	n1, n2,... = 1...155 lines (tab stops)
Effect:	Sets vertical tabs for a specific channel *n*. The tabs for this channel are cleared by ESC b *n* NUL or re-initialisation (or ESC R on IBM-compatibles). If *n*=0, any tabs set by ESC B are overridden. All other comments are as for the ESC B command (above).

Command:	Select vertical tab channel
Printers:	ESC/P ext
Syntax:	ESC / *n* (ASCII)
	1B 2F *n* (hex)
	27 47 *n* (dec)

Parameters: n = 0...7
Effect: Selects a vertical tab channel, to which all subsequent VT commands apply. Tabs can be changed with ESC B (for channel 0) or ESC b (any channel).

Command: Set vertical tab stop
Printers: Diablo
Syntax:
ESC -	(ASCII)
1B 2D	(hex)
27 45	(dec)

Parameters: None
Effect: Sets a vertical tab stop at the current line. Up to 63 vertical tab stops can be effective at any time.

Command: Absolute vertical tab
Printers: Diablo
Syntax:
ESC VT n	(ASCII)
1B 0B n	(hex)
27 11 n	(dec)

Parameters: n = 1...126
Effect: Move the print head to line n, measured from the absolute top of page. This command is ignored when the VMI is 0.

Command: Set VMI
Printers: Diablo
Syntax:
ESC RS n	(ASCII)
1B 1E n	(hex)
27 30 n	(dec)

Parameters: n = 1...126
Effect: Sets the Vertical Motion Index (VMI) to be (n-1) x $\frac{1}{48}$". This determines the line spacing for all relevant commands. The front panel settings are overridden by this command.

Line spacing

When text prints over the end of a line or an LF command is received, the printer is advanced by one line. By default, the distance from the top of one line to the next is $1/6$". This spacing is also used by commands that set tabs, perforation skip, page length, etc.

A number of commands exist to change the current line spacing. Any line-spacing command supersedes any previous command. Printer initialisation resets line spacing to its default. Spacing is given in terms of lines per inch (lpi) or in fractions of an inch.

The maximum depth of any printed line (with all pins used) is $27/216$" (= $9/72$" = $1/8$") for 9-pin printers or $24/180$" (= $8/60$") for other printers. Setting the line spacing to this amount will result in there being no gap or overlap for consecutive lines. This is particularly useful for graphics printing or images constructed from box-drawing characters in text mode.

Command:	Select $1/8$" line spacing	
Printers:	ESC/P 80, IBM Proprinter	
Syntax:	ESC 0	(ASCI
	1B 30	(he:
	27 48	(de•
Parameters:	None	
Effect:	Sets line spacing at 8 lpi for all future line feeds and associated commands	

Command:	Select $7/72$" line spacing	
Printers:	ESC/P ext, IBM Proprinter	
Syntax:	ESC 1	(ASC
	1B 31	(he
	27 49	(de
Parameters:	None	
Effect:	Sets line spacing at $7/72$" for all future line feeds and associated commands. This is just over 10 lpi (72 lines printed in each 7" vertically)	

Command:	Select ⅙" line spacing
Printers:	ESC/P 80, IBm Proprinter
Syntax:	ESC 2 (ASCII)
	1B 32 (hex)
	27 50 (dec)
Parameters:	None
Effect:	Sets line spacing at 6 lpi for all future line feeds and associated commands. This is the default that is adopted at power on or printer initialisation (unless the printer's default configuration is changed by dip switches or front panel settings).
	Variations: For IBM Proprinters in normal mode, effects the spacing selected by ESC A.

Command:	Select variable line spacing (medium units)
Printers:	ESC/P 81, IBM Proprinter
Syntax:	ESC 3 n (ASCII)
	1B 33 n (hex)
	27 51 n (dec)
Parameters:	n = 0...255 (fractions of inch)
Effect:	Epson: The line spacing is set to $^n/216$" for 9-pin printers or $^n/180$" for all other printers.

IBM: In normal mode, the line spacing is set to $^n/216$", where n is a multiple of 3. The units can be changed with ESC [\. In Alternate Graphics Mode, the units are $1/180$", as for Epson.

Command:	Select variable line spacing (large units)
Printers:	ESC/P 80, IBM Proprinter
Syntax:	ESC A n (ASCII)
	1B 41 n (hex)
	27 65 n (dec)
Parameters:	n = 0...85 (fractions of inch)
Effect:	The line spacing is set to $^n/72$" for 9-pin Epson-compatible printers or $^n/60$" for all other Epson-compatible printers.

For IBM Proprinters in normal mode, the line spacing is $n/72$" and the command must be followed by ESC 2, e.g. to set $1/6$" spacing ($=10/60$"), the command is ESC A FF ESC 2, where FF is decimal 12.

When in Alternate Graphics Mode, the command works identically to the Epson.

Command:	Select variable line spacing (small units)
Printers:	ESC/P ext
Syntax:	ESC + n (ASCII
	1B 2B n (hex
	27 43 n (dec
Parameters:	n = 0...255 (fractions of inch)
Effect:	The line spacing is set to $n/360$" for all future line feeds and associated commands.

Command:	Set vertical tab units
Printers:	IBM Proprinter
Syntax:	ESC [\ EOT NUL NUL NUL NUL n (ASCII
	1B 5B 5C 04 00 00 00 00 n (hex
	27 91 92 4 0 0 0 0 n (dec
Parameters:	n = 180 or 216 (decimal)
Effect:	Sets the units for the vertical spacing commands ESC J and ESC 3 to either $1/180$" or $1/216$" (the default).

Command:	Set lines per inch
Printers:	LaserJet
Syntax:	ESC & l n D (ASCII
	1B 26 6C n 44 (hex
	27 38 108 n 72 (dec
Parameters:	n = 0...8, 12, 16, 24, 48
Effect:	Sets the line spacing in terms of the number of lines per inch. This command has an effect on the Set Paper Size, Set Top Margin and Set Text Length commands. It remains in effect until the number of lines per inch is reset or the VMI is changed with the Set VMI command.

Vertical Movement Increment (VMI)

The distance that the printer position moves down a page when a new line is started is termed the Vertical Movement Increment (VMI). The value of the VMI can be changed with a LaserJet command or Diablo 630 command.

Command:	Set VMI	
Printers:	LaserJet	
Syntax:	ESC & l *n* C	(ASCII)
	1B 26 6C *n* 43	(hex)
	27 38 108 *n* 67	(dec)
Parameters:	*n* = 0...336	
Effect:	Sets the Vertical Movement Increment in terms of $1/48$". This command has an effect on the page length, top margin and text length. The command remains in effect until a new VMI is set or the number of lines per inch is changed. The default VMI is determined by the current font.	

Page printers

For page printers, the position at which a character is printed is not determined by the physical movement of a print head. The entire page is held in memory as it is being constructed, before it is physically printed. The printer maintains in memory values for the current position (horizontally and vertically). This position, which is known as the *active position*, is updated automatically every time you send a character. When a character is printed, the active position moves one character width to the right. When an end of line is reached, the active position moves to the start of the next line.

For printers that use the LaserJet commands, you can choose the current position on the page at any time. The position can be chosen either in absolute terms, measured from the left-hand margin at the top of the page, or relative to the current printer position. The units of movement can be given in lines or columns, decipoints or dots. A *decipoint* is $1/10$th of a printer's point (which in turn, is $1/72$"). There are therefore 720 decipoints to the inch. Alternatively, for most printers there are 300 dots per inch. When using lines, columns or decipoints, the print position will be taken to the nearest dot.

Distances can be given in absolute terms or relative terms. To move relative to the current position put a plus (+) or minus (-) in front of the parameter. A '+' value moves the position to the right or down the page, a '-' value moves the position to the left or up the page.

Command:	Move horizontally (by columns)	
Printers:	LaserJet	
Syntax:	ESC & a *n* C	(ASCII)
	1B 26 61 *n* 43	(hex)
	27 38 97 *n* 67	(dec)
Parameters:	*n* = number of columns	
Effect:	Moves the active position horizontally along the current line. The parameter is given in terms of columns, one column being the width of a space in the current font.	

Command:	Move horizontally (by decipoints)	
Printers:	LaserJet	
Syntax:	ESC & a *n* H	(ASCII)
	1B 26 61 *b* 48	(hex)
	27 38 97 *n* 72	(dec)
Parameters:	*n* = number of decipoints	
Effect:	Moves the active position horizontally along the current line. The parameter is given in terms of decipoints.	

Command:	Move horizontally (by dots)	
Printers:	LaserJet	
Syntax:	ESC * p *n* X	(ASCII)
	1B 2A 70 *n* 58	(hex)
	27 42 112 *n* 88	(dec)
Parameters:	*n* = number of dots	
Effect:	Moves the active position horizontally along the current line. The parameter is given in terms of dots.	

Command:	Move vertically (by lines)	
Printers:	LaserJet	
Syntax:	ESC & a n R	(ASCII)
	1B 26 61 n 52	(hex)
	27 38 97 n 82	(dec)
Parameters:	n = number of lines	
Effect:	Moves the active position vertically on the page. The parameter is given in terms of the current line spacing.	

Command:	Move vertically (by decipoints)	
Printers:	LaserJet	
Syntax:	ESC * p n V	(ASCII)
	1B 2A 70 n 56	(hex)
	27 42 112 n 86	(dec)
Parameters:	n = number of decipoints	
Effect:	Moves the active position vertically on the page. The parameter is given in terms of decipoints.	

Command:	Move vertically (by dots)	
Printers:	LaserJet	
Syntax:	ESC * p n Y	(ASCII)
	1B 2A 70 n 59	(hex)
	27 42 112 n 89	(dec)
Parameters:	n = number of dots	
Effect:	Moves the active position vertically on the page, the parameter is given in terms of dots.	

In all the above commands, a movement which takes the active position outside the printable area results in the current position being placed at the edge of the page. If you move over the bottom of the page, a form feed is forced and the current position placed at the top of the next page. For LaserJet printers, you can also specify that the print position moves down by half the current line height.

Command:	Half-line feed	
Printers:	LaserJet	
Syntax:	ESC =	(ASCII)
	1B 3D	(hex)
	27 61	(dec)

Parameters:	None
Effect:	Moves the active position down by half the height of the current line spacing.

Saving the active position

In some circumstances you might want to remember where on the page you had currently reached before some other operation took place. The Laser-Jet commands provide two instructions, one of which stores the current active position on a stack in memory, the other which retrieves the last active position that was stored on the stack. Placing values on the stack is generally referred to as *pushing* while retrieving values from the stack is termed *popping*.

Command:	Push/pop position	
Printers:	LaserJet	
Syntax:	ESC & f *n* S	(ASCII
	1B 26 66 *n* 53	(hex
	27 38 102 *n* 83	(dec
Parameters:	*n* = 0 (push)	
	1 (pop)	
Effect:	When *n* = 0 the current active position (horizontally and vertically) is stored on a stack in printer memory. When *n* = 1, the last active position to be stored is removed from the stack and the current position is restored to that point.	

Command:	Select graphics mode	
Printers:	Diablo	
Syntax:	ESC 3	(ASCII
	1B 33	(hex
	27 51	(dec
Parameters:	None	
Effect:	This command produces a crude form of graphics mode. Since it was originally created for daisywheel printers, it is still character-based. The result is that the following four commands, produce incremental	

movement, allowing you to place any character in any position:

SPC	Move right $\frac{1}{60}$"
BS	Move back $\frac{1}{60}$"
LF	Move down $\frac{1}{48}$"
ESC LF	Move up $\frac{1}{48}$"

These are the only commands that move the print head; the print head does not move automatically after printing each normal character. The command is cancelled by ESC 4.

Command:	Cancel graphics mode	
Printers:	Diablo	
Syntax:	ESC 4	(ASCII)
	1B 34	(hex)
	27 52	(dec)
Parameters:	None	
Effect:	Cancels the graphics mode selected with ESC 4.	

5 Character Sets and Fonts

character set is a collection of characters that are epresented by a sequence of numeric codes. For xample, the standard ASCII character set provides umeric representations for 128 control codes and haracters. However, there are many other characters that also need to be printed. As a result, there more than one character set available on most rinters. The font determines the way in which the aaracter set is printed.

efinitions

ae main problem with printer terminology is that e terms are derived from two different sources: aditional typewriters and typesetting. Each of ese has its own traditional terms and, mixed with e standard computer jargon, some confusion is evitable.

The definitions of typefaces, fonts, etc. tend to ry from one book or manual to another. The finitions used in this book are given below.

A *character set* determines what character or mbol is printed for a particular ASCII code. It es not determine the appearance or size of that aaracter. For example, the standard ASCII code h produces J while the Symbol character set ves a different character.

The *typeface* determines the overall appearance individual characters. For example, the Helvetica peface gives letters with no serifs while Times ds a serif to the end of each line. Other typefaces :lude Bookman and New Century Schoolbook.

The *type style* determines the slant, weight and ier similar features of the character. Type styles :lude bold, italic, shadowed, etc.

The *size* determines the height and width of the aaracter. For example, on dot matrix printers, the e may be pica or elite, six lines per inch or eight lines per inch; on a laser printer, the size is given in terms of point size.

Finally, the definition which causes the most confusion, is that of the *font*. In this book, the font taken to relate to a table held in the printer memory that determines precisely how the character will be printed. For dot matrix printers, type styles such as italic and condensed print are created by taking an existing table of dot information and modifying it. Therefore, the italic, bold and condensed versions of a character are merely variations of a single font; changing to a different typeface requires a different font. For most laser printers, on the other hand, there is a different table of information for each type style and each size. Therefore, 10-point bold, 10-point italic and 20-point bold are three different fonts for any of the typefaces. Finally, the introduction of *scalable fonts* means that a single table is required which can be mathematically adjusted to produce characters any size, slant and weight; in these cases this treated as a single font.

Confusion arises because some books will treat Helvetica as a single font, regardless of the variations of slant, weight and size, while a printer manual may treat every variation as a different font, regardless of whether it is produced by a formula or from a different table.

A *font family* is a group of fonts that have the same typeface. For example, Helvetica Bold 1 point and Helvetica Italic 8-point both belong to the Helvetica font family.

Character sets

Anything that does not form part of a control code is treated by the printer as a *character*. Characters include letters (both upper and lower case, numeric digits, punctuation marks, mathematical symbols and graphics symbols. The space (ASCII SPC, dec 32, 20h) is also usually classed as a 'character'.

All printers will treat codes in the range 32 to 126 as characters, unless they are part of a recognised command sequence. Those that can handle extended character sets will also accept codes in the range 128 to 255; otherwise, the eighth bit is used for parity checking or simply ignored (effectively, reducing the code value by 128). Codes in the range 0 to 31 and 127 are treated as *control codes* and acted upon where possible, otherwise ignored.

A *character set* is a collection of characters, usually corresponding to the codes 0 to 127 or 0 to 255. The most commonly-used character sets are the standard ASCII set (0 to 127) and extended ASCII (0 to 255). Other character sets may be supplied in printer ROM, as plug-in fonts or as downloaded user-defined character sets.

National variations

The ASCII character set in Figure 5.1 is the original set, as defined by the American Standards Organisation. Clearly, different countries have different needs. Therefore, the ASCII standard now encompasses several variations of the original character set, in which specific characters are replaced by characters more relevant to different countries. For each of the countries covered by the international standard, certain characters will vary. All other characters and codes are standard, regardless of nationality. The characters that vary and the countries to which these apply are listed in Figure 5.2.

A country-dependent character set can be selected in the following ways:

● By setting dip switches (this provides the default at power-on)

By selecting from the font-panel options (giving the user the opportunity to select a different set during printing)

ASCII character set

Dec	Hex	Char	Dec	Hex	Char	Dec	Hex	Char	Dec	Hex	Char
0	00	NUL	32	20	Space	64	40	@	96	60	`
1	01	SOH	33	21	!	65	41	A	97	61	a
2	02	STX	34	22	"	66	42	B	98	62	b
3	03	ETX	35	23	#	67	43	C	99	63	c
4	04	EOT	36	24	$	68	44	D	100	64	d
5	05	ENQ	37	25	%	69	45	E	101	65	e
6	06	ACK	38	26	&	70	46	F	102	66	f
7	07	BEL	39	27	'	71	47	G	103	67	g
8	08	BS	40	28	(	72	48	H	104	68	h
9	09	HT	41	29	)	73	49	I	105	69	i
10	0A	LF	42	2A	*	74	4A	J	106	6A	j
11	0B	VT	43	2B	+	75	4B	K	107	6B	k
12	0C	FF	44	2C	,	76	4C	L	108	6C	l
13	0D	CR	45	2D	-	77	4D	M	109	6D	m
14	0E	SO	46	2E	.	78	4E	N	110	6E	n
15	0F	SI	47	2F	/	79	4F	O	111	6F	o
16	10	DLE	48	30	0	80	50	P	112	70	p
17	11	DC1	49	31	1	81	51	Q	113	71	q
18	12	DC2	50	32	2	82	52	R	114	72	r
19	13	DC3	51	33	3	83	53	S	115	73	s
20	14	DC4	52	34	4	84	54	T	116	74	t
21	15	NAK	53	35	5	85	55	U	117	75	u
22	16	SYN	54	36	6	86	56	V	118	76	v
23	17	ETB	55	37	7	87	57	W	119	77	w
24	18	CAN	56	38	8	88	58	X	120	78	x
25	19	EM	57	39	9	89	59	Y	121	79	y
26	1A	SUB	58	3A	:	90	5A	Z	122	7A	z
27	1B	ESC	59	3B	;	91	5B	[	123	7B	{
28	1C	FS	60	3C	<	92	5C	\	124	7C		
29	1D	GS	61	3D	=	93	5D	]	125	7D	}
30	1E	RS	62	3E	>	94	5E	^	126	7E	~
31	1F	US	63	3F	?	95	5F	_	127	7F	△

Figure 2.7

- By sending a command sequence (either by the user from within the document, or by the programmer)

Note that selecting a new character set has no effect on the characters on-screen. For example, pressing the] key will normally produce] on both the screen and printer; selecting the Swedish character set results in Å being printed but the character on screen is still I and the user must still press the I key.

Command:	Select international character set
Printers:	ESC/P 81
Syntax:	ESC R *n* (ASCII)
	1B 52 *n* (hex)
	27 82 *n* (dec)
Parameters:	*n* = 0...13, 64
Effect:	Selects an international character set, affecting twelve standard ASCII codes. Fifteen character sets are widely available, as shown in Figure 5.2.

International Symbols

	35	36	64	91	92	93	94	96	123	124	125	126
decimal	35	36	64	91	92	93	94	96	123	124	125	126
hex	23	24	40	5B	5C	5D	5E	60	7B	7C	7D	7E
USA	#	$	@	[	\	]	^	'	{	|	}	~
France	#	$	à	°	ç	§	^	'	é	ù	è	¨
Germany	#	$	§	Ä	Ö	Ü	^	'	ä	ö	ü	ß
UK	£	$	@	[	\	]	^	'	{	|	}	~
Denmark I	#	$	@	Æ	Ø	Å	^	'	æ	ø	å	~
Sweden	#	¤	É	Ä	Ö	Å	Ü	é	ä	ö	å	ü
Italy	#	$	@	°	\	é	^	ù	à	ò	è	ì
Spain I	Pt	$	@	¡	Ñ	¿	^	'	z	ñ	}	~
Japan	#	$	@	[	¥	]	^	'	{	|	}	~
Norway	#	¤	É	Æ	Ø	Å	Ü	é	æ	ø	å	ü
Denmark II	#	$	É	Æ	Ø	Å	Ü	é	æ	ø	å	ü
Spain II	#	$	á	¡	Ñ	¿	é	'	í	ñ	ó	ú
Latin America	#	$	á	¡	Ñ	¿	é	ü	í	ñ	ó	ú
Korea	#	$	@	[		]	^	'	{	|	}	~
Legal	#	$	§	"	'	"	¶	'	©	®	†	™

Figure 5.2

Extended ASCII

The standard ASCII character set covers all of the most commonly used characters: letters (both upper and lower case), numeric digits, punctuation marks, mathematical symbols and other characters. However, when printing there are many other characters that we need to produce. To allow for these additional characters, the ASCII character set has been extended to produce the *Extended ASCII* character set.

The extended character set uses the other 128 possible values for a byte, from 80h to FFh (128-255). Unfortunately, there has been very little standardisation of this extended set, as a result of which many different character tables exist.

The most widely implemented extended ASCII set is the PC-8 character set, sometimes called the IBM-US set. This character set includes all the box-drawing characters as well as a variety of foreign letters. A variation of the PC-8 character set is usually implemented on PCs for displaying characters on the screen. Therefore, you can be fairly sure that an extended character printed on the screen will be reproduced on the printer if this set has been chosen. This set is shown in Figure 5.3.

There are several national variations of the PC-8 character set, for example, PC-8DN is a version for use in Denmark and Norway.

The ROMAN-8 character set is the default supplied with most Hewlett-Packard printers. This set does not have the box-drawing characters but does allow for a wide variety of foreign letters, including many different accented characters. The ECMA-94 Latin 1 character set replaces many of the foreign characters with symbols.

The most important thing to remember when trying to print a particular character is that it is the ASCII code that is important, not the appearance of the character on screen. For example, if you use Alt-201 to produce a character on screen and this appears as a foreign character, the printed character will be whatever character is represented by

ASCII extended character set

Dec	Hex	Char	Dec	Hex	Char	Dec	Hex	Char	Dec	Hex	Char
128	80	Ç	160	A0	á	192	C0	└	224	E0	α
129	81	ü	161	A1	í	193	C1	┴	225	E1	ß
130	82	é	162	A2	ó	194	C2	┬	226	E2	Γ
131	83	â	163	A3	ú	195	C3	├	227	E3	π
132	84	ä	164	A4	ñ	196	C4	─	228	E4	Σ
133	85	à	165	A5	Ñ	197	C5	┼	229	E5	σ
134	86	å	166	A6	ª	198	C6	╞	230	E6	µ
135	87	ç	167	A7	º	199	C7	╟	231	E7	τ
136	88	ê	168	A8	¿	200	C8	╚	232	E8	Φ
137	89	ë	169	A9	⌐	201	C9	╔	233	E9	Θ
138	8A	è	170	AA	¬	202	CA	╩	234	EA	Ω
139	8B	ï	171	AB	½	203	CB	╦	235	EB	δ
140	8C	î	172	AC	¼	204	CC	╠	236	EC	∞
141	8D	ì	173	AD	¡	205	CD	═	237	ED	φ
142	8E	Ä	174	AE	«	206	CE	╬	238	EE	ε
143	8F	Å	175	AF	»	207	CF	╧	239	EF	∩
144	90	É	176	B0	░	208	D0	╨	240	F0	≡
145	91	æ	177	B1	▒	209	D1	╤	241	F1	±
146	92	Æ	178	B2	▓	210	D2	╥	242	F2	≥
147	93	ô	179	B3	│	211	D3	╙	243	F3	≤
148	94	ö	180	B4	┤	212	D4	╘	244	F4	⌠
149	95	ò	181	B5	╡	213	D5	╒	245	F5	⌡
150	96	û	182	B6	╢	214	D6	╓	246	F6	÷
151	97	ù	183	B7	╖	215	D7	╫	247	F7	≈
152	98	ÿ	184	B8	╕	216	D8	╪	248	F8	°
153	99	Ö	185	B9	╣	217	D9	┘	249	F9	∙
154	9A	Ü	186	BA	║	218	DA	┌	250	FA	·
155	9B	¢	187	BB	╗	219	DB	█	251	FB	√
156	9C	£	188	BC	╝	220	DC	▄	252	FC	ⁿ
157	9D	¥	189	BD	╜	221	DD	▌	253	FD	²
158	9E	₧	190	BE	╛	222	DE	▐	254	FE	■
159	9F	ƒ	191	BF	┐	223	DF	▀	255	FF	

Figure 5.3

decimal 201 in the printer's character set. Therefore, the characters displayed on screen may bear
no relation to the final printout.

Character position

The foreign characters may move around from one
character set to another (for example, ñ is represented by A4h in the PC-8 set but B7h in the
Roman-8 set and F1h in ECMA-94). The box-drawing characters – if present – always occupy the
same positions, regardless of character set; for example, the top left-hand corner of the double box is
always C9h.

The dot patterns of the box-drawing characters
are always the same from one typeface to another
but will change in width and emphasis from one
font to another within any font family.

The first 32 extended codes (80h to 9Fh) may be
selected to be extended characters or to duplicate
the control codes.

Command:	Select extended printable characters
Printers:	ESC/P 84
Syntax:	ESC 6 (ASCII
	1B 36 (hex
	27 54 (dec
Parameters:	None
Effect:	Selects extended codes 80h-9Fh (128-159) to be printable characters rather than control codes, except when the italic set has been chosen (with ESC t NUL) on 24-pin and 48-pin printers. This extends the italic set, character graphics or user-defined characters, depending on the ESC t command currently in effect. This command is cancelled by either ESC 7 or ESC t.

Command:	Select extended control codes
Printers:	ESC/P 84
Syntax:	ESC 7 (ASCII
	1B 37 (hex
	27 55 (dec
Parameters:	None

Effect:	Duplicates the effect of the ASCII control codes 00h-1Fh (0-31) for extended codes 80h-95h (128-159). This code is needed only to cancel the effect of ESC 6 (or to override dip switches or front-panel settings). See also ESC t.

If extended characters are selected when the printer is in italic mode, the result is a set of 32 italicised characters for which there are no normal corresponding characters.

The default is determined by dip switch settings.

On some printers you can also select a group of special graphics characters for this range.

Command:	Select extended graphics characters	
Printers:	ESC/P ext	
Syntax:	ESC m n	(ASCII)
	1B 6D n	(hex)
	27 109 n	(dec)
Parameters:	n = 0 (control codes)	
	4 (graphics characters)	
Effect:	If n=0, the characters in the range 80h-9Fh (128-159) duplicate the control codes. This version of the command is identical to ESC 7. If n=4, these codes represent a group of 32 graphics characters. This option is not effective if the character graphics set has been selected (with ESC t SOH, dip switches or front-panel switches). See also ESC 6, ESC 7 and ESC t.	

Disabled control codes

Note that all Epson and compatible printers have a special 'feature' which results in normal control codes (00h to 1Fh) being disabled. This occurs when the following three escape sequences are sent to the printer:

ESC t 1   (Select graphics set; or use dip
               switches/front panel)

ESC 6	(Print 80h to 9Fh as characters, not control codes)
ESC >	(Set bit 9 of all bytes)

These codes do not have to be sent consecutively as long as there are no cancelling command, in between.

Since the printer no longer responds to any control codes, there is no way of sending any further instructions from the PC and the printer must be reset.

For 9-pin printers, the ESC 6 and ESC > commands are sufficient to result in all future control codes being printed as graphics or italic characters.

Command:	Print suppression	
Printers:	Diablo	
Syntax:	ESC 7	(ASCII)
	1B 37	(hex)
	27 55	(dec)
Parameters:	None	
Effect:	Prints spaces in place of all characters until the next CR is encountered.	

Extended character sets

As described earlier, the extended ASCII character set varies enormously from one printer to another. For Epson printers you can select from three alternatives for the extended set, using the dip switches front panel switches or ESC t command:

● Italic characters (ESC t 0)

● Graphics characters (ESC t 1)

● RAM-based characters (ESC t 2)

The italic characters are an italicised version of the standard ASCII characters. They do not exist as a character set in memory. When an extended character code is received the corresponding normal character is selected and italicised with a standard algorithm. For example, sending code CAh result

in the character for code 4Ah (i.e. J) being italicised
and printed.

The graphics character set exists in the printer
ROM and is similar to the PC-8 set. For example,
sending CAh results in X being printed.

The RAM-based characters are a user-defined set
that must first be downloaded from the PC. They
are then mapped onto the extended codes. For example, a new character can be defined and sent to
RAM as the letter J (4Ah). When the code CAh is
received, the printer selects the character at code
4Ah in RAM (the user-defined replacement for J).

In all these cases, sending the code 4Ah prints
'J'.

Command:	Select extended character table
Printers:	ESC/P 84
Syntax:	ESC t *n* (ASCII)
	1B 74 *n* (hex)
	27 116 *n* (dec)
Parameters:	*n* = 0 (italicised set)
	1 (character graphics)
	2 (user-defined)
Effect:	If *n*=0, the character set is an italicised version of the standard character set. Following an ESC 6 command on 9-pin printers, the codes 80h-9Fh (128-159) represent additional italic characters. For the ESC 7 command, and all 24-pin and 48-pin printers, these codes are duplicates of the 00h-1Fh control codes.
	If *n*=1, the extended set is the IBM-PC8 graphics set. Other graphics sets may be selected by the user via dip switches. The codes 80-9Fh represent either additional graphics characters (ESC 6 active) or the control codes (ESC > active).
	If *n*=2, the user-defined characters in RAM for codes 00h to 7Fh (0 to 127) are mapped onto the extended set. The codes 80h-9Fh represent

either the user-defined characters for codes 00h-31h (ESC 6 active) or the standard control codes (ESC 7 active). This option is not applicable to 9-pin printers. For more information, see Chapter 6.

See also ESC m.

Accents and overprinted characters

One approach to producing accented letters and other composite characters is to print one character, move the print head left and then overprint with a second character. For example, you can produce the character ô by sending the following ASCII characters to the printer:

o BS ^

Note that the backspace character on a printer (08h) moves the print head one space to the left but does not erase the previous character. You cannot send this character from the keyboard, since pressing backspace in most applications moves the cursor left and deletes the previous character; the backspace character is never incorporated in the text and therefore is not sent directly to the printer. The code must be specifically inserted by the software.

Drawing boxes

The PC-8 character set includes a large number of line and box drawing characters. These can be put together to generate any single- or double-line box or any combination of these. The individual characters have been designed so that the unfinished lines reach to the edge of the character grid. Thus, placing two well-matched characters side-by-side results in a continuous, unbroken line. These characters can be used to draw boxes both on the screen and on any printer which accepts extended ASCII characters of the PC-8 character set.

Figure 5.4 shows a variety of boxes drawn with these characters and the codes that are needed to put them together.

Remember that if you transmit these characters to the printer but have not selected the correct character set, the result will be a rectangle of other characters.

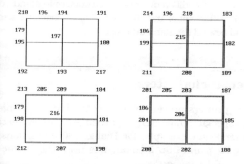

Figure 5.4 Box-drawing characters

Formulae

The printing of mathematical formulae leads to particular problems. In order to produce the superscript and subscript characters that are necessary (sometimes one immediately above the other), to draw lines and create symbols that stretch over more than one line, a great deal of programming is required. It is necessary to frequently change fonts, introduce graphics characters and so on. As a result, most applications do not even attempt to produce such formulae.

While displaying formulae on the screen is perfectly feasible, printing them becomes even more difficult. Some packages, such as WordPerfect 5 and Ventura Publisher, do manage to produce this feat to a limited extent. However, this generally involves two simple lines of text, one above another.

Symbol and Dingbat

Most laser printers (particularly PostScript-compatible printers) include two additional character sets which are very different to the standard ASCII set: Symbol and Dingbat. Each of these character sets produces an almost entirely different range of characters to standard ASCII. Both Symbol and ITC Zapf Dingbat character sets extend beyond the standard range.

Special characters

Some printers provide specific commands for printing special characters (particularly daisywheel printers). For example, for Diablo 360 emulations, the ESC Y and ESC Z commands print the characters ¬ and ¢ respectively.

Typefaces

Typefaces may be grouped together into *typeface families*. Broadly speaking, typefaces fall into the following four families:

- *Serif* typefaces end each unconnected line with a small tick (or serif).

- *Sans serif* typefaces do not have any extra mark at the end of the lines.

- *Script* typefaces end each letter in such a way that it will connect to the start of the next letter giving the appearance of handwriting.

- *Gothic* typefaces have much more ornate characters, with many of the lines doubled and additional connecting lines drawn in.

Typeface features

The appearance of a typeface is dependent upon a number of features:

- The overall shape: whether lines are curved, rounded, squared, not quite connected, etc.

- Serifs: if there are any, their shape and size

- Stress: whether this is angular, exaggerated or uniform

- Proportions: the relative size of capital height, descender height, lower-case x height, lower-case t height, slant adjust, fixed spacing and proportional spacing

Fonts can be classified by the following characteristics: orientation, character set, spacing (cpi or proportional), pitch (cpi), height (point size), style, weight, typeface. When searching for a font, the printer checks first the downloaded fonts (soft fonts), then any cartridge fonts and finally the internal fonts.

Font resolution

Scalable fonts are designed in three basic resolutions:

- *High resolution fonts* are designed for 1200 dpi on typesetting machines. These are not usually used on 300 dpi laser printers, since the time taken to compute the many extra formulae slows printing down considerably.

- *Medium resolution fonts* are designed for 300 dpi laser printers at all but the smallest point sizes.

- *Low resolution fonts* are specifically designed for small point sizes on 300 dpi laser printers. These fonts avoid the rounding errors that come into formulae when using small point sizes, ensuring that all parts of the letters are of the correct size. Such fonts are also sometimes known as *hinted fonts*.

Screen fonts

Different fonts are usually used for screen display and printer output. One of the reasons for this is that the screen display has a much lower resolution. Typically, a VGA screen on a PC has a horizontal resolution of 8 dpi. This contrasts with 120 dpi on a dot matrix printer and a minimum of 300 dpi on laser printers.

Another reason for requiring different fonts is the shape of the dots. While all dots on printed output are 'square', in that the resolution vertically is the same as that horizontally (that is, there are the same number of dots per inch across the page as down it), each pixel on a screen is actually rectangular. The screen pixel is tall and thin, the ratio of height to width generally being 4:3. This means that a character drawn on a screen, when printed using the same pattern of dots, will appear squashed. For this same reason, a true circle on the screen actually has more dots in its width than its height, so any screen dump which produces a dot-for-dot printout will produce a squashed circle.

If you add a new font to a software package, you will usually need to supply two files, one containing the font to be downloaded to the printer, the other containing a screen font.

Adding fonts

Fonts can be added to printers in two ways: as cartridges slotted into the printer or by downloading them from the PC.

When you select a font for printed output (for example, in a word processing or DTP program), the software will usually try to locate the matching screen font. If one cannot be found, it selects the nearest alternative.

Similarly, if you instruct a printer to print in a font that is not currently resident, it will usually default to a particular font (for example, Courier).

Fonts can be downloaded either before an application is run or when required for the printing of a document. If they are downloaded before the application is run, the time taken to print the document is greatly reduced, since the font will only ever have to be downloaded once. However, when more than one downloadable font is needed, the printer may run out of memory using this method.

When a font cartridge is loaded it is treated in the same way as a ROM-based font. The same algorithms may be applied to produce bold, italics, etc.

Changing typeface

When any printer is initialised it is set to print with a particular font. In most cases this is Times Roman 10cpi (or 10 point on a laser printer).

You can change the typeface (font family) with the following commands.

Command:	Select font family	
Printers:	ESC/P 83	
Syntax:	ESC k *n*	(ASCII)
	1B 6B *n*	(hex)
	27 107 *n*	(dec)
Parameters:	*n* = 0...8	
Effect:	Selects a typeface, as shown in Figure 5.5. If the selected typeface is not available, the printer defaults to Roman. These typefaces are only available in NLQ/LQ mode and will take effect when that mode is selected.	
Variations:	The type selected may vary considerably from one printer to another. For example, the table show the fonts selected by the Swift 24.	

	Font	
n	*Epson*	*Swift 24/24x*
0	Roman	Times Roman
1	Sans Serif	Helvetica
2	Courier	Helvetica
3	Prestige	Helvetica
4	Script1C	Font Card
5	OCR-B	
6	OCR-A	
7	Orator	
8	Orator-S	

igure 5.5

The user can also usually vary the default font that is used when the printer is initialised by setting the dip switches. When the printer is off-line, many printers allow the front-panel buttons to be used to change the typeface. Note that both dip switch settings and panel selections can be overridden by sending control codes directly to the printer.

On IBM Proprinters you can download fonts to the printer, if the optional FontSet module is installed.

Command:	Character font image download
Printers:	IBM Proprinter
Syntax:	ESC = (ASCII)
	1B 3D (hex)
	27 61 (dec)
Parameters:	None
Effect:	Begins a character font image download. This command is effective only if the FontSet module is installed.

For HP-compatible printers, two fonts are selected at a time: the primary and secondary fonts. The SO and SI commands switch between the two.

Command:	Select primary font
Printers:	LaserJet
Syntax:	SI (ASCII)
	0F (hex)
	15 (dec)
Parameters:	None
Effect:	Switches from the secondary font back to the primary font (the default font).

Command:	Select secondary font
Printers:	LaserJet
Syntax:	SO (ASCII)
	0E (hex)
	14 (dec)
Parameters:	None
Effect:	Switches to the secondary font for all future print operations.

Command:	Select symbol set – primary font	
Printers:	LaserJet	
Syntax:	ESC (n a	(ASCII)
	1B 28 n a	(hex)
	27 40 n a	(dec)
Parameters:	n and a define font	
Effect:	Selects a font according to the values given by the two parameters. The possible fonts that may be chosen are listed in Figure 5.6.	

LaserJet Symbol Sets

n	a	Character set
0	D	Norwegian 1 (ISO-60)
0	F	French (ISO-25)
0	G	German
0	I	Italian (ISO-15)
0	K	JIS ASCII (ISO-14)
0	N	ECMA-94/Latin 1 (ISO-100)
0	S	Swedish (ISO-11)
0	U	ANSI ASCII (ISO-6)
1	D	Norwegian 2 (ISO-62)
1	E	UK (ISO-14)
1	F	French (ISO-69)
1	G	German (ISO-21)
1	M	PC-8
2	K	Chinese (ISO-57)
2	S	Spanish (ISO-17)
2	U	International (ISO-2)
3	S	Spanish
3	S	Spanish (ISO-10)
4	S	Portuguese (ISO-16)
5	S	Portuguese (ISO-84)
6	S	Spanish (ISO-85)
8	M	PC-8 DN
8	U	Roman-8

Figure 5.6

Command:	Select symbol set – secondary font	
Printers:	LaserJet	
Syntax:	ESC) n a	(ASCII)
	1B 29 n a	(hex)
	27 41 n a	(dec)

Parameters:	*n* and *a* define font
Effect:	Selects a secondary font according to the parameters that are given. The possible fonts are listed in Figure 5.6.

Command:	Select typeface	
Printers:	LaserJet	
Syntax:	ESC (s *n* T	(ASCII)
	1B 28 73 *n* 54	(hex)
	27 40 115 *n* 84	(dec)
Parameters:	*n* = font number	
Effect:	Selects the typeface for the primary font. The font is determined by the parameter, the meaning of which is given in Figure 5.7.	

LaserJet Typefaces

n	Typeface
0	Gothic
1	Pica
2	Elite
3	Courier
4	Foundry
5	Press Roman
6	Letter Gothic
7	Script
8	Prestige
9	Caslon
10	Orator

Figure 5.7

Command:	Select typeface	
Printers:	LaserJet	
Syntax:	ESC) s *n* T	(ASCII)
	1B 29 73 *n* 54	(hex)
	27 41 115 *n* 84	(dec)
Parameters:	*n* = font number	
Effect:	Selects the typeface for the secondary font. The font is determined by the parameter, the meaning of which is given in Figure 5.7.	

Restoring defaults

For HP-compatible printers, you can restore the default settings for the current font.

Command:	Set primary font defaults
Printers:	LaserJet
Syntax:	ESC (n @ (ASCII)
	1B 28 n 58 (hex)
	27 40 n 88 (dec)
Parameters:	n = 0...3
Effect:	If n = 0 or 1, the default character set for the current orientation is selected for the primary font.
	If n = 2, the current primary character set is selected for the primary font, resulting in the font characteristics being recalculated.
	If n = 3, the default font is selected as the primary font and assigned its default values.

Command:	Set secondary font defaults
Printers:	LaserJet
Syntax:	ESC) n @ (ASCII)
	1B 29 n 58 (hex)
	27 41 n 88 (dec)
Parameters:	n = 0...3
Effect:	If n = 0, the default character set is selected for the primary font.
	If n = 1, the character set of the default primary font is put as that for the secondary font.
	If n = 2, the character set of the primary font is put as that for the secondary font.
	If n = 3, the secondary font becomes the default font and all characteristics are set to their defaults.

Font ID numbers

The Hewlett-Packard PCL commands allow you to assign a font ID number to a font once it has been selected. This ID identifies not only the typeface but also features such as the character size, style and weight. The advantage of assigning an ID number in this way is that the font can then be called up again without having to re-specify all of its characteristics. There are several stages involved.

1 The font characteristics must be set as required.

2 Use the SI code to select the primary font as the current font.

3 Assign a font ID using the ESC * c n D command, giving any number you like.

4 Use the ESC * c n F command with values of n = 4 or 5 to assign to the font as either temporary or permanent.

When you want to use a font, enter its ID number, then select either the ESC (n X or ESC) n X command.

Command:	Specify font ID	
Printers:	LaserJet	
Syntax:	ESC * c n D	(ASCII)
	1B 2A 63 n 44	(hex)
	27 42 99 n 68	(dec)
Parameters:	n = 0...32767	
Effect:	Assigns an ID number to the current font. The font can later be selected using this number. Any valid integer number may be used and you can assign up to 32 fonts at a time.	

Command:	Font & character control	
Printers:	LaserJet	
Syntax:	ESC * C n F	(ASCII)
	1B 2S 63 n 46	(hex)
	27 42 99 n 70	(dec)
Parameters:	n = 0...6	
Effect:	Deletes or assigns temporary fonts, depending on the value of the parameter.	

Command:	Download font as primary
Printers:	LaserJet

Syntax:	ESC (*n* X	(ASCII)
	1B 28 *n* 58	(hex)
	27 40 *n* 88	(dec)
Parameters:	*n* = font ID	
Effect:	Makes the font ID whose number is given the primary font. This command is only effective if the correct orientation has been selected for the font beforehand.	

Command:	Download font as secondary	
Printers:	LaserJet	
Syntax:	ESC) *n* X	(ASCII)
	1B 29 *n* 58	(hex)
	27 41 *n* 88	(dec)
Parameters:	*n* = font ID	
Effect:	Makes the font ID whose number is given the secondary font. This command is only effective if the correct orientation has been selected for the font beforehand.	

Changing print modes

Draft and NLQ printing are usually achieved by selecting different fonts. In some printers, NLQ is effected by repeat-printing each draft character and there is no NLQ font. Letter quality print is sometimes produced by both reducing the space between dots and doubling the number of dots.

When NLQ mode has been chosen, a font can be selected with ESC k.

For matrix printers, the following commands change between draft and NLQ/LQ modes.

Command:	Select draft quality or NLQ/LQ	
Printers:	ESC/P 82	
Syntax:	ESC x *n*	(ASCII)
	1B 78 *n*	(hex)
	27 120 *n*	(dec)
Parameters:	*n* = 0	(draft mode)
	1	(NLQ/LQ mode)
Effect:	Selects either draft mode or NLQ (9-pin) or LQ (24-pin, 48-pin) mode. When NLQ/LQ mode is selected, the	

> font is the last selected with ESC k or
> the default font. LQ mode is
> automatically selected for 24-pin and
> 48-pin printers when proportional
> spacing is turned on with ESC p.

Again, dip switches and panel switches provide the user with the opportunity to select a different mode for straight text (where no print-mode control codes are included).

For IBM-compatibles, a different command, ESC I, exists to select the print mode (including quality and pitch).

Command:	Select print mode	
Printers:	IBM Proprinter	
Syntax:	ESC I *n*	(ASCII)
	1B 49	(hex)
	27 73	(dec)
Parameters:	*n* = 0 - 22	
Effect:	Selects the quality, pitch and font, as shown in Figure 5.8. Any existing incompatible setting is cancelled automatically. Values not shown in the table have no effect.	

Print Mode

n	Mode
0	Draft 10 cpi Sans Serif
2	LQ 10 cpi Courier
3	LQ Proportional
4	Draft 10 cpi Downloaded
6	LQ 10 cpi Downloaded
7	LQ Proportional Downloaded
8	Draft 12 cpi (Derived from internal 10 cpi font)
10	LQ 12 cpi Prestige
12	Draft 12 cpi (Derived from downloaded draft 10 cpi font)
16	Draft 17 cpi (Derived from internal draft 10 cpi font)
18	LQ 17 cpi Courier
20	Draft 17 cpi (Derived from downloaded draft 10 cpi font)
22	LQ 17 cpi (Derived from downloaded LQ 10 cpi font)

Figure 5.8

Figure 5.9 shows how the effect can be derived from the bit values of the parameter byte.

Parameter bit values

Bit	Value if set	Effect when set	Effect when clear
0	1	Proportional	Monospaced
1	2	LQ	Draft
2	4	Downloaded	Internal
3	8	12 cpi	10 cpi
4	16	17 cpi	10 cpi

Figure 5.9

Printing speeds

Printing speeds for dot matrix, daisywheel and other non-laser printers are usually quoted in terms of characters per second (cps). For laser printers, where the entire printed page is the important feature, this speed is given in pages per minute (ppm). To translate from cps to ppm, assuming an average of 2,400 characters per page, divide by 40.

Character size

The size of a character is determined by its height and width. The way that this is measured depends upon whether it is from a laser printer or other printer.

Line printers

For dot matrix, thermal, daisywheel and other line printers, the size and ultimate appearance of the text is measured in terms of *lines per inch* and *characters per inch*.

This terminology has been handed down from the typewriter world. In general, these types of printer have very little ability to adjust the spacing between lines, therefore the number of lines fitted into each inch vertically must be selected from a very small range. Many such printers are only capable of producing output at six characters per inch. Most modern matrix printers can work with 6 cpi or 8 cpi.

If you are using double-height characters, this reduces to 3 cpi and 4 cpi. Some printers can also produce text with a height of 5 lpi.

It should be noted that the physical height of each character on the line is usually the same, regardless of the number of lines per inch (assuming you are not using double-height characters). Therefore, the effect of printing at 8 lpi is that the text appears more cramped, as there is less space between lines.

Note that for double-height text, you must always leave the first line blank, so that the second line can expand vertically to take up the space.

Character width

The width of characters for monospaced (or fixed-spaced) fonts is given in terms of the number of characters per inch (cpi). For normal text, the standards are 10 cpi and 12 cpi. In typewriter terms, 10 cpi is referred to as *pica*, whereas 12 cpi is known as *elite*.

Condensed text squashes the characters up producing 15 cpi. Enlarged text doubles the width of the characters, giving 5 cpi. Condensed and enlarged text do not affect the height of the characters.

The number of characters per inch should be chosen to suit the particular font that is being used; some fonts are naturally narrower than others and are therefore better suited to 12 cpi rather than 10 cpi. Using a narrower font at 10 cpi results in characters that have unsightly gaps between them.

Laser printers

Laser printers are not so restricted in the size of their characters. Since entire pages are made up a a time and dots can be placed anywhere, the characters can be virtually any height or width. 'Size' in laser printer terminology is taken from the typesetting world. Here the height of a character is

measured in terms of *points* and *picas*. There are
12 points to a pica and 6 picas to an inch (so there
is still some correspondence between these meas-
urements and those described above). This gives 72
points per inch.

The point size of a character determines its
height. The amount of space taken up by each line
is calculated from the point size plus the *leading*.
The leading is the size (in points) of the gaps between lines. Typically, the leading is 20% of the
character size. Therefore, 10-point characters will
have leading of two points, giving a total of 12
points for each line: this gives 6 lines per inch.
Other equivalents are:

Point size	Lines per inch
3 pt	20 lpi
4 pt	15 lpi
5 pt	12 lpi
6 pt	10 lpi
7½ pt	8 lpi
10 pt	6 lpi
12 pt	5 lpi
15 pt	4 lpi
20 pt	3 lpi

With 20% leading, available character space =
$^2/1.2$ = 60 points per inch. Therefore, Point size x lpi
60

On a 300 dpi printer, there are 4⅙th dots per
point (50 dots per pica).

Many fonts are designed to be printed at a
specific size. These are termed *fixed fonts*. If some
fonts are printed at a different size, by applying an
algorithm, they will usually appear rather blocked
and untidy. Some programs allow you to apply a
smoothing effect to the edges of such fonts, to
smooth out the step effect of the curves.

Scalable fonts are based not on a dot pattern but
on a formula and can therefore be printed at any
size, theoretically with the same degree of smoothness in each case.

It is possible to transfer dot matrix fonts to laser
printers, but rarely desirable. Because of the lower

resolution of the dot matrix, the effect when printed by the laser printer is rather poor.

Fixed spacing

Fixed-space (monospaced) text is printed so that each character takes exactly the same amount of space. For example, the same width is reserved for a 'W' and a full stop. Programming with fixed-space fonts is much easier, since you can calculate the position of any character on a line directly from the number of characters that precede it. This makes tasks such as full justification much more straightforward.

The space allocated to individual characters in fixed-space fonts is called the *pitch* and is measured in terms of the number of *characters per inch* (cpi). Most dot matrix printers provide fonts with two standard pitch sizes:

| Pica | 10 cpi |
| Elite | 12 cpi |

24-pin and 48-pin printers also provide a 15 cpi font. This should not be confused with condensed print, which is approximately 15 cpi when applied to a 10 cpi font.

Dot matrix character pitches (cpi)

Normal	Condensed	Wide	Condensed & Wide
10	17	5	8.5
12	20	6	10
15	n/a	7.5	n/a

By combining these fonts with the condensed and wide attributes, you can produce a variety of pitches (see Figure 5.10).

Usually, the height of 10 cpi and 12 cpi fonts are the same but 15 cpi characters are shorter (and therefore better-suited to printing at 8 lines per

Combined fonts and styles

	cpi	chars/line
10 cpi	10	80
10 cpi expanded	5	40
10 cpi condensed	17	136
10 cpi condensed expanded	8.5	68
12 cpi	12	96
12 cpi expanded	6	48
12 cpi condensed	20	160
12 cpi condensed expanded	10	80
15 cpi	15	120
15 cpi expanded	7.5	60
10 cpi high speed	12	96
12 condensed high speed	24	192

gh speed increses number cpi by 20% (reduces width by
5%)

gure 5.10

ch). This maintains readable proportions for the
xt. (Condensed characters retain their full height.)
Several commands exist to change the character
tch.

ommand:	Select 10 cpi text
inters:	ESC/P 81
yntax:	ESC P (ASCII)
	1B 50 (hex)
	27 80 (dec)
arameters:	None
fect:	Selects a pitch of 10 cpi (pica), the default for most printers. The ESC ! command also selects or cancels this pitch. See also ESC M, ESC g and ESC p.

Command:	Select 12 cpi text
Printers:	ESC/P 81
Syntax:	ESC M (ASCI
	1B 4D (hex
	27 77 (dec
Parameters:	None
Effect:	Selects a pitch of 12 cpi (elite). The command is cancelled by selecting a different pitch, using ESC P, ESC g o ESC p (proportional). This pitch can also be selected or cancelled with the ESC ! command.

Command:	Select 12 cpi text
Printers:	IBM Proprinter
Syntax:	ESC : (ASC
	1B 3A (he
	27 58 (de
Parameters:	None
Effect:	Selects a pitch of 12 cpi (elite). The command is cancelled by restoring pica pitch with DC4, as described in Chapter 6.

Command:	Select 15 cpi text
Printers:	ESC/P ext
Syntax:	ESC g (ASC
	1B 67 (he
	27 103 (de
Parameters:	None
Effect:	Selects a pitch of 15 cpi. The command is cancelled by ESC P, ES(M or ESC p (proportional). See also ESC !. Text at this pitch cannot be condensed.

The pitches that are available varies from or printer to another. Citizen, for example, have a ur que command for selecting their own variations.

Command:	Select pitch	
Printers:	Citizen	
Syntax:	ESC ~ 3 n	(ASCII)
	1B 7E 33 n	(hex)
	27 126 51 n	(dec)
Parameters:	n = 0 pica	
	1 elite	
	2 pica condensed	
	5 13.3 cpi	
	6 15 cpi	
	7 elite condensed	
Effect:	Selects pitch and optionally turns condensed mode on.	

Command:	Select character pitch – primary font	
Printers:	LaserJet	
Syntax:	ESC (s n H	(ASCII)
	1B 28 73 n 48	(hex)
	27 40 115 n 72	(dec)
Parameters:	n = 10, 12, 17	
Effect:	Selects the character pitch (10 cpi, 12 cpi or 17 cpi) for the primary font.	

Command:	Select character pitch – secondary font	
Printers:	LaserJet	
Syntax:	ESC) s n H	(ASCII)
	1B 29 73 n 48	(hex)
	27 31 115 n 72	(dec)
Parameters:	n = 10, 12, 17	
Effect:	Selects the character pitch (10 cpi, 12 cpi or 17 cpi) for the secondary font.	

Command:	Set/cancel compressed pitch	
Printers:	LaserJet	
Syntax:	ESC & k n S	(ASCII)
	1B 26 6B n 53	(hex)
	27 38 107 n 83	(dec)
Parameters:	n = 0 (cancel)	
	2 (set)	
Effect:	Selects compressed pitch (17 cpi) when n = 2; restores normal pitch (10 cpi) when n = 0. This command is different to many other PCL	

commands in that it affects both the
primary and secondary fonts.

Point size

For page printers, where text is not restricted to
using lines of limited size, the size of characters is
usually determined by the *point size*. The height of
the character is measured in terms of a number of
points, where there are 72 points to the inch.

For HP-compatible printers, you can specify the
point size. The font closest to that size is selected.

Command:	Set character height – primary font
Printers:	LaserJet
Syntax:	ESC (s *n* V (ASCII)
	1B 28 73 *n* 56 (hex)
	27 30 115 *n* 86 (dec)
Parameters:	*n* = point size
Effect:	Sets the point size for the font; the font that is closest in size will be selected.

Command:	Set character height – secondary font
Printers:	LaserJet
Syntax:	ESC) s *n* V (ASCII)
	1B 29 73 *n* 56 (hex)
	27 41 115 *n* 86 (dec)
Parameters:	*n* = point size
Effect:	Sets the point size for the font; the font that is closest in size will be selected.

Proportional spacing

The majority of non-laser printer fonts are mono
spaced (or fixed-spaced), which can lead t
unsightly text, since an 'i' and a 'W' are made to f
in precisely the same space.

To overcome this problem, some dot matri
printers allow you to use *proportional spacing*
where each character takes up only as much spac

as it needs. Therefore an 'i' takes up very much less space than a 'W'.

For dot matrix printers, you can usually apply proportional spacing to any typestyle: draft or LQ; normal width, condensed or double-width; pica or elite.

It is also possible to use proportional spacing on some daisywheel printers, as long as you have the correct type of print wheel fitted and put the printer into the correct mode.

On laser printers, almost all fonts are proportionally spaced. There is usually one font – for example, Courier – which is monospaced and when printed gives the appearance of typewritten work.

In order to make the characters appear neat, the printer must hold in ROM a *width table* for each font. This table defines for each character the amount of space it needs and is used to calculate the distance that must be moved by the print head after each character has been printed.

Command:	Select/cancel proportional spacing	
Printers:	ESC/P 83	
Syntax:	ESC p *n*	(ASCII)
	1B 70 *n*	(hex)
	27 112 *n*	(dec)
Parameters:	*n* = 0 (cancel)	
	1 (select)	
Effect:	Turns proportional spacing on or off. When proportional spacing is on, the amount of space allocated to each character depends on the character width. Character size approximates to that of 10 cpi text. For 9-pin printers, proportional spacing can be selected for either draft quality or NLQ. For 24-pin and 48-pin Epson-compatible printers, LQ mode is automatically selected while printing in proportional spacing; if the select font was Courier, LQ Roman is selected. For IBM emulations, the font is changed to LQ Courier regardless of the existing font.	

Proportional spacing may also be selected or cancelled with ESC !. Selecting a fixed-space pitch (ESC P, ESC M or ESC g) cancels proportional spacing.

Command:	Select/cancel proportional spacing
Printers:	IBM Proprinter
Syntax:	ESC P *n* (ASCI
	1B 50 (hex
	27 80 (dec
Parameters:	*n* = 0 (cancel)
	1 (select)
Effect:	Turns on or off proportional spacing. When switched off, the LQ 10cpi font is selected.

Command:	Select proportional/fixed space – primary font
Printers:	LaserJet
Syntax:	ESC (s *n* p (ASC
	1B 28 73 *n* 50 (he:
	27 40 115 *n* 80 (de
Parameters:	*n* = 0 (monospaced)
	1 (proportional)
Effect:	Turns proportional spacing either on or off for the primary font.

Command:	Select proportional/fixed space – secondary font
Printers:	LaserJet
Syntax:	ESC) s *n* P (ASC
	1B 29 73 *n* 50 (he
	27 41 115 *n* 80 (de
Parameters:	*n* = 0 (monospaced)
	1 (proportional)
Effect:	Selects proportional or fixed spaced printing for the secondary font.

Command:	Set proportional spacing
Printers:	Diablo
Syntax:	ESC P (ASC
	1B 50 (h
	27 80 (d

Parameters:	None
Effect:	Selects the proportional space font. The command is cancelled with ESC Q.

Command:	Cancel proportional spacing	
Printers:	Diablo	
Syntax:	ESC Q	(ASCII)
	1B 51	(hex)
	27 81	(dec)
Parameters:	None	
Effect:	Cancels proportional spacing, restoring the fixed space font.	

Spaces

Almost any output can be produced using proportionally spaced fonts, as long as the package is set up to expect them. The biggest problem arises with spacing on justified text or in tables with more than one column. Since a space takes up a very small gap (usually the width of the letter 'i'), the result is that text which was lined up on the right-hand margin or in columns in mono-spaced fonts will no longer line up in proportional fonts.

For text, the program should overcome this problem either by inserting extra spaces between words or by increasing the gap between letters, so that each line still ends at the right-hand margin.

For tables, the problem is overcome by the use of horizontal tabs. Any table that has been created with tabs between columns can be converted to a proportional spaced font with very little difficulty. However, if the columns have been created using spaces, then the spaces must be replaced with tabs. Alternatively, the software can keep track of the current position of the print head and either insert enough spaces to take it to the next tab stop or use the relevant command to move the print head to a tab stop.

Kerning

Proportional spaced text looks much more readable than monospaced text. Even so, there are improvements to be made. Certain pairs of characters do not look right, even when the right-hand edge of one character is directly next to the left-hand edge of the next. For example, the capital letters 'AW' when placed next to each other look as if they have a large space between them even though there is no gap between the character blocks. This problem is overcome by overlapping the character blocks, a process known as *kerning*. The result is that 'AW' becomes must easier to read.

In order to calculate the position for the print head, kerned text needs to take account of this overlap. The size of overlap for each pair of characters is given in a *kerning table*.

Ligatures

Some pairs of characters do not look right when printed normally. The most common example of this are the letters 'f i'. To give a smoother appearance you can join these special pairs together to form a single character. For example, the dot of the 'i' is omitted and the bar in the middle of the 'f' is extended to join up with the top of the it. This is not a method of printing two separate characters; it is a single character called a *ligature*.

The height of a character that does not have either ascenders or descenders is called the *height*. Such characters include c, e, m, n, o, r, s, u, v, w, x, z is called the x height.

6 Typestyles

Most dot matrix printers support a variety of typestyles. In general, you can use the typestyles below in any combination, although there are restrictions when working in high-speed draft modes. For line printers, typestyles are achieved by modifying existing character sets, rather than using new character sets. Page printers follow the same principles as matrix printers or use the PostScript language, described in Chapter 10.

Character sets, typefaces, typestyles and fonts

The character set determines which symbol is to be printed. It does not decide the appearance of the symbol or its size. For example, in the standard ASCII character set, the ASCII code 4Ah represents the letter J. The appearance of the letter when printed is determined by the typeface that is selected, and they include the following:

J J J J *J*

These represent the letter J in five different typefaces: Helvetica, Times, Bookman, New Century Schoolbook and Zapf Chancery. The appearance can be further modified by selecting a different typestyle:

J *J* **J** ***J***

These are the letter J for the Helvetica typeface given in four different styles: normal, italic, bold and bold italic.

Finally, you can change the size of the printed character as follows:

J J **J**

This is the letter J printed in 8 point, 10 point and 20 point sizes.

The *font* gives the precise definition of how the character will be printed. For example, the last let-

Helvetica	AaDdFfGgHhIiJjLlOoZz
Times	AaDdFfGgHhIiJjLlOoZz
Palatino	AaDdFfGgHhIiJjLlOoZz
Avante Garde	AaDdFfGgHhIiJjLlOoZz
Bookman	AaDdFfGgHhIiJjLlOoZz
Courier	AaDdFfGgHhIiJjLlOoZz
SchoolBook	AaDdFfGgHhIiJjLlOoZz
Zapf Chancery	AaDdFfGgHhIiJjLlOoZz
Symbol	AαΔδΦφΓγHηIιϑφΛλOoZζ
Dingbats	✿❂✚✳✦❖✧✳★✱☆✳✪✳✱●★ ❑✳■

Figure 6.1 Sample typefaces

ter in the example above is the letter J in Helvetica bold 20 point.

The Courier typeface is similar to that produced by a traditional typewriter; Times is the serif typeface used for headings in this book; and Helvetica is a *sans serif* typeface, with much more simple lettering. Example characters for a number of typefaces are given in Figure 6.1. Notice that some typefaces (for example, Symbol and Dingbats) are used for a completely different character set.

For dot matrix printers, there are different typefaces for draft modes and for near letter quality or letter quality (NLQ/LQ) modes.

The *typestyle* is the way in which the typeface is printed. Typestyles include normal (unmodified text), bold, italic, underlined and overscored.

Printer characters may be further modified by changing the *size*: a variety of graded sizes for laser printers; limited sizes (condensed, enlarged, double-height, etc.) for dot matrix printers.

The combination of typeface, typestyle and size is referred to as a *font*. For example, a font on a laser printer may be Times italic 10-point while a dot matrix printer may have Courier condensed. The set of all fonts for a typeface is termed the *font family*. Thus 'typeface' and 'font family' are synonymous. Font families include Courier, Times, Helvetica and so on.

The typeface consists of a character set, made up of dot patterns, stored in the printer's memory. The typestyle and size are effect by applying an algorithm to these dot patterns; they do not exist as separate character sets in memory. For example, italic characters are produced by shifting dots to the right, the shift increasing as you move further up from the baseline. There is no separate italic character set held in the printer's memory.

Some typestyles have no effect on the box-drawing graphic box and some mathematical symbols. These styles include italic, shadow and outline; underline and double-height styles have no effect on a subset of these characters.

Italic

Italic text is slanted and is achieved by shifting the dots of the character above the baseline to the right; those below the baseline are shifted left. The shift increases with distance from the baseline.

Command:	Select italic typestyle	
Printers:	ESC/P 82	
Syntax:	ESC 4	(ASCII)
	1B 34	(hex)
	27 52	(dec)
Parameters:	None	
Effect:	Turns italic style on. Italics can be turned off again with ESC 5. Certain characters are unaffected: box-drawing characters, graphics characters and some mathematical symbols. Italics may also be produced with the extended character set (see ESC t). The ESC ! command can be used to turn italics on or off.	

Command:	Cancel italic typestyle
Printers:	ESC/P 83
Syntax:	ESC 5 (ASCII)
	1B 35 (hex)
	27 53 (dec)
Parameters:	None
Effect:	Turns italic style off. This command has no effect on the italic extended character set, selected with ESC 5. See also ESC 4 and ESC !.

As an alternative to sending the codes to turn on and off italicisation, a program that prints to an Epson, with the italic character set selected, can produce italics by adding 80h to the character bytes. If adopting this method, the italic should be selected by means of ESC t 0, to avoid any problems with changed dip switch or front panel settings.

Some Epsons also have other graphics sets which can be selected only by means of the dip switch settings. In these cases, ESC t 0 overrides the settings and produces italicised standard characters.

Command:	Set character style – primary font
Printers:	LaserJet
Syntax:	ESC (s *n* S (ASCII)
	1B 28 73 *n* 53 (hex)
	27 40 115 *n* 83 (dec)
Parameters:	*n* = 0 (upright)
	1 (italic)
Effect:	When *n* = 1, an italic font is selected; when *n* = 0, a normal, upright font is chosen. This command affects the primary font.

Command:	Set character style – secondary font
Printers:	LaserJet
Syntax:	ESC (s *n* S (ASCII)
	1B 28 73 *n* 53 (hex)
	27 40 115 *n* 83 (dec)
Parameters:	*n* = 0 (upright)
	1 (italic)

Effect:	When *n* = 1, an italic font is selected; when *n* = 0, a normal, upright font is chosen. This command affects the secondary font.

Bold (emphasised)

Bold text is produced by repeating each dot a second time, a little to the right of the original (increasing the character *weight*). This produces a darker type.

Command:	Select bold type (emphasised)	
Printers:	ESC/P 80, IBM Proprinter	
Syntax:	ESC E	(ASCII)
	1B 45	(hex)
	27 69	(dec)
Parameters:	None	
Effect:	Turns bold type (emphasised) printing) on. Bold type is turned off with ESC F and can also be turned on or off with ESC !. Bold type and double-strike can be selected simultaneously.	

Command:	Cancel bold type (emphasised)	
Printers:	ESC/P 80, IBM Proprinter	
Syntax:	ESC F	(ASCII)
	1B 46	(hex)
	27 70	(dec)
Parameters:	None	
Effect:	Turns off bold type (emphasised printing). See also ESC E and ESC !.	

Command:	Set/weight	
Printers:	LaserJet	
Syntax:	ESC (s *n* B	(ASCII)
	1B 28 73 *n* 42	(hex)
	27 40 115 *n* 66	(dec)
Parameters:	*n* = -7...+7	
Effect:	This command can be used to embolden text for the primary font; it can also be used to make text 'lighter'. If *n* takes a positive value, the greater the value, the bolder will be the text. When *n* is negative, the	

characters become thinner. A value of
n = 0 produces a medium-weight
character.

Command:	Set/weight
Printers:	LaserJet
Syntax:	ESC) s *n* B (ASCII)
	1B 29 73 *n* 42 (hex)
	27 41 115 *n* 66 (dec)
Parameters:	*n* = -7...+7
Effect:	This command can be used to embolden text for the secondary font; it can also be used to make text 'lighter'. If *n* takes a positive value, the greater the value, the bolder will be the text. When *n* is negative, the characters become thinner. A value of *n* = 0 produces a medium-weight character.

Command:	Set bold printing mode
Printers:	Diablo
Syntax:	ESC O (ASCII)
	1B 4F (hex)
	27 79 (dec)
Parameters:	None
Effect:	Creates bold effect by printing each character twice, separated by 1/300". The command is cancelled by ESC &, ESC X or CR.

Command:	Set shadow printing mode
Printers:	Diablo
Syntax:	ESC W (ASCII)
	1B 57 (hex)
	27 87 (dec)
Parameters:	None
Effect:	Creates shadow effect by printing each character twice, separated by 2/300". The command is cancelled by ESC &, ESC X or CR.

Command:	Cancel bold/shadow printing mode	
Printers:	Diablo	
Syntax:	ESC &	(ASCII)
	1B 26	(hex)
	27 38	(dec)
Parameters:	None	
Effect:	Turns off bold or shadow printing, as set by ESC O and ESC W.	

Double strike

Double strike produces another form of bold type, which has a similar appearance. For many printers (such as Epsons), each character is printed a second time offset, the repeated dot being printed just below the original. (This, again, increases the character *weight*.) In some cases (for example, Citizen printers), double strike is produced by simply printing each line twice, without any dot offset. In all cases, the effect is darker type.

To increase the emphasis, combine both bold and double strike.

Command:	Select double-strike printing	
Printers:	ESC/P 80, IBM Proprinter	
Syntax:	ESC G	(ASCII)
	1B 47	(hex)
	27 71	(dec)
Parameters:	None	
Effect:	Turns double-strike printing on. The style is turned off with ESC H. Double-strike can also be turned on or off with ESC !. Double-strike can be combined with bold type. On 9-pin printers, double strike is effective in draft quality only.	

Command:	Cancel double-strike printing	
Printers:	ESC/P 80, IBM Proprinter	
Syntax:	ESC H	(ASCII)
	1B 48	(hex)
	22 72	(dec)
Parameters:	None	
Effect:	Turns off double-strike printing. See also ESC G and ESC !.	

Underline (underscore)

Underlining is achieved by filling in the entire bottom row of dot positions in the character matrix. Most programs offer a choice of full underlining or word underlining, where the underline is not applied to the space character. However, to apply word underlines only you must search the text for spaces and turn underlining on and off accordingly.

Command:	Select/cancel underlining
Printers:	ESC/P 80, IBM Proprinter
Syntax:	ESC - n (ASCII)
	1B 2D n (hex)
	27 45 n (dec)
Parameters:	n = 0 (cancel)
	1 (select)
Effect:	When n=1, underlining is selected, when n=0, underlining is cancelled. Underlining does not affect graphics and box-drawing characters but is applied to all other characters, including spaces. This is the simplest way of selecting underlining; the ESC (- command can also be used on some Epson-compatibles.

Command:	Set underlining mode
Printers:	Diablo
Syntax:	ESC E (ASCII)
	1B 45 (hex)
	27 69 (dec)
Parameters:	None
Effect:	Turns underlining on for all characters and spaces. The command is cancelled by ESC R or ESC X.

Command:	Cancel underlining mode
Printers:	Diablo
Syntax:	ESC R (ASCII)
	1B 52 (hex)
	27 82 (dec)
Parameters:	None
Effect:	Turns underlining off.

Command:	Start automatic underlining
Printers:	LaserJet
Syntax:	ESC & d D (ASCII)
	1B 26 64 44 (hex)
	27 38 100 68 (dec)
Parameters:	None
Effect:	Turns underlining of characters and spaces on. Underlining can be turned off with the command below.

Command:	End automatic underlining
Printers:	LaserJet
Syntax:	ESC & d @ (ASCII)
	1B 26 64 40 (hex)
	27 38 100 64 (dec)
Parameters:	None
Effect:	Turns off automatic underlining when this has been turned on by the command above.

Command:	Start underlining (general)
Printers:	LaserJet
Syntax:	ESC & d n D (ASCII)
	1B 26 64 n 44 (hex)
	27 388 100 n 68 (dec)
Parameters:	n = 1 (single fixed)
	2 (double fixed)
	3 (single float)
	4 (double float)
Effect:	Turns on underlining with either a single or a double underline and with the depth of the underline fixed or floating. When the depth is floating, it is determined by the particular font that is being used.

Strike-through (scoring)

Strike-through consists of a specific character (usually a dash) being overprinted on each character. The effect is achieved by superimposing the strike-through character on the character matrix before printing, not by printing two separate characters at the same position.

There is no specific strike-through command; rather, you must use a general command that also provides underlining and overscoring.

Command:	Select/cancel scoring
Printers:	ESC/P ext
Syntax:	ESC (- ETX NUL SOH *n1 n2* (ASCII)
	1B 28 4D 03 00 01 *n1 n2* (hex)
	27 40 45 3 0 2 *n1 n2* (dec)
Parameters:	*n1* = 1 underline
	2 strike-through
	3 overscore
	n2 = 0 turn off selected scoring
	1 continuous single line
	2 continuous double line
	3 broken single line
	4 broken double line
Effect:	Selects or cancels a particular style of scoring in one of three positions. Scoring does not affect does not affect graphics and box-drawing characters but is applied to all other characters, including spaces. You can apply all three types of scoring at the same time, by repeating the command with different parameters. Scoring and underlining (ESC -) are mutually compatible; both can be on at the same time and turning one off does not affect the other.

Overscore

Overscore consists of a single or double-line printed above the text. In a similar way to underline, it is achieved by filling in the dot positions in one or more lines across the top of the character matrix.

There is no specific overscore command for Epson-compatibles; overscoring is applied as an option of a general scoring command (see the ESC (command above).

Command:	Continuous overscore
Printers:	IBM Proprinter
Syntax:	ESC _ n (ASCII)
	1B 5F n (hex)
	27 95 n (dec)
Parameters:	n = 0 (Cancel)
	1 (Set)
Effect:	Switches continuous overscoring on (n = 1) or off (n = 0).

Condensed

Condensed type is narrower than normal type, typically producing 15 cpi for a standard 10 cpi typeface. The style is usually achieved by omitting every third column of dots.

Condensed mode has no effect on text that is already in subscript, superscript or 15 pitch.

Command:	Select condensed type
Printers:	ESC/P 80, IBM Proprinter
Syntax:	SI *or* ESC SI (ASCII)
	0F 1B 0F (hex)
	15 27 15 (dec)
Parameters:	None
Effect:	Selects condensed printing, with characters at roughly 60% of standard width for monospaced text and 50% for proportional text. Condensed mode cannot be selected when printing at 15 cpi or when proportional mode is selected on 9-pin printers. For Epson-compatibles, condensed printing can also be selected with ESC ! or (for more printers) front-panel settings.
Variations:	The ESC SI option is not used on IBM Proprinters.

Command:	Cancel condensed type
Printers:	ESC/P 80, IBM Proprinter
Syntax:	DC2 (ASCII)
	12 (hex)
	18 (dec)
Parameters:	None

Effect:	Cancels condensed printing and restores normal width printing. For Epson-compatibles, see also ESC !.
Variations:	For IBM emulations, this command also restores pica pitch.

Double-width

Double-width text stretches each character over twice the normal space by printing each dot twice, side-by-side. Double-width printing can be turned on for just a single line or for all lines. It is sometimes referred to as *expanded* print.

These commands can be applied to pica, elite and 15 cpi pitches.

Command:	Select double-width printing (one line)	
Printers:	ESC/P 80, IBM Proprinter	
Syntax:	SO *or* ESC SO	(ASCII)
	0E 1B 0E	(hex)
	14 27 14	(dec)
Parameters:	None	
Effect:	Turns on double-width printing for the remainder of the line. The command is cancelled by the next CR, LF, VT, FF, DC4 or ESC W0. See also ESC !.	
Variations:	The ESC SO option is not used on IBM Proprinters.	

Command:	Cancel double-width printing (one line)
Printers:	ESC/P 80, IBM Proprinter
Syntax:	DC4 (ASCII)
	14 (hex)
	20 (dec)
Parameters:	None
Effect:	Cancel single-line, double-width printing, as set by SO (or ESC SO). This command has no effect on double-width printing selected by ESC W or ESC !.

Command:	Select/cancel double-width printing (permanent)
Printers:	ESC/P 80, IBM Proprinter
Syntax:	ESC W n (ASCII)
	1B 57 n (hex)
	27 87 n (dec)
Parameters:	n = 0 (cancel)
	1 (select)
Effect:	Turns double-width printing on or off. The style remains in effect until cancelled by ESC W 0 or ESC ! and continue from one line to the next. See also SO and DC4.

You can combine condensed and double-width printing, to achieve a number of combinations.

Double-height printing

In a similar way to double-width printing, you can stretch characters vertically so that they take twice their normal height. Each dot is printed twice, one below the other. The result is that line spacing is effectively doubled for the duration of the command. The IBM Proprinter allows considerably more control over line spacing.

Command:	Select/cancel double-height printing
Printers:	ESC/P 84
Syntax:	ESC w n (ASCII)
	1B 77 n (hex)
	27 119 n (dec)
Parameters:	n = 0 (cancel)
	1 (select)
Effect:	Turns on double-height printing. Alternate lines are skipped to allow sufficient space. The command has no effect for text on the first line of any page (the first line can be skipped by starting each page with an LF).

Command:	Combined height and width
Printers:	IBM Proprinter
Syntax:	ESC [@ EOT NUL NUL NUL *n1 n2* (ASCII)
	1B 5B 40 04 00 00 00 *n1 n2* (hex)
	27 91 64 4 0 0 0 *n1 n2* (dec)
Parameters:	*n1* = 0 No change to height
	1 Normal height
	2 Double height
	Add 16 (decimal) for single-line
	spacing; add 32 (decimal) for
	double-line spacing
	n2 = 0 No change to width
	1 Normal width
	2 Double width
Effect:	Changes a combination of height,
	width and line spacing.

Combined effects

Citizen provides a unique command that allows you
to select height and width with a single escape sequence.

Command:	Combined height and width
Printers:	Citizen (all models)
Syntax:	ESC ~ 1 *n* (ASCII
	1B 7E 31 *n* (hex
	27 126 49 *n* (dec
Parameters:	*n* = 0 Normal height, normal width,
	single-line spacing
	1 Double height, double-line spa
	2 Quadruple height, quad-line
	spacing
	3 Double width
	4 Quadruple width
	5 Double height, double width,
	double-line spacing
	6 Quadruple height, quad width
	quad-line spacing
Effect:	Changes a combination of height,
	width and line spacing.

Outline and shadow printing

Two further typestyles are available on some printers. *Outline* printing produces characters with hollow centres. *Shadow* printing prints a line to the right and below where the character would normally be printed; the character itself is omitted. Both styles are selected with a single command.

Command:	Select/cancel outline and shadow printing
Printers:	ESC/P ext
Syntax:	ESC q *n* (ASCII)
	1B 71 *n* (hex)
	27 113 *n* (dec)
Parameters:	*n* = 0 Cancel outline and shadow
	1 Select outline
	2 Select shadow
	3 Select outline and shadow
Effect:	Selects or cancels outline, shadow or both styles. These styles do not affect graphics characters. The rightmost bits of the parameter byte determine the effect, as follows:
	Bit 0: Outline (0=off, 1=on)
	Bit 1: Shadow (0=off, 1=on)

Reverse printing

Reverse printing is a feature available only on some dot matrix printers, whereby white characters are printed on a black background. This is achieved by firing those pins that are not usually fired, and vice versa.

To join the blocks of one line with those of the line below (so that there is no white line across the page), change the line height with ESC A followed by 09h.

Command:	Reverse print
Printers:	Citizen
Syntax:	ESC ~2*n* (ASCII)
	1B 7E 32*n* (hex)
	27 126 50*n* (dec)
Parameters:	*n* = 0 (cancel)
	1 (select)
Effect:	When *n* = 1, prints white characters on black blocks; *n* = 0 cancels the effect.

Superscript and subscript

Superscript characters are printed at a higher position than normal, usually so that the bottom of the superscript character is just below the capital line. Subscript characters are printed at the bottom of the line. Superscript and subscript characters are usually smaller (in both height and width) than normal characters.

These styles are usually produced by raising or lowering characters from the printer's 15 cpi font. However, the pitch of the sub/superscript characters is not automatically reduced to 15 cpi, so there are relatively large gaps between characters.

On some printers (e.g. Epson), the height of the characters is about 66% of normal while for others (e.g. Citizen) it is 50%.

Command:	Select sub/superscript	
Printers:	ESC/P 81, IBM Proprinter	
Syntax:	ESC S *n*	(ASCII)
	1B 53 *n*	(hex)
	27 83 *n*	(dec)
Parameters:	*n* = 0 (superscript)	
	1 (subscript)	
Effect:	Selects either subscript or superscript printing, depending on the parameter value. Subscript characters are printed in the bottom half of the line, superscript characters in the top half. Sub/superscript can be cancelled either with ESC T or by repeating the command with the alternative value of *n*. Graphics and box-drawing characters are not affected.	

Command:	Cancel sub/superscript	
Printers:	ESC/P 81, IBM Proprinters	
Syntax:	ESC T	(ASCII)
	1B 54	(hex)
	27 84	(dec)
Parameters:	None	

Effect:	Cancels sub/superscript mode, restoring normal height characters.

Justification and centring

When printing text, it is sometimes desirable to produce the text *justified* or *centred*.

Justified text is text in which extra spaces are inserted to pad out the lines so that they are all of the same length. This gives a straight right-hand margin. Justified text is sometimes called *full-justified*.

Unjustified text (sometimes called *left-justified*) has no such extra spaces and is given a ragged right-hand margin.

Right-justified text has a straight right-hand margin but ragged left-hand margin. As for unjustified text, no extra spaces are inserted between letters or words but the start of each line is calculated so that the line always ends in the same position.

Centred text is printed so that the amount of space at either end of the line is the same, centring the text within the current margins.

A space typed at the keyboard is usually called a *hard space*. Additional spaces, inserted to create the justified effect, are usually referred to as *soft spaces*.

By default, all text is justified.

Command:	Select justification mode	
Printers:	ESC/P 83	
Syntax:	ESC a *n*	(ASCII)
	1B 61 *n*	(hex)
	27 97 *n*	(dec)
Parameters:	*n* =	0 (unjustified)
		1 (centred)
		2 (right-justified)
		3 (full-justified)
Effect:	When *n*=0, text is printed so that it lines up at the left margin, with a ragged right margin.	
	When *n*=1, the text is printed with an equal amount of space on either side.	

The spacing is calculated before the text in the buffer is printed. HT and ESC $ commands are ignored in this mode.

When *n*=2, each line is printed so that it ends precisely at the right margin. HT and ESC $ commands are ignored in this mode.

When *n*=3, the line is printed (as usual) when the buffer is full or when printing is forced by a CR, VT or FF character. The buffer is considered to be full when the end of a word (signified by a space character) takes the total width to between 75% and 125% of the distance between the margins. In all these cases the text is justified if the text length exceeds 75% of the line length. Justification is produced by changing the size of the space character, which may be anything from a quarter to twice its normal width. If full justification cannot be produced according to these rules, the text is printed left-justified.

The ESC a command must be at the start of a line, preceding text and commands are ignored.

Command:	Automatic justification mode
Printers:	Diablo
Syntax:	ESC M (ASCI
	1B 4D (hex
	27 77 (dec
Parameters:	None
Effect:	Turns on full justification of text. The line is printed when a CR or LF is received. Extra space is added between words. Unjustified text is restored with ESC X.

Command:	Automatic centring mode
Printers:	Diablo
Syntax:	ESC = (ASCII)
	1B 3D (hex)
	27 61 (dec)
Parameters:	None
Effect:	Centres the text between the current left and right margins. The text is printed when a CR, LF or ESC X command is received. Normal text is restored by ESC X.

Inter-character space

You can vary the amount of space between individual characters on a line. A nominal slice of space is included in the definitions of each character, as part of the character block. This cannot be reduced. However, you can specify that additional space is to be included after each character, giving the extra space in terms of dot widths.

When using justified text, the printer will automatically insert extra space either after each character or after each word, padding the text so that it fits the line. For proportional spacing, the space taken by the character itself varies for each character but the amount of space following is nominally the same.

Command:	Set inter-character space
Printers:	ESC/P 82
Syntax:	ESC SP n (ASCII)
	1B 20 n (hex)
	27 32 n (dec)
Parameters:	n = 0...127 units
Effect:	Inserts additional space between each pair of characters. The units for the parameter are $1/120$" for draft and NLQ modes, $1/180$" for LQ modes.

Additional inter-character spacing is turned off with the same command, specifying a width of 0 units.

Horizontal Movement Increment (HMI)

A similar procedure is adopted by Hewlett-Packard in their PCL commands and for Diablo 630 commands. By default, when a font is selected, a value known as the Horizontal Movement Increment (HMI) is set to be equal to the width of a space character in that font. For monospaced fonts, this width is used for each character that is printed. The HMI also determines the distance moved when a BS command is given; a multiple of the HMI determines the distance moved for tabs.

You can change the HMI, in which case characters will be printed closer together or further apart (for monospaced text); for proportionally spaced text, the HMI setting effects only spaces.

Command:	Set HMI	
Printers:	LaserJet	
Syntax:	ESC & k n H	(ASCII
	1B 26 6B n 48	(hex
	27 38 107 n 72	(dec
Parameters:	n = 1 ... 840	
Effect:	Sets the horizontal movement increment for the current font, in units of $1/120$". If necessary, up to two decimal places can be used in the value. The default HMI is reinstated when a new font is selected.	

Command:	Set inter-character spacing	
Printers:	Diablo	
Syntax:	ESC DC1 n	(ASCII
	1B 11 n	(hex
	27 17 n	(dec
Parameters:	n = 1...126	
Effect:	When n is less than 64, adds $n/120$" to the print head movement after each character is printed. When n is 64 or greater, subtracts $(n-64) \times 1/120$" from the print head movement. This is useful for proportional spacing, where the HMI setting affects only spaces.	

Cancelling print effects

The Diablo 360 command set has a single instruction for cancelling a range of printing effects.

Command:	Cancel printing effects	
Printers:	Diablo	
Syntax:	ESC X	(ASCII)
	1B 58	(hex)
	27 88	(dec)
Parameters:	None	
Effect:	Cancels the printing characteristics set by ESC DC1, ESC O, ESC W, ESC E, ESC M and ESC =.	

Selecting typestyle and pitch

Most of the time you will want to use the commands above to change just one feature of the printout at a time – bold, italic, pitch, etc. – but some printers include a command that allows you to change all elements of typestyle and character in one go.

Command:	Select typestyles and pitch	
Printers:	ESC/P 81	
Syntax:	ESC ! n	(ASCII)
	1B 21 n	(hex)
	27 33 n	(dec)
Parameters:	n = combined style parameter	
Effect:	Sets typestyles and pitch, replacing previous settings. Each bit in the parameter byte turns a feature either off (value=0) or on (value=1). The composition of the parameter byte is given in Figure 6.2. The only restriction is that if bit 1 is set (proportional on), the value of bit 0 (pitch) is ignored. Otherwise, any combination is allowed. If using this command, remember to set the bits for any features that are already on, otherwise they will be	

turned off. For example, if italic is on, setting $n=8$ will turn bold type on but will also turn italic off.

This command does not affect sub/superscript, print quality or font (see ESC S, ESC T, ESC X and ESC g). However, it does turn 15-pitch printing off: follow the command with ESC g to turn 15-pitch on again.

Variations: Proportional and italic bits ignored until ESC/P 83.

Citizen: Both pica and elite can be used in proportional mode.

Selecting Style with ESC !

Bit	Value	Style
0	1	Elite (0=pica)
1	2	Proportional
2	4	Condensed
3	8	Emphasised
4	16	Double strike
5	32	Expanded
6	64	Italics
7	128	Underline

Figure 5.2

IBM character sets

For the IBM Proprinter and compatibles two alter-native character sets are available for the extende ASCII characters. Character set 1 duplicates th control codes at the start of the extended set whil character set 2 contains a selection of Europea characters. You can choose one or the other wit dip switch settings or the ESC 7 and ESC 6 com mands.

Command:	Select character set 1
Printers:	IBM Proprinter
Syntax:	ESC 7	(ASC)
	1B 37	(he
	25 55	(de

Parameters:	None
Effect:	Selects the extended character set with duplicate control codes. This command is cancelled by ESC 6.

Command:	Select character set 2	
Printers:	IBM Proprinter	
Syntax:	ESC 6	(ASCII)
	1B 36	(hex)
	25 54	(dec)
Parameters:	None	
Effect:	Selects the European extended character set. This command is cancelled by ESC 7.	

Printable control code characters

You can also persuade an IBM Proprinter or compatible to interpret the control codes as printable characters, in order to extend the range of symbols that are printed. The character set thus produced is referred to by IBM as the 'All Characters Set'.

Command:	Print single character from all characters chart	
Printers:	IBM Proprinter	
Syntax:	ESC ^	(ASCII)
	1B 5E	(hex)
	27 94	(dec)
Parameters:	None	
Effect:	For the control codes, prints the symbol given; for all other codes, prints the corresponding character from character set 2. To print a string of such characters, use ESC \.	

Command:	Print continuously from all characters chart	
Printers:	IBM Proprinter	
Syntax:	ESC \ n1 n2	(ASCII)
	1B 5C n1 n2	(hex)
	27 92 n1 n2	(dec)

Parameters:	*n1* = Number of characters
	n2 = Number of blocks of 256 characters
Effect:	Prints a series of characters from the IBM 'All Characters Set'. For the control codes, prints the characters given; for all other codes, prints the corresponding characters from character set 2. The number of characters printed is given by *n1* + (*n2* x 256). For example, to print 288 such characters set *n1* = 32 (decimal) and *n2* = 1. To print just one character from the set, use ESC ^.

7 User-Defined Characters

For all but the daisywheel printers, characters are produced by printing a pattern of dots. All the printers store the pattern for each individual character in ROM, with one section of ROM set aside for each font. The patterns produced for any particular character are different from one font to the next. Different typestyles are produced either by selecting a different font or by applying an algorithm to an existing font.

In addition, most printers have an amount of RAM into which you may place your own patterns, giving you the opportunity to design your own characters.

This chapter describes the principles of character definition and how they are applied to Epson printers. Most other printers follow similar principles to these.

Designing characters

The principle for designing a new character is the same for all types of printer, although the mechanics vary from one group of printers to another. Any character is defined by filling in the cells in a rectangular grid. These cells are small enough and close enough together (especially for 24-pin and 48-pin printers) to produce smooth-looking characters, when viewed at a distance.

Figure 7.1 shows the grid for a 9-pin draft character. This has 8 rows of 11 columns (only eight pins can be used). The cells that might be selected for a particular character are filled in. However, the pins themselves are round and overlap from one cell to the next horizontally. Since the print head consists of a column of pins, the cell height vertically must match the size of the pin; however, the head is usually moved along the row in units of half this distance, resulting in an overlap. For this reason, any character cannot use two cells that are adjacent horizontally; the second cell is ignored if defined. The illustration in Figure 7.2 shows a better approximation of the area that will actually be covered by the pins.

Although the grid varies for different types of printer, the method is always the same: the cells to

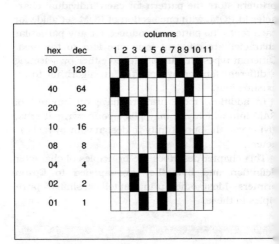

Figure 7.1 9-pin draft letter J

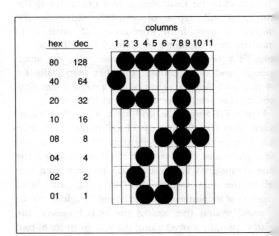

Figure 7.2 9-pin draft letter J – as printed

be filled in must be selected and a series of data codes can be calculated.

When defining characters, the following rules should be remembered:

● No two horizontally-adjacent cells should be filled in.

● Two or more columns on the right of the grid should be left blank if you want a space between the user-defined character and any following character.

Two or more rows at the top and bottom of the grid are usually used for ascenders and descenders. The position of the baseline is particularly important.

Descenders are the parts of certain lower case letters (j, p, q, y) which are printed below the base line. For some earlier dot matrix printers, there were no descenders, the entire character being printed above the base line.

Calculating the data code

For each column of cells in the grid, there will be one or more bytes of data. Each bit in the data byte corresponds to one cell; if the cell is filled in, the bit takes a value of 1; otherwise, it is 0. The left-most bit of the first (or only) byte corresponds to the top cell.

For example, in the first column of the example grid the second cell from the top is filled in; all others are blank. The byte corresponding to this column therefore has a binary value of 01000000, which is 40h (64 decimal). The calculations for the next three data bytes are as follows:

Col. 2	*Binary:*	10100000	
	Hex:	80 + 20	= A0
	Decimal:	128 + 32	= 160
Col. 3	*Binary:*	00000010	
	Hex:	02	= 02
	Decimal:	2	= 2

Col. 4   *Binary*:   10100101
           Hex: 80 + 20 + 04 + 01 = A5
           Decimal: 128 + 32 + 4 + 1 = 165

The entire user-defined character therefore re
quire the following 11 data bytes:

Hex: 40 A0 02 A5 00 89 02 BC 40 88 00
Decimal: 64 160 2 165 0 137 2 188 64 136 0

In most cases, there are more than eight row:
and therefore two or more bytes are used. The firs
byte relates to the top eight rows, the next byte i
for the next eight rows, and so on. Each byte i
filled from left to right, so if the number of row
that is not a multiple of eight, only the higher bit
of the byte will be used. The low-order bits will al
ways be 0 in such cases.

Attribute bytes

In most cases you need to specify one or more *a
tribute bytes* for each character that is bein
defined. The use of these bytes varies, depending o
the printer, but specifies features such as:

● Pins used to produce the character

● Number of columns to be used

● Number of blank columns before and after th
  character

The attribute byte is split in some cases, with th
binary value of a group of bits specifying a pa
ticular feature.

Typestyles

When characters have been downloaded to RAN
any of the usual typestyles can be applied to ther
where these are derived from algorithms or a phys
cal printer function. For example, user-define
characters can be underlined, regardless of wheth
the underline is created by adding dots to the pa
tern or overprinting the character with a
underscore. Other such typestyles include bo
type, double-strike, italic, condensed, doub
height, double-width and overscore.

Some character attributes must be selected *before* the characters are downloaded. These attributes include draft or NLQ, fixed or proportional spacing, and full size or sub/superscript. The same combinations are available as for the standard ROM-based fonts and are printer-dependent.

This is particularly important when copying a ROM-based set to RAM. The attributes must be set *before* the copy is made.

Alternatives for creating characters

To produce user-defined characters, you do not necessarily have to define an entire character set. The following possibilities exist:

● One or more characters can be downloaded into ROM as replacements for particular characters in a built-in font.

  User-defined characters can be used to extend the character set, providing characters that could not otherwise be printed.

● An entire character set can be downloaded to ROM.

The way in which user-defined characters are used depends upon the amount of free RAM in the printer.

Replacement characters

The easiest way to replace part of a character set is to copy the ROM patterns to RAM and then overwrite the relevant characters. The RAM character set is then selected. This is feasible only if the RAM is sufficient to hold an entire set.

Command:	Copy ROM-based characters to RAM	
Printers:	ESC/P 82	
Syntax:	ESC : NUL *n* NUL	(ASCII)
	1B 3A 00 *n* 00	(hex)
	27 58 0 *n* 0	(dec)
Parameters:	*n* = font number	

Effect:	Copies the characters from the specified font into character RAM. One or more characters may then be replaced (using ESC &) and the RAM character set can be used for printing (after it has been selected with ESC %). The font numbers are the same as those used for the ESC k command (see Figure ?.?). In draft quality mode, the only valid value for *n* is 0. The Orator and Orator-S fonts cannot be copied to RAM, nor can any font that has been italicised with ESC 4.

Additional characters

For an extended character set, the program mus' switch to the RAM set when the additional charac- ters are needed, then switch back to ROM when the standard characters are required again, using the ESC % command below. The same principle is ap plied when you want to replace certain character: but the printer RAM is not large enough to copy the entire character set.

Command:	Select/deselect RAM-based character:	
Printers:	ESC/P 82	
Syntax:	ESC % *n*	(ASCII
	1B 25 *n*	(hex
	27 37 *n*	(dec
Parameters:	*n* = 0 (ROM-based characters)	
	1 (RAM-based characters)	
Effect:	When *n*=1, all future text is printed with the characters in RAM (as set by ESC : or defined by ESC &). When *n*=0, printing reverts to the ROM-based characters (using whatever font was previously selected).	

For a large number of additional character: when RAM is limited, you may need to downloa characters repeatedly, re-using RAM characte positions for more than one additional character. I this way, the character set can be expanded to any size.

New character sets

To use an entirely different character set, download the entire set of patterns to RAM, then select the RAM set using the ESC % command described above. The size of the new character set is limited only by the amount of free RAM in the printer.

Character range

The number of characters that can be defined depends on the printer model.

9-pin

For most 9-pin printers, you can redefine 191 characters in the following code ranges:

20h-7Eh, A0h-FFh	(hex)
32-126, 160-255	(decimal)

If you want to use more characters than this, you must use the ESC I command to expand the range, allowing you to use some of the control codes (those which do not have a printer-specific use) and the corresponding extended ASCII area. The additional codes are:

00h-06h, 10h, 11h, 15h-17h, 19h, 1Ah, 1Ch-1Fh, 80-9Fh	(hex)
0-6, 16, 17, 21-23, 25, 26, 28-31, 128-159	(decimal)

This expands the range to a maximum of 241 characters.

Command:	Expand/reduce user-defined character set	
Printers:	Epson 9-pin (ESC/P ext)	
Syntax:	ESC I *n*	(ASCII)
	1B 49 *n*	(hex)
	27 73 *n*	(dec)

Parameters:	n =	0 (reduce range)
		1 (expand range)
Effect:		When n=1, an additional 50 characters can be user-defined. A setting of n=0 restricts the user-defined characters to the original range.

LX printers

Epson LX printers are restricted to user-defined characters in the range 3Ah-3Fh (58-63).

24-pin and 48-pin

For all other printers, a maximum of 96 characters can be defined, in the range 20h-7Fh (32-127).

However, this can be expanded to 128 characters by mapping the user-defined characters onto the range 80h-FFh (128-255) using the ESC t 2 command.

Downloading characters

Once the user-defined characters have been defined (consisting of single characters or a complete set) the procedure for downloading the RAM is as follows:

1 Select the required attributes (draft/NLQ, fixed/proportional, full size/subscript), using the commands in Chapters 5 and 6.

2 If required, select the ROM-based character set (ESC k) and copy the complete set to RAM (ESC :).

3 Download the new characters to RAM, using the commands described below.

You are then free to use the new characters. Such characters will remain available until either they are replaced or the printer is re-initialised.

Command:	Download user-defined characters	
Printers:	ESC/P 82	
Syntax:	ESC & NUL *n1 n2 data*	(ASCII)
	1B 26 00 *n1 n2 data*	(hex)
	27 38 0 *n1 n2 data*	(dec)
Parameters:	*n1* = first character to define	
	n2 = last character to define	
	data = attribute and character data	
Effect:	Downloads one or more user-defined characters to printer RAM. The first two parameters, *n1* and *n2*, specify the start and end of a continuous sequence of user-defined characters. If the characters to be defined are not consecutive, use more than one ESC & command. If only a single character is to be defined, set *n1=n2*. The composition of the *data* parameters varies according to the printer type and is detailed below.	

9-pin draft

For 9-pin printers in draft mode, the main features are as follows:

Grid size:	11 columns x 8 rows
Attribute bytes:	1
Maximum total bytes:	12
Spacing:	Fixed, proportional

The grid is shown in Figure 7.3. The *data* consists of a single attribute byte, followed by eleven bytes of data (one for each column). Note that only eight of the nine pins can be used for draft characters.

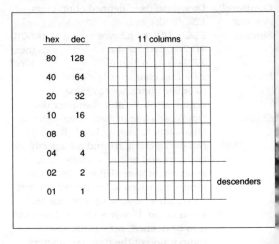

Figure 7.3 9-pin draft grid

Attribute byte

The attribute byte for each user-defined character is divided into three sections as follows:

Bits Meaning

0-3   Last column used (01h-0Ah, 1-10)

4-6   First column used (0-7)

7   Which pins are used:

    0   Bottom 8 pins

    1   Top 8 pins

The first and last columns are only relevant for proportional characters. For fixed-space characters these are ignored and should be set to 0, giving a value for the attribute byte of either 00h (bottom eight pins used) or 80h (top eight pins used). The choice of proportional of fixed-space characters is made before the ESC & command is issued.

9-pin NLQ

For NLQ mode, 9-pin user-defined characters have the following limits:

Grid size:	12 columns x 18 rows
Attribute bytes:	1
Max total bytes:	39
Spacing:	Fixed only

The NLQ grid is shown in Figure 7.4. The *data* string for each character takes the following form:

```
NUL attribute NUL definition
```

NLQ characters require two passes of the print head. The printer prints the even-numbered rows (0, 2, 4, etc.), the paper is advanced vertically by half the cell height, and the odd-numbered rows are printed. In this case, each dot overlaps onto the cells above and below, as well as those at either side.

For Epson FX printers and compatibles, the character *may* include horizontally adjacent cells.

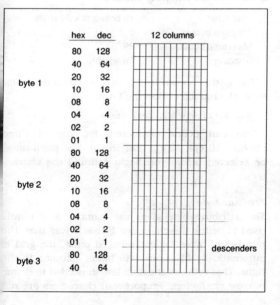

Figure 7.4 9-pin NLQ grid

Attribute byte

The attribute byte states the number of columns used to define the character. Data bytes need not be specified for blank columns on the right-hand side of the grid; however, these are assumed to be blank by the printer. You cannot reduce the size of the characters (proportional spacing is not permitted) but this does reduce the number of bytes needed to define the character.

Character definition

The *definition* consists of three bytes for each column used. For example, if columns 0-7 are used (and columns 8-11 are blank), the value of the attribute byte is 8 and 24 data bytes are required.

The right-most six bits of the third byte in each case are ignored and should be set to 0 (so the byte may only take values 00h, 40h, 80h, C0h).

24-pin draft

User-defined characters for 24-pin printers in draft mode have the following limits:

Grid size:	12 columns x 24 rows
Attribute bytes:	1
Max. total bytes:	39
Spacing:	Fixed only

The grid is shown in Figure 7.5. The *data* string for each character takes the form:

```
NUL attribute NUL definition
```

You can define characters for any of three pitches: 10 cpi, 12 cpi and 15 cpi. The pitch must be selected before you begin defining the characters.

Attribute byte

The attribute byte gives the number of columns used to define the character. If this is less than the number of bytes for the selected pitch, the grid is automatically filled out with blank columns to the right. This reduces the data length needed to define narrow characters. Proportional characters are not

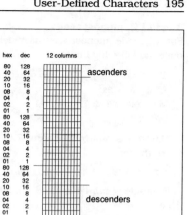

Figure 7.5 24-pin draft grid

allowed. The maximum character width and the bytes needed for each pitch are:

Pitch	Char. width (cols)	Max. bytes
10 cpi	12	36
12 cpi	10	30
15 cpi	8	24

Character definition

The *definition* consists of three bytes for each column used. For example, if the character uses 7 columns (including blank columns to the left but not those to the right), the definition *must* contain 21 bytes.

24-pin LQ, monospaced

For LQ mode, monospaced user-defined characters have the following limits:

Grid size:	36 columns x 24 rows
Attribute bytes:	1
Max. total bytes:	111
Spacing:	Fixed

The grid is shown in Figure 7.6. The *data* string takes the form:

```
NUL attribute NUL definition
```

Characters can be defined for 10 cpi, 12 cpi and 15 cpi.

Attribute byte

The attribute byte gives the number of columns used to define the character, and works in the same way as for draft mode, described above.

The maximum character width and bytes for each print are:

	Char. width	
Pitch	(cols)	Max. bytes
10 cpi	36	108
12 cpi	30	90
15 cpi	24	72

Character definition

The *definition* consists of three bytes for each column specified in the attribute byte. This includes any blank columns to the left of the character (for which the definition bytes are 00 00 00). Any undefined columns to the right are filled out with blanks automatically, expanding the character space to the required width.

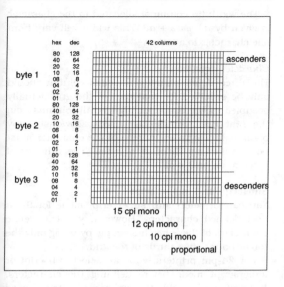

Figure 7.6 24-pin LQ grid

24-pin LQ, proportional

For LQ mode on 24-pin printers, you can also define proportional-spaced characters. The limits are:

Grid size:	42 columns x 24 rows
Attribute bytes:	3
Max. total bytes:	129
Spacing:	Proportional

The grid is shown in Figure 7.6. The *data* string takes the form:

    a1 a2 a3 definition

where *a1*, *a2* and *a3* are three attribute bytes.

Attribute bytes

For proportional characters, three attribute bytes must be specified:

a1	Blank columns to left
a2	Actual character width
a3	Blank columns to right

The width (in columns) allocated to the character is given by $a1 + a2 + a3$. This width will vary from one character to another.

Character definition
The three *definition* bytes for each column should only be specified for that part of the grid actually occupied by the character (that is, all columns from the first used to the last used). Obviously, any blank columns in the middle of the character must be specified as three zero bytes. The number of bytes must be $3 \times a2$.

Subscript and superscript
You cannot select sub/superscript mode for 9-pin user-defined characters. However, you can define characters of these heights simply by using only the top or bottom two-thirds of the grid.

For 24-pin printers, you can select subscript or superscript mode before defining the characters. For draft mode and letter quality mode monospaced characters, the main difference from full-size user-defined characters is that only 16 rows of the grid can be used. When printing superscripts or subscripts in these modes, the printer uses only the top or bottom 16 wires respectively. Therefore, only two definition bytes are needed for each character, rather than three (reducing the maximum number of bytes per character to 27 for draft and 75 for LQ).

For 24-pin LQ proportional modes, the grid is reduced in both directions, to 28 columns by 16 rows. Again, only two bytes are needed, so the maximum number of bytes per character is 59. In all other respects, the operation of the ESC & command is identical to that of the full-size equivalent.

48-pin printers
The process of defining characters for 48-pin printers is identical to that of 24-pin printers. The same grids are used to design the characters, the format of the ESC & command is identical and the same number of bytes of data are required. All that happens is that the character is mapped onto a larger grid and the printer then interpolates between cells to create a smoother image.

Using user-defined characters

A user-defined character is printed as follows:

1 Select the required attributes (if necessary) and typestyle (italic, bold, etc.)

2 Switch to the RAM-based character set (unless this has already been selected), using ESC % 1.

3 Send the required character codes to the printer.

4 Switch back to the ROM-based set (ESC % 0).

5 Turn off unwanted typestyles and attributes.

8 Graphics Printing

Much of the time the data we send to the printer is intended to produce text-based printouts. For this purpose, the data consists of a string of ASCII characters, with additional commands interspersed to determine how the final text will appear.

However, just as the PC display can be used in either text or graphics mode – to produce either text-based output or images based on the setting of individual pixels – so the printer can be put into a graphics mode.

In this mode, the data that is sent to the printer does not produce a specific series of ASCII codes, which in turn are converted into the patterns needed to represent characters. Instead, the data determines the precise position of each dot that is printed, building up an image on the paper.

Thus, by specifying which of the potential dots on the page will be 'on' and which will be 'off', you can encourage your printer to produce an extremely detailed and recognisable picture.

You can create some basic 'graphics' by combining specific combinations of characters, of course. For example, the box-drawing characters and other graphics symbols can be used to design simple boxes and other shapes. Similarly, it is possible – though arduous – to create a set of user-defined characters that will slot together to form a particular graphic. However, such methods operate entirely in text mode and are very limited in their output.

The best graphics are created by bit-image graphics. This chapter describes the principles used for Epsons and IBM Proprinters. Similar methods are applied on other types of printer.

Bit-image graphics

The idea of bit-image graphics is to define the specific lots that are to be printed. Each column of dots, produced by the print head at one position, is defined by one or more bytes of data. Each bit defines one dot: a 1 prints the dot, 0 omits it. The most significant bit of the first byte defines the top dot of the column, the least significant bit of the last byte defines the bottom dot. Data is sent on a column-by-column basis.

Aspect ratio

The aspect ratio is the ratio of horizontal dot density (number of dots per inch) to vertical dot density. For example, a horizontal density of 120 dpi and a vertical density of 60 dpi gives a ration of 2:1. Increasing the horizontal density to 240 dpi gives a ratio of 4:1; the result, if the same image data is sent, is an image that is thinner but with the same height.

The ratio is determined by the number of pins, the addressing mode and the density chosen by the command.

Addressing modes

You can use bit-image graphics for most types of IBM and Epson-compatible dot matrix printers. For each type of printer, there is one or more *addressing mode* available. This determines the number of pins used in that mode and hence the vertical dot density.

8-pin mode

8-pin addressing mode is used for 9-pin printers where only the top eight pins are used. It can also be used for 24-pin printers, where every third pin is used, and for 48-pin printers, with every eighth pin used.

9-pin mode

This modes uses all pins of a 9-pin printer.

24-pin mode

This mode is applied to 24-pin and 48-pin printers for 48-pin printers, only every second pin is used.

48-pin mode

The final mode uses all pins of a 48-pin printer.

Vertical dot density

The vertical dot density depends on the addressing mode and the type of printer. The possible densities are given in Figure 8.1. The table also shows the number of bytes needed to define a column of data in each mode.

Addressing Mode	Vertical density (dpi)			Bytes/ column
	9-pin	24-pin	48-pin	
8-pin	72	60	60	1
9-pin	72	-	-	2
24-pin	-	180	180	3
48-pin	-	-	360	6

Figure 8.1 Addressing modes

Bit-image commands

The command to send the carriage data takes the form:

    ESC n n1 n2 data

The first parameter, *d*, determines the addressing mode and density, as shown in Figure 8.2. (Note that some of the ESC * commands have other equivalents.)

The parameters *n1* and *n2* determine the number of columns for which data is being supplied. The number of columns is given by *n1* + (*n2* x 256).

The number of bytes of data must be the number of columns times the number of bytes per column (as shown in Figure 8.1). For example, for 20 columns of bit-image printing, in 24-pin addressing mode, you require 3 x 20 = 60 bytes of data.

Following receipt of this data, the printer returns to text mode. The image is only printed when the line is complete.

Command	Addr Mode	Density	Horizontal dpi
ESC * 0 ESC K	8	Single	60
ESC * 1 ESC L	8	Double	120
ESC * 2 ESC Y	8	High speed double	120
ESC * 3 ESC Z	8	Quad	240
ESC * 4	8	CRT I	80
ESC * 5	9	Plotter	72
ESC * 6	8	CRT II	90
ESC * 7	9	Double plotter	144
ESC * 32	24	Single	60
ESC * 33	24	Double	120
ESC * 38	24	CRT III	90
ESC * 39	24	Triple	180
ESC * 40	24	Hex	360
ESC * 64	48	Single	60
ESC * 65	48	Double	120
ESC * 70	48	CRT IV	90
ESC * 71	48	Triple	180
ESC * 72	48	Hex	360

Figure 8.2 Epson bit-image commands

9 Colour Printing

Colour printing is still a luxury that the majority of individuals and businesses cannot afford. However, there are a few colour printers available, and this chapter provides a brief introduction to the topic.

Colour theory

Essentially, colour is the sensation that is generated by the brain as a response to light of different wavelengths hitting our eyes.

The retina at the back of the eye has two different types of mechanism for receiving light: rods and cones. Rods take no account of the colour of the light but are able to determine the intensity; cones decide the colour that we perceive.

Cones come in three basic types, each of which can identify a single colour. These three types operate at wavelengths of 460, 530 and 650 nanometers. These wavelengths correspond to blue, green and red light respectively. The more 'blue' the light, the greater the signal passed by the 460nm cone. All colours are created by mixing these three *primary colours* in different amounts.

Additive colours

When the colours are mixed, new colours are perceived. Equal combinations of two colours give us a *secondary colour*. Red and blue create magenta; blue and green create cyan; greed and red produce yellow. All three colours together give white light; the absence of all three gives us black (no light). The effect is the same whether the lights are shown on a white surface or on our eyes.

This is the same principle used on computer monitors, which produce RGB (Red-Green-Blue) output. All 'dots' on the screen set their colour by adding three separate dots at various intensities.

Subtractive colours

The principles are reversed when mixing different colours inks (or other substances, such as paint). Here the primary colours are determined by the light colours they absorb. The primaries are the secondary colours from the additive process: magenta, cyan and yellow. Magenta absorbs green light and reflects blue and red; cyan absorbs red light and reflects green and blue; yellow absorbs blue light and reflects red and green.

When two of these colours are mixed equally, they absorb two of the light colours. Magenta and cyan absorb green and red, reflecting blue, giving a blue colour. Similarly, cyan and yellow reflects green, yellow and magenta reflects red.

All three primaries mixed together should theoretically reflect nothing, giving a colour of black. In practice, it is usual to include a genuinely black ink in the printing process as one of the 'colours', to ensure that all colour variations can be produced, including pure black. This method of mixing the colours is called *four-colour* printing. It is often abbreviated to CMYK (Cyan-Magenta-Yellow-blacK).

These alternative principles – RGB and CMYK - are available in PostScript printing (see Chapter 10). Four-colour printing is also used on many dot matrix colour printers.

Dot matrix colour printing

A growing number of printers include the ability to print in colour. In many cases, this is simply a question of offering a machine that can use a wide ribbon with two or more bands of coloured ink along it. Selecting a different colour for printing becomes a question of raising or lowering the ribbon so that the required band lines up with the print head.

Command:	Select colour	
Printers:	ESC/P ext	
Syntax:	ESC r n	(ASCII)
	1B 72 n	(hex)
	27 114 n	(dec)
Parameters:	n = 0 black	
	1 magenta	
	2 cyan	
	3 violet	
	4 yellow	
	5 orange	
	6 green	
Effect:	Selects a colour for printing, where the correct ribbon type has been installed by the user.	

10 PostScript

PostScript is a *page description language*. Its purpose is to provide a series of instructions that define the contents of a page – including text, graphics and bit images – in a form that can be understood by a PostScript printer. The instructions are stored in a PostScript file. The main aim behind PostScript was that it should become a standard language, so a program written for one printer should produce identical output on any other Post-Script printer. In this, the language's originators, Adobe, have been largely successful.

PostScript files

PostScript has the advantage that the page-description programs are stored in ASCII files; i.e. the files are straight text, with no formatting characters or other codes. The only special characters are the CR LF codes at the ends of lines and the final Ctrl-Z (end-of-file) character.

This means that any PostScript file can be inspected, edited and re-saved. If you have an application program with a PostScript driver – a word processor, for example – you can produce output for a PostScript printer and then redirect this to a file rather than the printer port. (Most applications allow printer output to be redirected to a file or later printing.) This file can be viewed or edited with any text editor or a word processor that allows you to work with ASCII files (almost all do).

The first thing you will notice is that the ASCII file is very large, no matter how little you asked the program to print. This is because the printer needs a great deal of information to define the fonts it can use, the type of graphics that will be needed, and so on. Most general-purpose word processors include all these extra instructions at the start of the file, regardless of whether or not they are actually used in the document. The result is that a lot of unnecessary instructions are sent to the printer, and printing is much slower than it need be. In fact,

PostScript programs can be extremely small and compact.

Having inspected – or changed – a PostScript file you can force the printer to print the document by typing a simple command at the DOS prompt. For example, for a file called TEXT.C00 (C00 is a standard extension applied by many applications), the DOS command is:

```
COPY TEXT.C00 PRN:
```

This assumes that the printer is attached to the standard parallel port. In this way, you can transport PostScript files from one PC to another and print documents without having to run the original application program.

Compatibility

Perhaps the greatest advantage of PostScript is that of compatibility. You can be reasonably satisfied that a document produced for one PostScript printer will produce an identical result on any other PostScript printer.

There are, of course, exceptions. In some cases these are minor: a rounded box produced by one printer may be more rounded at the corners on a second. The result may be that the box clips the edge of any graphic inside it, even though there appeared to have been plenty of white space inside the box on the first printout. Such minor irritations are easily catered for once you know to expect them.

More serious are problems arising from different versions of PostScript. Since its first release, there have been many versions of PostSript, all sequentially numbered. Although a file produced for a printer with a low version number will work on any printer with a higher number, the reverse is not necessarily true, particularly if the more advanced recently introduced features are used. Never assume that a file will work on another PostScript printer until you have tried it.

Finally, even though an *application* may support a feature, that doesn't mean a printer can print it. For example, including colour PostScript commands will only be effective if you know that your printer has a colour-printing capability.

Version numbers

Each new enhancement of Adobe's PostScript language is given a new version number – and there have been a great number of enhancements since the first version appeared in 1986. The latest version number is now above 50. However, most enhancements are only minor and should not cause any real problems.

The main changes came at version 23, and later PostScript files are unlikely to produce a satisfactory result when run with versions that have a lower number, unless the programs are very simple.

More recently, Adobe has introduced a much enhanced version of PostScript, known as *Level 2*.

Encapsulated PostScript Files (EPSF)

For standalone applications, the use of PostScript as described above is adequate. However, if you want to create PostScript files that can be used by other qualifications and incorporated into larger documents, you will need to create *Encapsulated PostScript Files* (EPSF).

There are some minor restrictions on EPSF code but the main differences are:

Additional %% comments are required at the top of the file; these tell the importing program how large the printed image will be, for example.

- The origin of the image is determined by the importing application, and all drawing and text within the EPSF is relative to that origin (rather than taking a fixed position on the page).

Program structure

The overall structure of a PostScript program is usually divided into three main sections: the prologue, the main program and the trailer.

The prologue

The first part is the *prologue*, which describes the program and its function, the creator and so on. Following these first few titles, the dictionaries and routines are defined.

In fact, programs will operate quite happily with no prologue.

Although you can start and end a PostScript program with any comments you like (for Level 1 versions), certain comments are expected.

It is usual to use double % symbols for these recognised comments. It should also be noted that these conventions are mandatory for Level 2 PostScript files. The %% option is also used for a variety of other purposes, such as defining the resources required by the program; therefore you should avoid the use of %% except where you are incorporating a recognised structuring statement.

The main program

The prologue is followed by the instructions for creating the output, one page at a time. As a rule, the code for each page will be enclosed in a matching pair of save and restore operators. The save operator stores on the stack a copy of the current working memory (the printer's *virtual memory*); restore rewrites the working memory from the stack using the values put there at the last save. This means that you do not have to include instructions to move the drawing point back to the top of the page, clear the stack and so on; all of this is done for you automatically. All variables are reset to their defaults. Effectively, this allows you to start again from scratch, with no danger of problems being caused by uncleared variables. Following the restore are the instructions that actually print the page.

The save and restore operators are not restricted to use at page ends; you can also use them within a page definition if you want to perform some action and then get back where you started.

The trailer

The final part of the program is called the *trailer* and is simply there to signify the end of the program.

PostScript instructions

Each element of the output of the printed page is defined by one or more instructions in the file. For example, there will be an instruction in the file for each line of text, including information on how the text is to be formatted. Other instructions will define the font to be used, the orientation of the paper, and so on.

For graphics images, the picture must be broken down into a series of simple instructions. For instance, drawing a box consists of instructions to move to a particular point on the page and then draw four different lines. Other instructions may be used to draw circles, ark, ellipses and so on; there are also commands to fill areas, and produce shading and other effects.

Paths

Each of these instructions only define the *path* to be created on the paper. They have the effect of building up in the printer's memory an image of part of the final printed page. At any time you can transfer the path to the overall image in memory; this process is referred to as *stroking* the path. A final PostScript command is needed to perform the task of transferring this image to the paper.

The PostScript file is transmitted to the printer in the normal way. Each PostScript printer contains a high-powered microprocessor that is dedicated to the task of handling the incoming file. The Post-

Script file is treated as a program, a list of com
mands. The PostScript *interpreter* reads each line o
the file and carries out the action required of it.

PostScript Programming

Programming in PostScript is similar to that of an
other programming language, once you hav
grasped the general principles. The main feature
are outlined here and there are several good tutori:
books available on the topic. The core PostScript in
struction set is given at the end of this chapter.

Interpreted languages

PostScript is an *interpreted* language. With such
language, each line is dealt with in turn. Therefor
you must ensure that everything is defined before
is needed; you cannot use the contents of a variabl
before the variable has been defined, for exampl
You can define subroutines, which may be re-use
many times, but each time the subroutine is calle
it will be re-interpreted.

Interpreted languages tend to be slower tha
compiled languages, though there is no time waste
in the compilation stage. For compiled languages,
program called a *compiler* reads the program befo:
it is executed, converting the program into anoth
form, building up lists of variables and routine
identifying syntax errors and so on; the resulta:
program runs much faster than one that is inte
preted but the compilation takes time.

Instructions

Each instruction usually consists of data and :
operator. The operator is a key word that tells th
interpreter what to do with the data. For exampl
the following two instructions move the drawi
point to co-ordinates (20,30) and then draw a li
to (40,50):

```
20 30 moveto
40 50 lineto
```

(Note that these instructions alone are not enough to draw the line physically; see the section of 'Graphics' below.)

The PostScript interpreter reads the file from the beginning, ignoring line ends (in effect, treating them as spaces). Therefore you can put each instruction on a separate line, combine instructions on one line or split an instruction over several lines. For example, the code above could equally well be written:

```
20 30 moveto 40 50 lineto
```

Or:

```
20 30
moveto
40
50 lineto
```

All these are equally acceptable to the interpreter (though not so easy for us to read and understand).

The stack

All data is stored on a *stack*. This is part of the printer's memory set aside for the purpose, in which data is stored on a 'last in first out' principle. The result is a 'pile' of data items, all new data being added at the top. If you want to get at some data lower down, you must first remove all those items above it.

PostScript is unusual in that an item of data in the program is, in effect, an instruction to store that piece of data on the stack. Therefore you can include data values in the program without necessarily following them with an instruction. For example, this line puts four values on the stack, with the value 30 at the top:

```
40 50 20 30
```

Any command that requires values as input simply takes the next available values from the stack. The values above could be removed by adding the following two instructions:

```
moveto lineto
```

The first instruction (moveto) takes 30 and 20 off the stack and acts accordingly, the next removes 50 and 40.

These two lines of instruction could thus be combined:

```
40 50 20 30 moveto lineto
```

This is equivalent to the earlier example. The main point is that if you want to store data for later use, the sets of values must be added to the stack *in reverse order*.

Putting values on the stack

Some instructions put their results on the stack, as well as removing values from it. For example, the sub instruction takes two values off the stack, subtracts one from the other and puts the result onto the stack.

The following instruction puts two values (8 and 5) on the stack, then subtracts the second from the first, leaving only the result (3) on the stack:

```
8 5 sub
```

Clearing the stack

Although many PostScript instructions remove values from the stack and use them, you can also use the pop instruction to remove values and discard them. Each pop instruction removes one item from the top of the stack.

Variables

The stack alone is not enough for most purposes. You must also define *variables* (like almost all other programming languages).

The syntax for a numeric variable is:

 /variable definition def

For example, to define the variable 'counter' with an initial value of 10, the instruction is:

```
/counter 10 def
```

This variable can be used in the program; for example:

```
counter 1 sub
```

The result is that counter - 1 (i.e. 9) is placed on the stack. The value of counter can be changed by further def statements. The definition may itself be a series of PostScript instructions. For instance, to reduce the value of counter by 1, the definition would be:

```
/counter counter 1 sub def
```

This is equivalent to the BASIC statement:

```
counter% = counter% - 1
```

A variable may be redefined (i.e. assigned a new value) as often as you like within a program. The example above could be used in a loop and followed by a conditional statement (see below).

Strings and arrays

Two other types of variable can be defined:

String variables, which may hold items of text

Array variables, which can hold a series of indexed values, either integer or string

Procedures

PostScript allows you to define procedures – sections of code that may be called repeatedly from other parts of the program – in much the same way as any other programming language. The syntax is similar to that for variable definition:

/*procedure* { *definition* } def

The *definition* may spread over many lines and may call other procedures and use variables, provided all those have been defined earlier in the program.

For example, to draw a rectangle around the inside of an A4 sheet, you might define the following subroutine:

```
/drawborder

{
   300 300 moveto
   300 2100 lineto
   3200 2100 lineto
   3200 300 lineto
   300 300 lineto
} def
```

Whenever the instruction 'drawborder' is en countered, a rectangle will be drawn on the paper.

Comments

You can include comments anywhere within a pro gram to explain what is going on, a wis precaution, particularly for complex programs. Any thing following a % symbol is regarded as comment and ignored by the interpreter (up to th end of the current line). Comments can take entir lines or be added at the ends of lines.

Conditional operations

PostScript allows you to carry out an actio depending on the result of a comparison. The com parison is made with operators such as gt (great than) and le (less than or equal to). These general act on two items of data from the stack.

The operator is followed by a section of code, curly brackets, and the if operator. The brackete code will take effect only if the compariso produced a 'true' result.

For example, suppose that you have a procedu called StartNewPage and are holding the number lines of text printed so far in a variable called line Then you can invoke the procedure by checking th number of lines printed against the maximum r quired. This is done using the ge (greater than equal to) operator, as follows:

```
lines 66 ge
{ % start a new page
  StartNewPage
  } if
```

The ge operator takes the two values (lines and 66) off the stack and performs the comparison. If lines has reached 66, a value of 'true' is placed on the stack; otherwise, the value returned is 'false'. Therefore the subroutine StartNewPage is only called if the value of lines is 66 or more.

Boolean values

Conditional operators rely heavily on *boolean* values. A boolean can take only two possible values: 'true' and 'false'. Mathematically, 'false' is represented by zero and 'true' is any non-zero value (usually -1 or 1).

The conditional operator and if statement do not necessarily have to be used together. The effect of an operator such as ge is to put a value of 'true' on the stack if the result of the comparison is true or 'false' if it is not; this value can be picked up by *any* subsequent instruction. The if statement takes the top value from the stack and processes the bracketed instructions if the value is non-zero; the value may have been put there by any other instruction.

Alternative options

You can also select between two alternative sets of instructions, using the ifelse instruction. For example:

```
linestoprint 0 gt
{%Print more text
   ...}
{%Finished printing
         ...}ifelse
```

The first set of instructions is executed if the condition is true, the second if it is false.

Repeated operations

A group of instructions can be repeated a number of times with the for operator, which has the syntax:

start *step stop* {*instructions*} for

The start value is the initial value of an unnamed loop counter, *step* is the amount by which the counter is to increase each time through the loop and *stop* is the value at which the loop should end. For example:

```
5 1 8 {drawbox} for
```

The drawbox procedure is executed four times. Although the counter is not stored in a variable, its value is placed on the stack each time through the loop and is therefore available for the instructions to use.

Similarly the forall operator repeats instructions for all elements of an array and repeat executes a loop a specified number of times.

Text

There are several steps to be taken when printing text. To start with, the font to be used must be defined (if it is different to that last used). Fonts are defined initially in the program prologue. PostScript recognises names such as Helvetica, Helvetica-bold and so on.

A series of operators are needed to select the precise font:

- findfont identifies the font to use

- scalefont sets the point size

- setfont implements the changes by making the chosen font the *current* font

For example, to choose the Helvetica 10-point font for all following printing (until the next change of font), use:

```
Helvetica findfont 10 scalefont setfont
```

To print a string of text, this must be enclosed in normal brackets and followed by the show operator For example:

```
300 300 moveto   % start 1" down and across
(This is the first line) show
                 % print first line
300 350 moveto   % move down ⅙"
(This is the 2nd line) show

                 % print second line
```

It is important to realise at this stage that a new PostScript program will be generated by the application each time a document is printed. Therefore the program contains the actual text to be printed on each occasion; unlike most programming tasks, it does not have to be a generalised program that allows for all eventualities. Most PostScript programs are used once and then thrown away.

The show instructions are used to build up an image of the printed page in memory; the physical printing only takes place when the showpage operator is encountered. This usually takes place at the end of the program (or at the end of a page, for multi-page documents).

Before issuing the showpage command, a system variable, #copies, may be given a value. This variable determines the number of copies to print. (All system variable names begin with the # symbol.) For example:

```
/# copies 2 def % Set number of copies to 2
showpage        % Print two sheets
```

Extended ASCII

Extended ASCII characters can be included in the text in the form \nnn, where nnn is a three-digit decimal ASCII code. For example, in the PostScript Helvetica font, the £ sign is represented by ASCII 156 (decimal), so can be included in a document as 156. A line of text may appear as follows:

```
(The cost will be \15628.05 inc. VAT) show
```

This will print as:

```
The cost will be £28.05 inc. VAT
```

Dictionaries

All names found in a PostScript program are held in dictionaries. This includes all user-defined variable names, as well as the PostScript operators themselves. There may be many dictionaries but these will usually include:

- userdict, which holds the user-defined names

- systemdict, which defines all PostScript operators

- statusdict, which stores all machine-dependent values or configuration data

- errordict, which is used for error handling

The fonts are also stored in dictionaries.

A dictionary does not just hold a set of names; it also includes the definitions that are associated with these names. For instance, userdict contains the variables and their current values, and the procedures and their full definitions. Each dictionary is a series of pairs; the first item is a key word, the second its definition.

The dictionaries are all stored on the dictionary stack. When the PostScript interpreter encounters a name in the program – including PostScript operator – it searches down through the dictionaries, starting at the top of the stack, until it finds a match.

Since systemdict is always at the bottom of the stack, the system operator can be redefined in other dictionaries, so care in naming is essential.

The userdict dictionary is created automatically but you can also define your own dictionaries. For example:

/shapes 8 dict def

This defines a dictionary called shapes, which can hold eight definitions. This dictionary declaration is usually followed by the definition of the dictionary items; for instance:

```
Shapes begin      % Define dictionary items
  /Rectangle {...} def       % Define rectangle
  /Oval {...} def            % Define an oval
  ...                 % Define 6 more items
end               % End definition
```

The dictionary definitions should come at the start of the program, as part of the prologue, so that they are placed on the stack before the main routines begin.

Co-ordinates

The PostScript co-ordinate system determines your current position on the paper in terms of a pair of (x, y) co-ordinates. The x co-ordinate is the distance up the page, counted from the bottom. The co-ordinates are given in terms of the dots that are printed: in most cases at a scale of 300 dots per inch. Thus (0, 0) is the point in the bottom left-hand corner of the page; (600,300) is a point two inches across and one inch from the bottom.

The program keeps track of where you are. For example, the show operator prints the text on the stack, starting at the current position. After adding the text to the image in memory, the current position will be just beyond where the text ended.

You can modify the co-ordinate system with several instructions:

- The translate operator moves the origin to a new point.

- The scale operator changes the x and y scales (independently).

- The rotate operator rotates the co-ordinate system (in degrees) anticlockwise.

For example, 1 2 scale leaves the x-axis as it is but the y-axis is doubled; everything is printed with twice the height. The 90 rotate instruction turns the page on its side, for landscape printing.

If you change the co-ordinates for a particular graphic or item of text, remember to change them back when you have finished. Alternatively, use save before the changes and restore when the action has been completed.

Matrices

The modification that has been applied to the co-ordinate system is determined by the Current Transformation Matrix (CTM). This matrix is applied to all co-ordinates before anything is actually printed. Whenever a further transformation is executed (a translate, scale or rotate operation), the effect is that a new matrix, representing this transformation, is multiplied by the CTM to give a new CTM.

Although it helps to have an understanding of matrix multiplication, this is not essential here. The important point is that each transformation further modifies the current origin, scale and grid angle but at any time you can recover an earlier version of the CTM with restore operator.

Graphics

PostScript allows you to draw lines of various types. You can select the position to start the line with one of two operands:

- moveto moves to a specific point on the page

- rmoveto moves to a point relative to the current position

Types of line-drawing operators include the following:

- lineto draws a straight line between two specific points

- rlineto draws a line to a new point relative to the current point

- arc produces an arc of a circle

- curveto generates a Bézier curve

These are the fundamental instructions but there are several others.

Bézier curves

The curves are perhaps the most complicated to program and to predict, yet allow you to produce any curve you need. The curveto operator requires four pairs of co-ordinates: the start and end point for the curve plus two points in the middle.

When the curve is drawn it starts working towards the direction of the first intermediate point the line then curves around towards the second point before finally arriving at the end point, coming from the direction of the second intermediate.

The effects of this behaviour are dramatically different, depending on the positioning of the intermediate points.

Completing the graphics

The instructions above define a *path* to be followed by the line; they do not actually add the graphics to the current page. This is achieved by the stroke operator. Each graphics element, or group of elements, should be concluded with this instruction.

Graphics information should be saved at the start of any new part of the output with the gsave operator. Afterwards the graphics settings can be restored with grestore. This includes the settings of translations, rotations, current point and many more. The principle is the same as that for save and restore.

You can save and restore the graphics settings at any time, of course. You can also *nest* pairs of commands; for example:

```
gsave       % Save before main graphics
...         % Instructions for start of graphics
...         % e.g. to rotate page
Rectangle   % Draw a rectangle
gsave       % Save graphics again
...         % Draw another graphic
grestore    % Restore main graphics settings
...         % Other graphics commands
...         % With other gsave...grestore if
               necessary
grestore    % Cancel all graphics settings
```

As for the save...restore operators, these graphics operators allow you to get back to any earlier position without having to redefine everything.

You can vary the shade of the graphics with the setgray operator. This has the syntax:

```
level setgray
```

The value of *level* determines the level of grey to be applied, and must lie in the range 0 to 1. A *level* of 0 produces black graphics, while 1 represents white. For example:

```
0.25 setgray    % Dark grey
0.75 setgray    % Pale grey
0 setgray       % Restore full black printing
```

Of course, the printer can only produce dots of black, so they 'grey' colour is created by varying the density of the dots that are printed. The closer together the dots are, the darker the grey that is produced.

Inserting graphics

If you have developed a re-usable graphics image – for example, a logo or a letter head – this can be saved separately as a PostScript file. You can include this in further documents simply by inserting it in the middle of another PostScript file.

The inserted file should always be enclosed in pairs of save...restore or gsave...grestore operators to ensure that any changes made within the file do not affect the later parts of the document.

Reducing the graphics area

You can make sure that a graphic stays within a specific area using the clip operator. This defines a rectangle, in which all future graphics will be restricted. The following graphics instructions only add new points and lines to the current path if they are within the clip area. For example, if a line is drawn that is partly out of the clip area, the line will be drawn so that it stops at the boundary of the clip area.

Any clip operations should be enclosed within a pair of gsave...grestore operators, so that the clip area is restored to the full page afterwards.

Bit-mapped graphics

Graphics images do not necessarily have to consist of lines, curves and rectangles. You can also print *bit-mapped images*, where each bit of a set of bytes determines whether or not a particular point is to be printed. For example, if the value 1 represents

black and 0 is white, the binary value 10101010
(i.e. AAh) will print alternate dots; the binary value
11100000 (E0h) prints a row of three dots then
skips the next five dots.

The imagemask operator maps a series of such binary values onto a specified area. The operator has
the syntax:

> *width height black* [*matrix*] {*data*} imagemask

The *width* and *height* determine the rectangle
into which the image is to fit. The dots are filled
from left to right and bottom to top (unless the co-
ordinate system has been changed).

The *black* value is the bit value for which a point
is to be printed; for example, if *black* is 1 then a '1'
in the binary data results in the dot being printed;
set *black* to 0 to reverse the image.

The *matrix* represents any transformation that is
to be carried out on the co-ordinate matrix. The
data can be actual hex values (*not* decimal or
genuine binary), a procedure that generates the
values or an instruction to include another file. In
particular, you may want to include an existing
IMG image file.

Note that any bits representing 'white' do not affect any existing graphics; they simply skip that
point. Therefore any underlying graphics are not
cancelled by the bit image, merely overlaid.

To increase the size of the image, use the scale
operator before the imagemask instructions.

Grey-scale images

Following similar principles to imagemask, the image
operator allows you to draw each 'point' in a different shade of grey. The shade of grey is
determined by 1, 2, 4 or 8 bits for each point. This
results in 2, 4, 16 or 256 levels of grey respectively.
For example, to get 16 levels of grey requires 4 bits
per point, so each byte of data represents two
points only.

The syntax of the operator is:

> *width height bits* [*matrix*] {*data*} image

The main difference is the *bits* value, which determines the number of bits required per point. To get the full effect you should apply a scale factor beforehand.

Note that the use of grey-scale images significantly reduces the speed of print, because of the vastly increased number of calculations required to produce the image.

PostScript Operators

This section describes the core set of PostScript operators. In each case, the syntax gives the values that are taken from the stack. The values put back on the working stack are also shown. For example, the syntax of the add operator is shown as:

Syntax:	*num1 num2* add
To stack:	*num3*

This means that two numbers, *num1* and *num2*, are removed from the stack. A third value, *num3*, the result of the addition, is put back to the stack.

When an operator uses the stack values in this way, you can either include the values as part of the instruction or make sure that the values have been put on the stack by some previous operation (remembering that if one set of values is needed later than another set, these must be put on the stack *earlier*). For example:

```
23 34 add  % adds 34 to 23
add        % adds the top two values of
             the current stack
```

The effect is that the top two values of the stack

This means that two numbers, *num1* and *num2*, are removed from the stack. A third value, *num3*, the result of the addition, is put back on the stack.

Operator:	[
Syntax:	[
To stack:	*mark*
Effect:	Places a *mark* on the stack for use by other operators or to define the start of a matrix. Identical to the mark operator.

Operator:	]
Syntax:	]
To stack:	(Nothing)
Effect:	Identifies the end of an array

Operator:	=
Syntax:	*item* =
To stack:	(Nothing)
Effect:	Prints a text version of the *item* that is on the stack, directing the output to the standard output file.

Operator:	==
Syntax:	*item* ==
To stack:	(Nothing)
Effect:	Prints a text version of the *item* on the top of the stack, in the format in which it was placed on the stack. The output is sent to the standard output file. For example, arrays are printed in square brackets and text is enclosed in round brackets.

Operator:	abs
Syntax:	*num1* abs
To stack:	*num2*
Effect:	Converts *num1* to its absolute value, *num2*. Positive values are unchanged, negative values are made positive.

Operator:	add
Syntax:	*num1 num2* add
To stack:	*num3*
Effect:	Adds the top two numbers from the stack, *num1* and *num2*, and puts the result (*num3*) on the stack.

Operator:	aload
Syntax:	*array* aload
To stack:	*val1 ... valn array*
Effect:	Puts the values of the named array (*val1* to *valn*) on the stack, followed by the array name itself.

Operator:	anchorsearch
Syntax:	*string1 string2* anchorsearch
To stack:	*string3 string2* true (if matching)
	string1 false (if not matching)
Effect:	Compares *string2* with the start of *string1*. If they are the same, then *string3*, the non-matching part of *string1*, is put on the stack, followed by the sub-string and a 'true' value. If they are not the same, then *string1* is put on the stack, followed by a 'false' value.

Operator:	and
Syntax:	*num1 num2* and
To stack:	*num3*
Effect:	If *num1* and *num2* are booleans and both are 'true', the *num3* is 'true'; otherwise, *num3* is 'false'. If the two numbers, *num1* and *num2*, are compared bit-by-bit to create *num3*. A boolean 'and' operation is carried out: each bit in *num3* is only set to 1 if both corresponding bits in *num1* and *num2* are also 1.

Operator:	arc
Syntax:	*x y radius angle1 angle2* arc
To stack:	(Nothing)
Effect:	Draws an arc of a circle, centred at (*x,y*), with the given *radius*. The arc is drawn anti-clockwise, starting at an angle of *angle1* and ending at *angle2*. Use the scale and rotate operators beforehand to produce the arc of an ellipse.

Operator:	arcn
Syntax:	*x y radius angle1 angle2* arcn
To stack:	(Nothing)
Effect:	Has the same effect as arc but the arc is drawn clockwise rather than anti-clockwise, starting at *angle1* and ending at *angle2*. The arc is part of a circle of specified *radius*, centred on (*x,y*). Use scale and rotate to draw an elliptical arc.

Operator:	arcto
Syntax:	*x1 y1 x2 y2* arcto
To stack:	*x3 y3 x4 y4*
Effect:	Two imaginary lines are drawn, from the current point to (*x1,y1*) and from (*x1,y1*) to (*x2,y2*). An arc is drawn inside the angle created by these two lines, so that it is at a tangent to the lines. The co-ordinates of the tangent to the arc are put on the stack.

Operator:	array
Syntax:	*n* array
To stack:	*array1...arrayn*
Effect:	Creates a blank array of *n* items and places them on the stack.

Operator:	ashow
Syntax:	*x y string* ashow
To stack:	(Nothing)
Effect:	Prints the *string* on the current page, in the current font and colour, starting at the current point. This operator is similar to show but after each character, the printing position is moved by relative co-ordinates (*x,y*).

Operator:	astore
Syntax:	*item1...itemn n* astore
To stack:	*array*
Effect:	Takes *n* objects off the stack and puts them back as an *array*

(consisting of the *n* elements *item1* to *itemn*).

Operator:	atan
Syntax:	*num1 num2* atan
To stack:	*angle*
Effect:	Stores on the stack an *angle* (in degrees) whose tangent is given by *num1/num2*.

Operator:	awidthshow
Syntax:	*x1 y1 char x2 y2 string* awidthshow
To stack:	(Nothing)
Effect:	Prints the *string* with a relative displacement of (*x1,y1*) after each character has been printed. In addition, any occurrence of *char*, a particular character, result in a further displacement of (*x2,y2*). The effect is that of combining the ashow and awidthshow operators.

Operator:	begin
Syntax:	*dictionary* begin
To stack:	(Nothing)
Effect:	Makes *dictionary* the current directory and puts it at the top of the dictionary stack.

Operator:	bind
Syntax:	*procedure1* bind
To stack:	*procedure2*
Effect:	Compiles the procedure, *procedure1*, into an executable format and puts this back on the stack as *procedure2*. The advantage is that the interpreter does not need to read and convert the procedure each time it is called. The disadvantage is that the executable code is fixed, so any variables that are used by the procedure and have changed will be ignored. Each time the procedure is called in future, the effect is identical. This process

should be used for self-contained, frequently-called procedures, to speed up the printing process.

Operator:	bitshift
Syntax:	*integer1 num* bitshift
To stack:	*integer2*
Effect:	Shifts the bits in *integer1* to the left *num* times, if *num* is positive, or to the right if *num* is negative. For example, when *num* has a value of 2 the effect is to shift left twice (i.e. equivalent to multiplication by 4); when *num* is -1 the bits shift right once, equivalent to division by 2. The resulting integer, *integer2*, is put back on the stack.

Operator:	bytesavailable
Syntax:	*filename* bytesavailable
To stack:	*num*
Effect:	Returns the number of bytes still to be read from the open file specified by *filename*. If there are no bytes still to be read in the file, or the number cannot be ascertained for some reason, the value of *num* is returned as -1.

Operator:	cachestatus
Syntax:	cachestatus
To stack:	*bitmapused bitmapmax fontused fontmax numchars maxchars charbytesmax*
Effect:	When memory is used as a font cache, the following values relating to the current situation are returned:

bitmapused	Number of bytes of the bit-map used
bitmapmax	Maximum number of bytes for the bit-map
fontused	Number of bytes used for the font

fontmax	Maximum number of bytes for the font
numchars	Number of characters cached
maxchars	Maximum number of characters that can be cached
charbytesmax	Maximum number of bytes to be used in the creation of each character, if the character is to be cached

The only value that can be changed is *charbytesmax* (see the setcachelimit operator).

Operator:	ceiling
Syntax:	*number* ceiling
To stack:	*integer*
Effect:	Rounds the given *number* up to the nearest integer (unless it is already an integer). The result is always greater than or equal to the original value; for example, 4.8 is rounded up to 5 and -4.8 is rounded up to -4.

Operator:	charpath
Syntax:	*string clip* charpath
To stack:	(Nothing)
Effect:	Puts an outline of the *string* as it would be printed in the current path (i.e. each character has a black outline but is white inside). This outline can be printed as it is or used to define a clipping area for the clip operator.
	The *clip* value determines how the path is to be used. A value of 1 indicates that the path can be clipped or filled but it cannot be stroked; with a value of 0 the path can be stroked

(i.e. printed) but may not be clipped or filled.

Operator:	clear
Syntax:	clear
To stack:	(Clears)
Effect:	Clears the stack completely, leaving it empty and discarding all values.

Operator:	cleatomark
Syntax:	cleartomark
To stack:	(Clears to mark)
Effect:	Takes all items from the stack down to, and including, the first mark it finds (put there by the [or mark operator).

Operator:	clip
Syntax:	clip
To stack:	(Nothing)
Effect:	Creates a path to be used for clipping; any future graphics stroked to the paper are only drawn if they are within the clip path. This instruction defines the current path as the clip path. If a clip path already exists, the new clip path is those areas that are within both the existing *and* the current path. The clip path can be cancelled (allowing graphics over the whole page) or a previous clip path re-used, by careful use of gsave and grestore.

Operator:	clippath
Syntax:	clippath
To stack:	(Nothing)
Effect:	Discards the current path and replaces it with a new one which matches the current clip path. If you follow this with a stroke instruction, the effect is to draw an outline of the clip path as it is at present.

Operator:	closefile
Syntax:	*filename* closefile
To stack:	(Nothing)
Effect:	Closes the named file, having first written away any outstanding data (for output files).

Operator:	closepath
Syntax:	closepath
To stack:	(Nothing)
Effect:	Draws a line from the current point to the start of the current path. If all lines in the path are consecutive, this will create a completely enclosed area. The path is not printed until you use the stroke operator.

Operator:	concat
Syntax:	*matrix* concat
To stack:	(Nothing)
Effect:	Combines the *matrix* that is at the top of the stack (or specified in the instruction) with the Current Transformation Matrix to create a new transformation matrix.

Operator:	concatmatrix
Syntax:	*matrix1 matrix2* concatmatrix
To stack:	*matrix3*
Effect:	Combines *matrix1* with *matrix2* to create a new matrix, *matrix3*, which is stored on the stack. There is no effect on the Current Transformation Matrix.

Operator:	copy
Syntax:	*n* copy
	object1 object2 copy
To stack:	*item1...itemn*
	object2
Effect:	Where the item at the top of the stack is an integer, the operand places a copy of the *n* items below on top of the stack. Where the item at the top

is a composite object (array, string or dictionary), the contents of *object1* are copied onto *object2*.

Operator:	copypage
Syntax:	copypage
To stack:	(Nothing)
Effect:	Sends a copy of the current page to the printer but does not clear the page (unlike showpage). Therefore you can print the page at various stages of the process of building up the final output.
	The number of copies printed is determined by the #*copies* system variable.

Operator:	cos
Syntax:	*angle* cos
To stack:	num
Effect:	Returns the cosine of the specified *angle* (which should be given in degrees).

Operator:	count
Syntax:	count
To stack:	num
Effect:	Counts the number of items on the stack and puts the answer on the top of the working stack.

Operator:	countdictstack
Syntax:	countdictstack
To stack:	num
Effect:	Counts the number of items on the dictionary stack and puts the answer on the top of the *working* stack

Operator:	counttomark
Syntax:	counttomark
To stack:	num
Effect:	Counts the number of items on the stack up to (but not including) the

mark nearest the top. The answer is put on the stack.

Operator:	currentcacheparams
Syntax:	currentcacheparams
To stack:	*mark threshold maximum other ...*
Effect:	Puts a mark on the stack and then stores the following cache parameters:

threshold	The number of bytes above which any character data is compressed for storing in cache memory
maximum	The maximum number of bytes that may be used for storing the bit image data for any character
other	Other parameters that are stored by different versions of PostScript

The cache parameters are set up with setcacheparams.

Operator:	currentcmykcolor
Syntax:	currencmykcolor
To stack:	*cyan magenta yellow black*
Effect:	Returns the current settings of the four colours set by the setcmykcolor operator.

Operator:	currentdash
Syntax:	currentdash
To stack:	*array num*
Effect:	You can specify that any lines are to be drawn with a pattern of dashes (using the setdash operator). This operator puts on the stack the *array* that currently defines the pattern of

dashes and the number of points that
are drawn at the start of the line
before the pattern begins.

Operator:	currentdict
Syntax:	currentdict
To stack:	*dictionary*
Effect:	Puts a copy of the current dictionary (from the top of the dictionary stack) on the working stack.

Operator:	currentfile
Syntax:	currentfile
To stack:	*filename*
Effect:	Puts the *filename* of the current input file on the top of the stack

Operator:	currentflat
Syntax:	currentflat
To stack:	*num*
Effect:	Returns the value used to determine how 'flat' curves are. A low value indicates that curves are made of many very small straight lines, giving a smooth appearance; a high value indicates that fewer straight lines are used, so that curves will have more 'flat' sections and appear less smooth.

Operator:	currentfont
Syntax:	currentfont
To stack:	*fontname*
Effect:	Puts on the stack the name of the current font, as determined by setfont.

Operator:	currentgray
Syntax:	currentgray
To stack:	*num*
Effect:	Puts on the stack the grey-level setting of the current 'colour', as set by setgray. If the colour has been set by setcmykcolor, the brightness is returned.

Operator:	currenthsbcolor
Syntax:	currenthsbcolor
To stack:	*hue saturation brightness*
Effect:	Returns the settings of the values that determine the current colour, as set by sethsbcolor.

Operator:	currentlinecap
Syntax:	currentlinecap
To stack:	*num*
Effect:	Returns the code (0 to 2) that determines the shape of line endings, as set by setlinecap.

Operator:	currentlinejoin
Syntax:	currentlinejoin
To stack:	*num*
Effect:	Returns the code (0 to 2) that determines the way in which consecutive lines are joined, as set by setlinejoin.

Operator:	currentlinewidth
Syntax:	currentlinewidth
To stack:	*num*
Effect:	Returns the current line width, as set by setlinewidth

Operator:	currentmatrix
Syntax:	*matrix1* currentmatrix
To stack:	*matrix2*
Effect:	Replaces the matrix at the top of stack with the Current Transformation Matrix.

Operator:	currentmiterlimit
Syntax:	currentmiterlimit
To stack:	*num*
Effect:	Returns the current limit of the mitres that can be used to join lines, as set by *setmiterlimit* (in the range 0 to 2).

Operator:	currentpacking
Syntax:	currentpacking
To stack:	num
Effect:	Indicates the current array packing mode, as set by setpacking.

Operator:	currentpoint
Syntax:	currentpoint
To stack:	x y
Effect:	Returns the (x, y) co-ordinates of the current point.

Operator:	currentrgbcolor
Syntax:	currentrgbcolor
To stack:	red green blue
Effect:	Returns the three components of the current colour, as set by setrgbcolor.

Operator:	currentscreen
Syntax:	currentscreen
To stack:	frequency, angle, procedure
Effect:	Returns the current halftone settings, as determined by setscreen.

Operator:	currenttransfer
Syntax:	currenttransfer
To stack:	procedure
Effect:	Returns the procedure that transfers the current grey-scale settings to the printer, as defined by settransfer.

Operator:	curveto
Syntax:	x1 y1 x2 y2 x3 y3 curveto
To stack:	(Nothing)
Effect:	Draws a Bézier curve, starting at the current point. The curve starts in the direction of (x1, y1), then increasingly veers away towards (x2, y2) and ends up at (x3, y3), coming directly from (x2, y2).

Operator:	cvi
Syntax:	value cvi
To stack:	integer

Effect:	Converts a *value*, which may be a real number or a string, to an *integer*. Real numbers are truncated; the numeric part of any string is stored as an integer.

Operator:	cvlit
Syntax:	*item1* cvlit
To stack:	*item2*
Effect:	Converts an executable item on the stack to a literal format; the item can be converted back to executable format with cvx.

Operator:	cvn
Syntax:	*string* cvn
To stack:	*name*
Effect:	Converts a *string* into an object *name*.

Operator:	cvr
Syntax:	*value* cvr
To stack:	*real*
Effect:	Converts a value, which may be an integer or a string, into a real number. In the case of a string, the numeric part of the string is converted to a real number.

Operator:	cvrs
Syntax:	*num base name* cvrs
To stack:	*string*
Effect:	Converts the decimal number, *num*, to a number of a given *base*, storing the result in a variable, whose *name* is given, and also putting the *string* containing the result on the stack. This operator does not produce a numeric representation of the result.

Operator:	cvs
Syntax:	*item name* cvs
To stack:	*string*
Effect:	Converts an *item* – which may be numeric, an existing name or an

operator – into a *string*, also storing it in a variable with the given *name*.

Operator:	cvx
Syntax:	*item1* cvx
To stack:	*item2*
Effect:	Converts the literal item at the top of the stack into an executable format; the item can be converted back with cvlit.

Operator:	def
Syntax:	*name value* def
	name {*definition*} def
To stack:	(Nothing)
Effect:	Assigns the *value* to the variable with the given *name* or determines the *definition* of a variable or procedure with the given *name*. The curly brackets are only necessary if the *definition* consists of more than one value or word.

Operator:	defaultmatrix
Syntax:	*matrix1* defaultmatrix
To stack:	*matrix2*
Effect:	Removes one matrix, *matrix1*, from the stack and places the Default Transformation Matrix on the stack (*matrix2*)

Operator:	definefont
Syntax:	*name font* definefont
To stack:	*font*
Effect:	Assigns the specified *font* to the given *name* and also places it on the stack. This new name can then be used with operands such as setfont.

Operator:	dict
Syntax:	*num* dict
To stack:	*dictionary*
Effect:	Generates a *dictionary* of *num* elements and places it on the working

stack. Initially, all elements of the
dictionary are blank.

Operator:	dictstack
Syntax:	*array1* dictstack
To stack:	*array2*
Effect:	Replaces the array at the top of the stack with a new array, in which each element is a dictionary, copied from the dictionary stack. The size of the array required can be determined by countdictstack.

Operator:	div
Syntax:	*num1 num2* div
To stack:	*num3*
Effect:	Divides *num1* by *num2* and places the result, which is stored as a real number (*num3*), on the stack.

Operator:	dtransform
Syntax:	*x1 y1* dtransform
	x1 y1 matrix dtransform
To stack:	*x2 y2*
Effect:	Transforms the displacement (*x1,y1*) by the *matrix* or, if no *matrix* is specified, by the Current Transformation Matrix. The resultant displacement, (*x2, y2*), is stored on the stack. This displacement can be used in any instruction that acts relative to the current point. The transformation can be reversed by the idtransform operator.

Operator:	dup
Syntax:	*item* dup
To stack:	*item item*
Effect:	Duplicates the top item on the stack.

Operator:	echo
Syntax:	*boolean* echo
To stack:	(Nothing)

Effect:	Switches echoing on or off. When echoing is on (with *boolean* 'true'), everything from the standard input file is echoed to the output file. By default, echoing is off (*boolean* 'false').

Operator:	end
Syntax:	end
To stack:	(Nothing)
Effect:	Deletes the current dictionary from the dictionary stack. The dictionary now at the top of the stack becomes the current dictionary.

Operator:	eoclip
Syntax:	eoclip
To stack:	(Nothing)
Effect:	Makes the current path into the current clip path, combining it with any existing clip path (as for the clip operator). However, the area defined as the inside of the path is determined by an 'even-odd' rule, rather than by the overall outside boundary. In effect, this means that if there is one closed path within another, the inside of the inner path is considered to be 'outside' the clip path.

Operator:	eofill
Syntax:	eofill
To stack:	(Nothing)
Effect:	Fills the current path with the current colour. The area to be filled is defined by the 'even-odd' rule, as described for eoclip above. Otherwise the effect is identical to that of clip.

Operator:	eq
Syntax:	*item1 item2* eq
To stack:	*boolean*

Effect:	Returns a 'true' value if the top two items on the stack are equal, otherwise the result is 'false'.

Operator:	erasepage
Syntax:	erasepage
To stack:	(Nothing)
Effect:	Clears the current page, without printing anything.

Operator:	errordict
Syntax:	errordict
To stack:	*dictionary*
Effect:	Copies the errordict dictionary to the stack.

Operator:	exch
Syntax:	*item1 item2* exch
To stack:	*item2 item1*
Effect:	Exchanges the top two items on the stack.

Operator:	exec
Syntax:	*item* exec
To stack:	(Nothing)
Effect:	Executes the item at the top of the stack.

Operator:	execstack
Syntax:	*array1* execstack
To stack:	*array2*
Effect:	Creates an array of all executable items that have not yet been used. These are placed on the top of stack and can be executed with the exec operator.

Operator:	executeonly
Syntax:	*item1* executeonly
To stack:	*item2*
Effect:	Converts the item at the top of the stack – which may be a file, string or array – into an executable object. Such an object can be executed by

the exec operator but no other action can be carried out on it.

Operator:	exit
Syntax:	exit
To stack:	(Nothing)
Effect:	Exits the current program loop (e,g for, loop, repeat) immediately, without executing any further instructions. The program resumes at the instruction following the end of the loop.

Operator:	exp
Syntax:	*num1 power* exp
To stack:	*num2*
Effect:	Raises the given number (*num1*) to the *power* specified. The result (*num2*) is put on the stack.

Operator:	false
Syntax:	false
To stack:	*false*
Effect:	Puts a boolean 'false' value on the stack.

Operator:	file
Syntax:	*filename type* file
To stack:	*file*
Effect:	Opens a file, with the specified *filename*. The *type* may be (r) for a read-only file or (w) for a write file. In the case of a write file, the file is created. The file is added to the stack and remains open until a closefile operator is encountered or an end-of-file character is written to the file. A restore operator also closes the file if the corresponding save came before the file was opened.

Operator:	fill
Syntax:	fill
To stack:	(Nothing)
Effect:	Completes the current path by joining the current point to the start of the path and then fills the path with the current colour. Everything within the path is changed to this colour, even if the colour is white (i.e. no colour). Another, slightly different method of filling a path is provided by the eofill operator.

Operator:	findfont
Syntax:	*fontname* findfont
To stack:	*font*
Effect:	Puts the *font* specified by *fontname* on the working stack.

Operator:	flattenpath
Syntax:	flattenpath
To stack:	(Nothing)
Effect:	Every curve is made up from a sequence of straight lines, the number of lines being determined by the setflat operator. The more lines there are, the smoother the curves; fewer lines result in 'flatter' curves. With this operator, any section of the current path that was created by curveto is replaced by a series of straight lines, the number depending on the current setting for setflat.

Operator:	floor
Syntax:	*number* floor
To stack:	*integer*
Effect:	Rounds the given *number* down to the nearest *integer* (unless it is already an integer). The result is always less than or equal to the original value; for example, 4.8 is rounded down to 4 and -4.8 becomes -5.

Operator:	flush
Syntax:	flush
To stack:	(Nothing)
Effect:	When data is directed to the standard output file, it is usually held in a buffer in memory and only physically written to the file when the buffer is full. The fush operator clears the buffer by directing all data in the buffer to the file. Other operators have a similar effect; for example, closefile automatically flushes the buffer before closing the file.

Operator:	flushfile
Syntax:	*filename* flushfile
To stack:	(Nothing)
Effect:	The file that has been named is flushed. If the file is being used for output, the effect is the same as that of flush; all data currently held in a buffer in memory is directed to the buffer. For input files, all data up to the end-of-file character is read in and ignored.

Operator:	FontDirectory
Syntax:	FontDirectory
To stack:	*dictionary*
Effect:	Copies the font dictionary to the stack. Entries in this dictionary are made with definefont; the findfont operator searches this dictionary for a specific font. (The two capital letters in the operator name are essential.)

Operator:	for
Syntax:	*start step stop* {*instructions*} for
To stack:	(Nothing)
Effect:	Repeats the *instructions* a specific number of times. A count is kept of the number of times the loop is executed, starting with the count on *start* and increasing the count by *step* after each loop. This count is

placed on the stack at the start of each loop and may be used by the instructions; if the count value is not used, then successive values will be left on the stack.

The loop ends when the count exceeds the *stop* value or when an exit operator is encountered. For example, 12 2 16 {*instructions*} for results in a loop that is executed three times (with the count set to 12, 14 and 16 for successive loops).

If the *instructions* consist of a single procedure name, the curly brackets may be omitted.

Operator:	forall
Syntax:	*objectname* {instructions} forall
To stack:	(Nothing)
Effect:	The object that is named may be a string, an array or a dictionary. The *instructions* in curly brackets are repeated for each element of the object. In each case, the element value is put on the stack and is available to be used by the instructions; if the elements are not used, they will be left on the stack when the loop has finished. If the object is a string, the values put on the stack are the integer ASCII values for individual characters, rather than the characters themselves.
	The loop ends when all elements have been used in turn or an exit operator is encountered.
	If the *instructions* consist of a single procedure name, the curly brackets may be omitted.

Operator:	ge
Syntax:	*item1 item2* ge
To stack:	*boolean*
Effect:	If *item1* is greater than or equal to *item2*, then a value of 'true' is put on

the stack; otherwise the value returned is 'false'.

Operator:	get
Syntax:	*object offset* get
To stack:	*value*
Effect:	Retrieves a *value* from the *object*. The object may be a string, array or dictionary name. The *offset* determines which value is to be retrieved, with the first item in the object being assigned an *offset* of 0. For example, to get the third character of a string the *offset* would be 2.
	For strings, the *value* returned is the ASCII value that represents the required character, rather than the character itself. For dictionaries, the *offset* must be a name from the dictionary and the corresponding definition is returned.

Operator:	getinterval
Syntax:	*offset count* getinterval
To stack:	*object2*
Effect:	This operator is similar to get but this time more than one value is retrieved. The object to be searched (*object1*) can be either a string or an array. The values retrieved start at *offset* (with the first itme in the object being assigned an *offset* of 0). The number of values retrieved is determined by *count*. After the operand has been executed the stack contains an array or string that holds the required items. For example, string1 2 4 getinterval results in a four-character string being extracted from string1, beginning at the third character. In the case of strings, an actual string is transferred to the stack (not the ASCII values, as is the case with get).

Operator:	grestore
Syntax:	grestore
To stack:	(Nothing)
Effect:	Restores the graphics state to the way it was before the corresponding gsave operator was executed. Each gsave operator puts the current graphics parameters on the graphics stack; each grestore operator uses one set of parameters and clears them from the stack. If the graphics stack is empty, the graphics parameters are reset to their defaults.

Operator:	grestoreall
Syntax:	grestoreall
To stack:	(Nothing)
Effect:	Removes successive sets of parameters from the graphics stack until either a set is found which was put there by save (rather than gsave) or the last set of parameters is reached. In either case the set that is found is restored but is not removed from the stack.

Operator:	gsave
Syntax:	gsave
To stack:	(No)
Effect:	Puts a copy on the graphics stack of all the parameters that determine the current graphics state (current point, current colour, etc.). This state can be recovered with grestore.

Operator:	gt
Syntax:	*item1 item2* gt
To stack:	*boolean*
Effect:	If *item1* is greater than (but not equal to) *item2*, then a value of 'true' is put on the stack; otherwise the value returned is 'false'.

Operator:	identmatrix
Syntax:	*matrix1* identmatrix
To stack:	*matrix2*
Effect:	Replaces the matrix on the stack (*matrix1*) with the identity matrix [1 0 0 1 0 0]. When this matrix is combined with any other matrix it has no effect (rather like multiplying by 1).

Operator:	idiv
Syntax:	*integer1 integer2* idiv
To stack:	*integer3*
Effect:	Divides one integer (*integer1*) by another (*integer2*) and rounds down the result to the nearest integer (*integer3*). This is then placed on the stack.

Operator:	idtransform
Syntax:	*x1 y1* idtransform
	x1 y2 matrix idtransform
To stack:	*x2 y2*
Effect:	Transforms the displacement (*m1,y1*) by the inverse of the given *matrix* or, if no *matrix* is specified, by the inverse of the Current Transformation Matrix. The resultant displacement can be used in any instruction that acts relative to the current point. The effect is the inverse of that achieved by the dtransform operator.

Operator:	if
Syntax:	*boolean {instructions}* if
To stack:	(No)
Effect:	If the *boolean* value is 'true' the *instructions* are executed, otherwise they are ignored. To choose between two sets of instructions, use ifelse.

Operator:	ifelse
Syntax:	*boolean* {*instructions1*} {*instructions2*} ifelse
To stack:	(No)
Effect:	If the *boolean* value is 'true' the first set of instructions is executed; otherwise the second set is executed. Only one set of instructions is ever executed. This operator provides an extension to the *if* operator.

Operator:	image
Syntax:	*width height bits matrix* {*instructions*} image
To stack:	(No)
Effect:	The *instructions* read or create a set of hexadecimal data representing a bit-mapped image. This is printed in an area defined by the *width* and *height*. The image may be further transformed by the *matrix*. The number of *bits* used to create each element of the image must also be given and may be 1, 2, 4 or 8; this gives a choice of 2, 4, 16 or 256 grey-scale levels for each element of the image. For a pure black-and-white image, use imagemask.

Operator:	imagemask
Syntax:	*width height boolean matrix* {*instructions*} imagemask
To stack:	(Nothing)
Effect:	As for the image operator, the *instructions* read or create a set of hexadecimal data representing a bit-mapped image. This is printed in an area defined by *width* and *height*, and further transformed by the *matrix*. The *boolean* value determines whether each bit with value 1 represents a black point ('true') or a white point ('false'). For grey-scale images, use the image operator.

Operator:	index
Syntax:	*count* index
To stack:	*item*
Effect:	Retrieves an *item* from the stack, and copies it to the top of stack. The item is found by counting the items below the *count* value. The first value below the *count* value is numbered 0, the next is 1 and so on. For example, 4 index retrieves the fifth item below the '4' on the stack.

Operator:	initclip
Syntax:	initclip
To stack:	(Nothing)
Effect:	Initialises the clip path to the default (the entire paper area), forgetting any previous clip path.

Operator:	initgraphics
Syntax:	initgraphics
To stack:	(Nothing)
Effect:	Initialises the graphics state to its default. Several parameters are affected, including the Current Transformation Matrix, the line width, colour, clip path, current path and point, dash pattern and line joining parameters (end style, join style and mitre limit).

Operator:	initmatrix
Syntax:	initmatrix
To stack:	(Nothing)
Effect:	Initialises the Current Transformation Matrix, restoring it to its default values (i.e. all translations, scales and rotations are cancelled).

Operator:	invertmatrix
Syntax:	*matrix1 matrix2* invertmatrix
To stack:	*matrix2*
Effect:	The matrix that is returned to the stack (*matrix2*) has its values

replaced by the inverse of *matrix1*.
The inverse of a matrix is such that
when combined with the original
matrix, the result is the identify
matrix; i.e. there is no effect. The
inverse matrix reverses any
transformation performed by the
original matrix.

Operator:	itransform
Syntax:	*m1 y1* itransform
	x1 y1 matrix itransform
To stack:	*x2 y2*
Effect:	Transforms the co-ordinates (*x1,y1*) by the inverse of the matrix or, if no *matrix* is given, by the inverse of the Current Transformation Matrix. The resultant co-ordinates, (*x2,y2*), are placed on the stack. This operator reverses the effects of transform.

Operator:	known
Syntax:	*dictionary name* known
To stack:	*boolean*
Effect:	Determines whether the given *dictionary* contains a definition with the specified *name*. If it does, a 'true' value is put on the stack; otherwise, a 'false' is returned.

Operator:	kshow
Syntax:	*procedure string* kshow
To stack:	(No)
Effect:	Prints the *string* one character at a time, after each character returning to the stack the ASCII values of the character that has been printed and the next in the string. The *procedure* is then executed. This procedure can perform any operation you like but should use or discard the two ASCII values; otherwise, these values will build up on the stack.

Operator:	le
Syntax:	*item1 item2* le
To stack:	*boolean*
Effect:	If *item1* is less than or equal to *item2*, then a value of 'true' is put on the stack; otherwise, the value returned is 'false'.

Operator:	length
Syntax:	*object* length
To stack:	*num*
Effect:	Returns the 'length' of the given *object*, as an integer. In the case of a string, this is the number of characters; for an array it is the number of elements and for a dictionary the number of names that are defined.

Operator:	lineto
Syntax:	*x y* lineto
To stack:	(No)
Effect:	Draws a straight line from the current point to the point with co-ordinates (*x,y*).

Operator:	ln
Syntax:	*num1* ln
To stack:	*num2*
Effect:	Returns the natural logarithm of the number, *num1*.

Operator:	load
Syntax:	*name* load
To stack:	*value*
Effect:	Puts on the stack the *value* corresponding to the given *name*, if the name can be found in any of the dictionaries. Each dictionary is searched in turn, starting from the top of the dictionary stack. If there is more than one occurrence of the *name*, only the *value* for the first one that is found will be put on the stack.

Operator:	log
Syntax:	*num1* log
To stack:	*num2*
Effect:	Returns the logarithm (to base 10) of the specified number, *num1*.

Operator:	loop
Syntax:	{*instructions*} loop
To stack:	(No)
Effect:	Repeats the set of *instructions* (which may be a single procedure) until an exit or stop operator is found. The exit operator results in execution resuming with the first instruction after loop; the stop operator causes execution to continue at the instruction following the corresponding stopped operator (after the stack has been cleared).

Operator:	lt
Syntax:	*item1 item2* lt
To stack:	*boolean*
Effect:	If *item1* is less than (but not equal to) *item2*, then a value of 'true' is put on the stack; otherwise, the value returned is 'false'.

Operator:	makefont
Syntax:	*font1 matrix* makefont
To stack:	*font2*
Effect:	Creates a new font (*font2*) and puts it on the stack. The font is created by transforming the original font (*font1*) by the *matrix*.

Operator:	mark
Syntax:	mark
To stack:	*mark*
Effect:	Places a mark at the top of the stack. This mark can be used by a variety of operators, such as cleartomark and counttomark. The effect is the same as that of the [operator.

Operator:	matrix
Syntax:	matrix
To stack:	*matrix*
Effect:	Puts an identity matrix [1 0 0 1 0 0] on the stack. The identity matrix, when used as a transformation, has no effect.

Operator:	maxlength
Syntax:	*dictionary* maxlength
To stack:	*num*
Effect:	Puts on the stack the maximum number of definitions (*num*) allowed in the specified *dictionary*.

Operator:	mod
Syntax:	*integer1 integer2* mod
To stack:	*integer3*
Effect:	Performs integer division of *integer1* by *integer2* and puts the remainder (*integer3*) on the stack.

Operator:	moveto
Syntax:	*x y* moveto
To stack:	(Nothing)
Effect:	Makes (*x,y*) the current point but does not draw a line.

Operator:	mul
Syntax:	*num1 num2* mul
To stack:	*num3*
Effect:	Multiples *num1* by *num2* and stores the result on the stack (*num3*).

Operator:	ne
Syntax:	*item1 item2* ne
To stack:	*boolean*
Effect:	If *item1* is not equal to *item2*, then a value of 'true' is put on the stack; if the two items are equal, the value returned is 'false'.

Operator:	neg
Syntax:	*num1* neg
To stack:	*num2*
Effect:	Negates the number, *num1*, and stores the result (*num2*) on the stack.

Operator:	newpath
Syntax:	newpath
To stack:	(Nothing)
Effect:	Discards everything in the current path and starts a new path. Any lines and other graphics in the path will now be ignored and will not be printed when the stroke operator is executed.

Operator:	not
Syntax:	*num1* not
To stack:	*num2*
Effect:	Performs a logical 'not' operation on the item. If *num1* is a boolean, then a value of 'true' becomes 'false' and vice versa. If *num1* is an integer, each bit of the integer is reversed (1s become 0s and 0s become 1s).

Operator:	null
Syntax:	null
To stack:	*null*
Effect:	Puts a null value on the stack.

Operator:	nulldevice
Syntax:	nulldevice
To stack:	(Nothing)
Effect:	The current output device (by default, the printer) becomes the null device (equivalent to NUL: in DOS). Any future output is therefore ignored. This operator also affects the clip path, Current Transformation Matrix, etc.

Operator:	or
Syntax:	*num1 num2* or
To stack:	*num3*
Effect:	Performs a logical 'or' on the two values, *num1* and *num2*. If these values are booleans, the result (*num3*) is 'true' if either *num1* or *num2* (or both) are 'true'; only if both are 'false' is the value returned 'false'. If the values are integers, the 'or' operation is carried out on a bit-by-bit basis. Each bit in *num3* is set to 0 if either of the corresponding bits in *num1* and *num2* is 1, or if both are 1. The resultant bit is 0 only if both corresponding bits are 0.

Operator:	packedarray
Syntax:	*item1 ... itemn n* packedarray
To stack:	*parray*
Effect:	Creates a packed array (*parray*), which is stored on the stack, consisting of *n* elements. These *n* elements are taken from the stack and put into the array.

Operator:	pathbox
Syntax:	pathbox
To stack:	*x1 y1 x2 y2*
Effect:	Puts on the stack two pairs of co-ordinates which identify the smallest rectangle that would completely enclose the current path. The bottom left corner of the rectangle is (*x1,y1*) and the top right is (*x2,y2*).

Operator:	pathforall
Syntax:	*procedure1 procedure2 procedure3 procedure4* pathforall
To stack:	(Nothing)
Effect:	For each element of the current path, the operator places certain values on the stack and executes one of the four procedures. The action that is

taken depends on the category of element, which may be one of the following:

move   Puts the co-ordinates of the point moved to on the stack and executes *procedure1*.

line   Puts the co-ordinates of the point the line or arc was drawn to on the stack and executes *procedure2*.

curve   Puts the co-ordinates of the two intermediate points and those of the final point (i.e. *x1 y1 x2 y2 x3 y3*) on the stack and executes *procedure3*.

close path Executes *procedure4*.

It is up to the programmer to decide the action to be taken by these procedures and to clear the stack in each case.

Operator:	pop
Syntax:	pop
To stack:	(Nothing)
Effect:	Discards the item that is currently at the top of the stack.

Operator:	print
Syntax:	*string* print
To stack:	(Nothing)
Effect:	Sends the *string* to the current output file. This may be used for debugging purposes, for example. It does not affect the page that is

currently being prepared for output
to the printer.

Operator:	pstack
Syntax:	pstack
To stack:	(Nothing)
Effect:	Copies the entire contents of the working stack to the output file (*not* to the page that is being printed). The items are written in text form, starting from the top of the stack and working down. This command is useful for debugging purposes.

Operator:	put
Syntax:	*object element item* put
To stack:	(Nothing)
Effect:	Puts an *item* in an *object*, which may be a string, an array or a dictionary. The position in which the *item* is placed is determined by the *element* number.

For strings, the *element* number is
the character number, counting from
the left; the first character is
numbered 0. The *item* must be an
ASCII value representing the
character to be inserted in the string.
For arrays, the *item* is a value to be
inserted in the array, with *element*
numbers in the array counted from 0.
For dictionaries, the *element* is an
entry in the dictionary; the *item* is the
definition that is to replace the
existing definition for that element. If
the named *element* cannot be found,
a new entry is created.
For strings and arrays, you can
replace a number of elements at once
with the putinterval operator. You can
retrieve a value from one of these
objects with the put operator.

Operator:	putinterval
Syntax:	object1 element object2 putinterval
To stack:	(Nothing)
Effect:	Replaces the contents of *object1*, which may be a string or an array, with the contents of *object2*, starting at the given *element*.
	For strings, part of the string, starting at the given *element*, is overwritten by the second string. For arrays, the contents of the array, starting at the given *element*, are overlaid by the contents of the second array. See also the put operator.

Operator:	quit
Syntax:	quit
To stack:	(Nothing)
Effect:	Stops the program.

Operator:	rand
Syntax:	rand
To stack:	*integer*
Effect:	Puts a psuedo-random number on the stack. The value is determined according to the current settings of the random number generator, which are set by the srand operator.

Operator:	rcurveto
Syntax:	*x1 y1 x2 y2 x3 y3*
To stack:	(Nothing)
Effect:	Draws a Bézier curve relative to the current point. Each pair of co-ordinates is an offset measured from the current point, rather than an absolute position. Full details of Bézier curve-drawing are given for the curveto operator.

Operator:	read
Syntax:	*filename* read
To stack:	*character true* (successful)
	false (end of file)

Effect:	Reads a *character* from the file with the given *filename*. If the read is successful, the character is put on the stack, followed by a boolean 'true'. If the read is unsuccessful, usually because the end-of-file has been reached, a boolean 'false' is put on the stack.

Operator:	readhexstring
Syntax:	*filename string1* readhexstring
To stack:	*string2 boolean*
Effect:	Reads a group of hex values from the named value and places them in the named string, *string1*. The string that is read, *string2*, is put on the stack. If the data that was read is enough to fill *string1*, then the *boolean* is 'true'; otherwise, if there was insufficient data in the file, the *boolean* is 'false'.

Operator:	readline
Syntax:	*filename string1* readline
To stack:	*string2 boolean*
Effect:	Reads a line of text from the named file and puts it in *string1*. The line that is read is put on the stack (*string2*). If the line that is read is the same length as the original *string1*, the *boolean* is 'true'; if the line that is read is shorter than *string1*, the boolean is 'false'; if the line from the file is too long, an error is given. Note that the end-of-line character read from the file is not put into the string.

Operator:	readonly
Syntax:	*object* readonly
To stack:	*object*
Effect:	Makes the *object* – a string, array, dictionary or file – read-only; after this instruction, no changes can be made to the object. Once an object has been made read-only, it remains

in that state for the remainder of the program.

Operator:	readstring
Syntax:	*filename string1* readstring
To stack:	*string2 boolean*
Effect:	Reads a group of ASCII characters (including control characters, such as CR, LF and HT) from the named file into the string (*string1*). The text that is read is stored on the stack (*string2*). If the string was completely filled with the new text, the *boolean* is 'true'; if the end-of-file was reached before the string was filled, the *boolean* is 'false'.

Operator:	repeat
Syntax:	*integer {instructions}* repeat
To stack:	(Nothing)
Effect:	The *instructions* or named procedure are executed for the number of times specified by the *integer*. You can leave the repeat loop early by executing an exit operator, usually as a result of some conditional instruction.

Operator:	resetfile
Syntax:	*filename* resetfile
To stack:	(Nothing)
Effect:	Clears the buffer for the named file. Data is always read into and written out of a buffer in memory in blocks. If data has been read from an input file but not yet used, this is discarded; data waiting to be sent to an output file (which would normally be written when the buffer is full) is also removed.

Operator:	restore
Syntax:	*state* restore
To stack:	(Nothing)

Effect:	Restores the printer's working memory to the state it was in when saved on the stack by the save operator. This restores features such as the current point and current font to their values before the save.

Operator:	reversepath
Syntax:	reversepath
To stack:	(Nothing)
Effect:	Reverses the current path. The individual elements are placed in the path in reverse order, and each element acts in the opposite direction.

Operator:	rlineto
Syntax:	*x y* rlineto
To stack:	(Nothing)
Effect:	Draws a line from the current point to another point relative to the current point. The offset of the new current point is given by (*x,y*) co-ordinates.

Operator:	rmoveto
Syntax:	x y rmoveto
To stack:	(Nothing)
Effect:	Moves to a new point, relative to the current point. The (*x,y*) co-ordinates give the position of the new point relative to the current point.

Operator:	roll
Syntax:	(*items*) *num1 num2* roll
To stack:	rolled-items
Effect:	Rotates the *num1* objects at the top of the stack by an amount *num2*. If *num2* is positive the top items move to the bottom and the rest move up; if *num2* is negative the 'roll' is in the opposite direction. For example, suppose that the top of the stack is currently as follows:

item0 item1 item2 item3 item4 item5

The result after 5 2 roll would be:

> *item0 item4 item5 item1 item2 item3*

In effect the top two items are each 'rolled' to the bottom of this part of the stack. If the instruction is 5 -1 roll, the effect is:

> *item0 item2 item3 item4 item5 item1*

The item at the bottom of this part of the stack is 'rolled' to the top.

Operator:	rotate
Syntax:	*angle* rotate
	angle matrix rotate
To stack:	*matrix*
Effect:	If a matrix is specified in the instruction, then the matrix is rotated anti-clockwise by the angle specified and then returned to the stack.When a matrix is specified, there is no effect on the Current Transformation Matrix. If no matrix is given, then the Current Transformation Matrix is rotated by the specified *angle* and nothing is returned to the stack.

Operator:	round
Syntax:	*num1* round
To stack:	*num2*
Effect:	Rounds the number (*num1*) to the nearest integer, returning the result (*num2*) to the stack as a real number. For example, if *num1* is 4.8, then *num2* will be 5; if *num1* is 4.3, then *num2* will be 4. In the case of a number ending in .5 the value is always rounded up; therefore 4.5 is rounded up to 5.

Operator:	rrand
Syntax:	rrand
To stack:	*num1*

Effect:	Returns the number (*num1*) which is the seed of the current pseudo-random number generator. If the same number is used repeatedly by srand, then the same sequence of pseudo-random numbers will be generated.

Operator:	run
Syntax:	*filename* run
To stack:	(Nothing)
Effect:	Runs a PostScript program contained in the named file. This command will cause an error if the specified file does not contain a valid PostScript program.

Operator:	save
Syntax:	save
To stack:	(Nothing)
Effect:	Saves the current *state* to the stack. This includes details such as the current point, Current Transformation Matrix and various other current values. The state may later be restored to its original values by the restore operator. Note that a save operator encompasses all the values that are saved by the gsave operator.

Operator:	scale
Syntax:	*num1 num2* scale
	num1 num2 matrix scale
To stack:	*matrix*
Effect:	Scales the given *matrix* by an amount *num1* on the x-axis and *num2* on the y-axis. The scale matrix is then returned to the stack. If no *matrix* is given, then the Current Transformation Matrix is scaled by these amounts.

Operator:	scalefont
Syntax:	*font1 scale* scalefont
To stack:	*font2*
Effect:	Scales the font that is specified (*font1*) by the given *scale* factor. The scale is applied to both x and y axes, with the result that the characters of the font are larger but have the same proportions. The new font is placed on the stack. The setfont operand can be used to convert this to the current font.

Operator:	search
Syntax:	*string1 string2* search
To stack:	*string3 string4 string5 true* (if successful)
	string1 false (if not successful)
Effect:	This operator searches *string1* to see if it contains *string2*. If the search is a success, three new strings are placed on the stack:

string3	The end of *string1*, following *string2*
string4	The part that matches (*string2*)
string5	The beginning of *string1* before the match

A boolean 'true' is also put on the stack.

If *string1* does not contain *string2*, then *string1* is returned to the stack, followed by a boolean 'false'.

Operator:	setcachedevice
Syntax:	*x-width y-width x1 y1 x2 y2* setcachedevice
To stack:	(Nothing)
Effect:	This operand is used by the PostScript font generator. It is used to pass values to that generator for each character, *x-width* and *y-width* being

the width and height of the character and (x1, y1) and (x2, y2) being the bottom left and top-right corners of a box that encloses the character.

Operator:	setcachelimit
Syntax:	*num* setcachelimit
To stack:	(Nothing)
Effect:	Gives the maximum size in bytes to be allowed for the bit image for any character to be cached. Bit image characters that use more than this number of bytes must be generated each time they are used, rather than being retrieved from the cache each time.

Operator:	setcacheparams
Syntax:	*mark num1 num2* setcacheparams
To stack:	(Nothing)
Effect:	This operator sets the size in bytes for bit-image characters (*num1*) above which the data used to generate the character is compressed before being stored. It also gives the maximum size in bytes (*num2*) for any individual character. The lower the value of *num1*, the more characters that will have to be compressed and the greater the number that may be cached. If the two numbers are the same, no characters are compressed but the number of characters that can be cached is more limited. Therefore a balance has to be found between caching characters and the savings to be made by not compressing them. The *mark* is placed on the stack because different versions of PostScript require different numbers of parameters. It is as well to check the particular version on which your program will be running for the number of parameters needed, although any

surplus parameters will be discarded, while default values are given parameters to any that are not supplied.

The currentcacheparams operator returns the current settings of these various parameters.

Operator:	setcharwidth
Syntax:	*width height* setcharwidth
To stack:	(Nothing)
Effect:	Gives the *width* and *height* of a character being built by the PostScript font generator. A character specified in this way cannot be cached but must be generated each time it is needed, the advantage being that various operators (such as those to produce grey-scales) can be used in the generation.

Operator:	setdash
Syntax:	*array num* setdash
To stack:	(Nothing)
Effect:	Specifies the pattern of dashes that are to be used when drawing lines, giving a broken line effect. The first element of the *array* gives the length of the first part of the line in dots, the second element is the number of dots to be skipped, the third is the number of dots in the next segment of the line, and so on. In this way, you can define any pattern, with a number of different-sized line segments (for example, dashes that are alternately long and short). The *offset* determines the distance along the line before the dash pattern begins. For a path that is made up of several individual lines, the pattern restarts with each new section of the path.
	To cancel the dash pattern and resume normal printing (with

continuous lines) repeat the
instruction but with an empty array.

Operator:	setflat
Syntax:	*num* setflat
To stack:	(Nothing)
Effect:	Determines the smoothness or otherwise of curves. Every curve is made up of a number of individual straight lines: the more lines you use, the smoother will be the appearance of the curve. The value of *num* can be anything from 0.2 (in a smooth curve) to 100 (giving a very 'flat' curve). While the ideal is to produce as smooth a curve as possible, this dramatically increases the processing time taken to produce each page.

Operator:	setfont
Syntax:	*font* setfont
To stack:	(Nothing)
Effect:	Makes the specified *font* into the current font, which is used for all future text. The font can be selected and changed by operators such as findfont, makefont and scalefont. To find out what is the current font, use the currentfont operator.

Operator:	setgray
Syntax:	*num* setgray
To stack:	(Nothing)
Effect:	Selects a colour for all future graphics actions, printing as a shade of grey. Setting the number (*num*) to 0 produces black output while 1 produces white (in other words, the dots are not printed). Any other shade of grey in between is selected by choosing a number less than 1. The lower the number, the darker the printout. Darker shades of grey are actually produced by filling in more dots.

For colour printers, you can use the setrgbcolor, sethsbcolor or setcmykcolor commands.

Operator:	sethsbcolor
Syntax:	*hue saturation brightness* sethsbcolor
To stack:	(Nothing)
Effect:	Selects a new colour for all future graphics actions. The three parameters, each in the range 0-1, are combined to create the colour. Other systems of generating colour can also be used, as determined by the setgray, setrgbcolor and setcmykcolor operators.

Operator:	setlinecap
Syntax:	*num* setlinecap
To stack:	(Nothing)
Effect:	Selects the style of ending to be applied to any lines drawn on the page. Three values are permissible for the number (*num*):

- **0** Square end

- **1** Rounded end, centred on the point at the end of the line

- **2** Square end, finishing beyond the end of the line and projecting by half the line width

When determining how to end lines, you should also take into account the way in which two lines are joined (as determined by setlinejoin) and whether or not the line is made up of dashes (as determined by setdash). The default is 0: square ends with the line finishing at the last point that is drawn.

Operator:	setlinejoin
Syntax:	*num* setlinejoin
To stack:	(Nothing)
Effect:	Determines the way in which two consecutive lines in the same path

are joined. The value of the number
(*num*) must be one of the following:

0 The edges of the lines are
continued until they meet at a
point

1 The gap at the ends of the lines
is filled in with a rounded curve

2 The gap where the lines meet is
filled in with a straight edge

The way in which lines are joined will
only have any noticeable effect if you
are using fairly thick lines.

Operator:	setlinewidth
Syntax:	*num* setlinewidth
To stack:	(Nothing)
Effect:	Determines the width of all future lines, measured in dots. If a scale factor has been applied to the Current Transformation Matrix (with the scale operator), then the line width, will be scaled accordingly; that is, vertical and horizontal lines will not have the same width and lines at an angle will have a width in proportion to the angle. It should also be noted that, as far as PostScript is concerned, the line is drawn from one point to another; the extra dots that are filled on either side of the line are there purely to pad the line out to its full size; therefore, for thick lines, two lines joined together at an angle will have an untidy gap where they meet unless you use setlinejoin to change the joining style. If the width is set to 0, the line will be drawn with a thickness of just one dot. The width currently in use can be determined with the currentlinewidth operator.

Operator:	setmatrix
Syntax:	*matrix* setmatrix
To stack:	(Nothing)
Effect:	Replaces the Current Transformation Matrix with the matrix that is specified. This will be used in all future operations until replaced or altered. If you precede this instruction with the defaultmatrix operator then the Current Transformation Matrix will be restored to its original default. You can copy the Current Transformation Matrix to any other matrix with the currentmatrix operator.

Operator:	setmiterlimit
Syntax:	*num* setmiterlimit
To stack:	(Nothing)
Effect:	When two lines are joined and the setlinejoin value is set to 0 (the default) the outer edges of the two lines are extended until they meet, creating a point. This is termed a 'mitre'. The greater the angle between the two lines, the larger will be this protruding point. This operator sets the limit above which the two lines are not mitred but a straight line is drawn between the ends of the lines and the triangle filled in (as if the setlinejoin operand had been given with a value of 2). The larger the value of the number (*num*), the greater the angle that can be drawn before the mitre is flattened. The value of the number must be at least 1 and the default is 10; this has the effect of flattening any mitres for lines where the inside angle is less than about 11 degrees.

Operator:	setpacking
Syntax:	*boolean* setpacking
To stack:	(Nothing)

Effect:	If the *boolean* is 'true', any executable arrays that are created in future are packed; a *boolean* of 'false' disables this array packing.

Operator:	setrgbcolor
Syntax:	*red green blue* setrgbcolor
To stack:	(Nothing)
Effect:	Determines the 'colour' for all future graphics and text operations. On most printers, the effect is to choose a shade of grey. The colours are created by choosing values for each of the three parameters in the range 0-1. This relates to the additive colour scheme, referred to in Chapter 9. Other colour schemes can be selected with setgray, sethsbcolor setcmykcolor.

Operator:	setscreen
Syntax:	*frequency angle procedure* setscreen
To stack:	(Nothing)
Effect:	The process of converting a picture into a pattern of dots is known as *screening*. The final appearance varies greatly depending on the way the dots are selected for each colour. As described in Chapter 9, a half-tone produced in this way varies according to the number of dots-per-inch (the *frequency*) and the *angle* of the halftone. The *procedure* is used to find the way in which the dots are selected. This is a rather complex operator, which will not usually be required. A default half-tone method is automatically selected by all printers. You can check the current parameters with the currentscreen operator.

Operator:	settransfer
Syntax:	*procedure* settransfer
To stack:	(Nothing)

Effect:	Maps the current grey value to the printer. The current grey value can be determined with currentgray and the transfer method with currenttransfer.

Operator:	show
Syntax:	*string* show
To stack:	(Nothing)
Effect:	Adds the specified *string* to the current page. The text is printed in the current font (which can be changed with setfont) and the current shade of grey (as determined by setgray or one of the colour operators). Other variations can be achieved with the ashow and widthshow commands. The text is printed starting at the current point.

Operator:	showpage
Syntax:	showpage
To stack:	(Nothing)
Effect:	Prints the current page, as set up. The number of copies that are printed is determined by the #copies system variable. Once the page is complete, everything is cleared from memory and you can start a new page. To print the page as it stands and then continue adding to it, use copypage. Note that you can also clear the page at any time with erasepage.

Operator:	sin
Syntax:	*angle* sin
To stack:	*num*
Effect:	Returns the sine of the given *angle*, where the angle is specified in degrees.

Operator:	sqrt
Syntax:	*num1* sqrt
To stack:	*num2*

Effect:	Returns (as *num2*) the square root of the number (*num1*) that is specified. Attempting to give a negative value to *num1* results in an error.

Operator:	srand
Syntax:	*integer* srand
To stack:	(Nothing)
Effect:	Selects the *seed* for the pseudo-random number generator. Once the *seed* has been set a sequence of numbers can be chosen with the rand operator. The *seed* is merely an integer to determine how the first number in the sequence is generated. If you use the same seed more than once, you will produce the same sequence of numbers. You can check the current seed with the rrand operator.

Operator:	stack
Syntax:	stack
To stack:	(Nothing)
Effect:	Writes the contents of the stack, starting with the item at the top and working down, to the current output file. This operator is used for debugging purposes and has no effect on the printed page. To send just one item from the top of the stack, use the = operator.

Operator:	status
Syntax:	*filename* status
To stack:	*boolean*
Effect:	Determines whether the given file is open or not. If the file is open, the *boolean* is 'true'; if the file is closed, the *boolean* is 'false'. A file is opened with the file operator and closed with closefile.

Operator:	stop
Syntax:	stop
To stack:	(Nothing)
Effect:	Interrupts the execution of a part of the program that was executed with the stopped operator. After clearing all surplus items off the stack, a *boolean* value of 'true' is placed on the stack and execution continues with the next instruction after the stopped operator.

Operator:	stopped
Syntax:	*item* stopped
To stack:	*boolean*
Effect:	Executes the named *item*. If during execution of these instructions, a stop operator is found, a *boolean* value of 'true' is put on the stack. If no such operator is found, a 'false' is placed on the stack. This operator is normally used for debugging purposes.

Operator:	store
Syntax:	*name value* store
To stack:	(Nothing)
Effect:	Defines a dictionary entry. If any of the dictionaries on the dictionary stack contains an entry with the given *name* then the *value* that is specified is given as the new definition of that entry. Only the first item that is found with that *name* is redefined. If none of the dictionaries contains such an entry, a new entry and definition are placed in the current dictionary.

Operator:	string
Syntax:	*integer* string
To stack:	*string*
Effect:	Creates a blank *string* of length as specified by the *integer*. This string

can be filled by various other operators.

Operator:	stringwidth
Syntax:	*string* stringwidth
To stack:	*x, y*
Effect:	The (*x,y*) co-ordinates that are returned to the stack are the relative offset of the new point from the current point if the show operator were to be used with the *string* specified. In other words, they give the distance from the start of the string to the end. The *y* value will be non-zero if the string is not being printed horizontally; i.e. the Current Transformation Matrix includes a rotation.

Operator:	stroke
Syntax:	stroke
To stack:	(Nothing)
Effect:	Draws everything held in the current path on the page, so that it will be printed when the show operator is issued. To do so, it uses the current line width and current colour. After the lines in the current path have been drawn, the path is cleared ready to start again. Note that commands such as setlinecap, setdash, setlinejoin, setlinewidth and setmiterlimit will have their current values used when the stroke operator is executed. Therefore, if you want to draw lines in different thicknesses, you must use stroke each time you want to change the width.

Operator:	strokepath
Syntax:	strokepath
To stack:	(Nothing)
Effect:	Creates a path that completely surrounds the current path and then makes this the current path. You can

use this path for clipping and filling but not necessarily for adding to the page with the stroke operator.

Operator:	sub
Syntax:	*num1 num2* sub
To stack:	*num3*
Effect:	Subtracts *num2* from *num1* and puts the result (*num3*) on the stack.

Operator:	systemdict
Syntax:	systemdict
To stack:	(Nothing)
Effect:	Puts the name of the systemdict dictionary on the stack.

Operator:	token
Syntax:	*filename* token
	string1 token
To stack:	*item true* (filename: if foun
	string2 item true (string: if foun
	false(if not found)
Effect:	This operator reads text from the specified *filename* or string (*string1*) and assumes that they are valid PostScript instructions. When a complete *item* has been read in, it is stored on the stack. If the item is a string rather than a file the section o the string (*string2*) that is used in the creation of the *item* is put on the stack. This is followed by the *item*. In both cases a boolean 'true' is also pu on the stack. If the file or string is no sufficient to create an item, then a boolean 'false' is put on the stack.

Operator:	transform
Syntax:	*x1 y1* transform
	x1 y1 matrix transform
To stack:	*x2 y2*
Effect:	The co-ordinates (*x1*, *y1*) are transformed by the specified *matrix* produce a new pair of co-ordinates

($x2$, $y2$). If no *matrix* is given, then the co-ordinates ($x1$, $y1$) are transformed by the Current Transformation Matrix to produce the new co-ordinates ($x2$, $y2$). To move a point back where it started after such a transformation, you can use the inverse transformation operator itransform.

Operator:	translate
Syntax:	*x y* translate
	x y matrix translate
To stack:	*matrix*
Effect:	Translates the *matrix* by the *x* and *y* values given. If no *matrix* is specified then the Current Transformation Matrix is translated by the amount *x* and *y* on the x-axis and y-axis respectively.

Operator:	true
Syntax:	true
To stack:	*true*
Effect:	Puts a *boolean* 'true' on the stack. This is usually needed to carry out some comparison or perform a conditional operation.

Operator:	truncate
Syntax:	*num1* truncate
To stack:	*num2*
Effect:	Rounds any positive number down to the next integer and any negative number up to the next highest integer, in effect removing anything after the decimal point. For example, 4.8 is truncated to 4 and -4.8 is truncated to -4.

Operator:	type
Syntax:	*item* type
To stack:	*name*

Effect:	Puts on the stack a *name* which indicates the type of the *item* that is specified.

Operator:	userdict
Syntax:	userdict
To stack:	*dictionary*
Effect:	Places the userdict *dictionary* on the stack for use by other operators that require the name of the dictionary.

Operator:	usertime
Syntax:	usertime
To stack:	*integer*
Effect:	Returns the number of milliseconds since the interpreter was switched on (as an *integer*). The actual value has no real meaning but it can be used to give an assessment of the relative speeds of different sections of program.

Operator:	version
Syntax:	version
To stack:	*string*
Effect:	Puts the version number of the PostScript interpreter on the stack in the form of a *string*.

Operator:	vmstatus
Syntax:	vmstatus
To stack:	*num1 num2 num3*
Effect:	Puts on the stack the following three values:

num1	The number of copies of the system state that have been stored with the save operator but have yet to be restored.
num2	The amount of virtual memory (VM) that is currently being used.

	num3	The total virtual memory available.

Note that the memory is given in multiples of eight bytes. These figures can be used for debugging purposes.

Operator:	wcheck
Syntax:	*object* wcheck
To stack:	*boolean*
Effect:	Checks to see if the *object* – a string, array, file or dictionary – may have new values written to it. A *boolean* 'true' will be returned if the *object* can be changed. A *boolean* 'false' will be returned if the object has been made read-only (for example, by the readonly operator). If the *object* is a packed array then the *boolean* will automatically be 'false', since such arrays are always read-only.

Operator:	where	
Syntax:	*name* where	
To stack:	*dictionary true*	(if name found)
	dictionary false	(if name not found)
Effect:	This operator searches through all the dictionaries for the given *name*. If it is found, the name of the dictionary is placed on the stack along with a *boolean* 'true'. If the name cannot be found in any dictionary, the operator returns a 'false' value.	

Operator:	widthshow
Syntax:	*x y character string* widthshow
To stack:	(Nothing)
Effect:	Prints the string in the same way as the show operator but after printing the specified *character* adds (*x*, *y*) as an offset to the current position. For example, you might justify text by adding an offset each time the space character is printed. The *character* must be given as an ASCII code.

Operator:	write
Syntax:	*filename integer* write
To stack:	(Nothing)
Effect:	Outputs the character whose ASCII value is given in the *integer* to the file with the given *filename*. The file must already by open.

Operator:	writehexstring
Syntax:	*filename string* writehexstring
To stack:	(Nothing)
Effect:	Converts each character in the named *string* to its two-digit hexadecimal format and outputs this to the file of the given name.

Operator:	writestring
Syntax:	*filename string* writestring
To stack:	(Nothing)
Effect:	Outputs the specified *string* to the file whose *filename* is given.

Operator:	xcheck
Syntax:	*item* xcheck
To stack:	*boolean*
Effect:	If the named *item* is executable, a *boolean* 'true' is put on the stack; otherwise, a *boolean* 'false' value is returned.

Operator:	xor
Syntax:	*num1 num2* xor
To stack:	*num3*
Effect:	Performs a logical 'exclusive or' on the two numbers. If the numbers are both booleans, then the resultant boolean (*num3*) will be true if either *num1 or num2* is 'true' but not both. If *num1* and *num2* are integers, they are compared on a bit-by-bit basis. Each bit in *num3* is set to 1 if one or other of the corresponding bits in *num1* and *num2* is 1 but not if both bits are 0 or both bits are 1.

11 The Printer Ports

Data is sent to the printer via either a parallel port or a serial port. These are connectors, attached to the computer's motherboard, into which cables to the printer can be plugged. Most computers are fitted with both types of port; some printers have two ports but the majority have at least a parallel port. Data is transmitted by sending pulses along an array of wires to the port, where they proceed along the printer cable to arrive at corresponding pins on the printer. Once there, the data is handled by the printer's own internal software and treated either as control information or data.

How the data actually makes its way from the computer's memory to the pins on the output port is not of particular interest; what is important is that the data arrives at the port in the correct format, that the cable between the two machines delivers the data to the correct pins on the receiving port, and that the printer knows what to do with it when it arrives.

The last part of this procedure – processing the data correctly – relies upon the application program sending the correct codes, as described earlier in this book. The other activities – getting the data to the port and transmitting it to the other end of the cable – are the subject of this chapter.

Programming the ports

There are essentially four ways of sending data to a printer:

- Put the data directly into the memory registers corresponding to the output ports

- Use a BIOS operating system interrupt to transmit the data

- Use an operating system interrupt to transmit the data

- Use an application program to do the work for you

Which of these methods you adopt depends on how your applications are being generated. If you are writing in assembler code, you will need to consider one of the first three options. If you are using a high-level language then you can rely on the language's PRINT command (or equivalent) to do the hard work on your behalf; then all you need to concern yourself with is that the correct port is being addressed and that the connecting cable is properly set up.

Output registers

The hardware ports (serial and parallel) are the physical points to which the printer cable is connected. Corresponding to these are some internal *registers* (sometimes also called *ports*, rather confusingly). These are internal locations into which data can be written or from which data can be read (in some cases). Once you have put data into a register, the system hardware does the rest for you, completing the task of getting the data from there onto the physical pins.

Although you can program the ports directly – using the assembler IN and OUT instructions – this is not usually recommended. Generally, it is far simpler to use the interrupts. For any form of programming, it is wise to use as high a level of language as possible, as long as this does not significantly affect the efficiency of the application.

BIOS interrupts

The next method of communicating with the hardware ports is to use the ROM BIOS interrupts. The BIOS is the Basic Input/Output System and is held in a ROM chip on the PC's motherboard. The programs of the BIOS are executed whenever the computer is switched on. It is these programs that load and execute the operating system (such as MS-DOS).

The BIOS also contains routines called *interrupts* that allow you to carry out various hardware-specific tasks. The operating system has its own interrupts, all of which are based on these BIOS interrupts. An interrupt is simply a section of machine code, stored anywhere in memory, but with the address of the code held in a particular location at the start of memory. Each interrupt is given a number, which acts as an index to this block of interrupt addresses. For example, if you issue interrupt 05, the ROM BIOS routines find the 6th address in the block – the interrupts are numbered from 00 – and execute the code that is located at that address.

The interrupt is executed with an assembler INT instruction. Before doing so, you are usually required to store any values that will be needed by the interrupt code (such as the data byte to be printed) in the processor's working registers (AX, BX, etc.) Any response from the interrupt is stored in these same registers.

The interrupts that are of interest here are 17h for the parallel port and 14h for the serial port. Also worth noting is interrupt 05h, which is used by the PrtSc feature.

Operating system interrupts

The operating system (MS-DOS or PC-DOS) also performs its input/output activities through a selection of interrupts. These simply set up and call the BIOS interrupts. The advantage of using the operating system in this way is that you can be more certain that your program will work in exactly the same way on any other PC with the same operating system.

Another important difference is that the operating system interrupts always refer to the *standard* port (initially the first port). To work with another port you must use the DOS MODE command before you run the application (see below).

MS-DOS and PC-DOS are identical in this respect and all printer actions are obtained through functions of interrupt 21h.

High-level languages

This is the easy way out but perfectly respectable in the vast majority of circumstances. If you want to print a piece of text, you simply use an instruction such as this, from BASIC:

```
LPRINT "Item of text"
```

Life is much easier with these commands and, although a minor amount of flexibility is lost, you should stick to this level unless you are writing the rest of the program in assembler.

Standard ports

The DOS operating system always directs its output to the *standard port*, which may be referred to in DOS commands as PRN:. By default this is the first parallel port, LPT1: but you can redirect printer output to any other port with the MODE command.

The parallel ports are labelled LPT1:, LPT2: and LPT3:, while the serial ports are COM1: and COM2:. The first seral port is also known as AUX:.

The MODE command allows you to set up various features of these ports and the way in which they will be used.

Parallel ports

For parallel ports, the command to set up the port takes the form:

```
MODE LPTn:[characters],[lines],[PorN]
```

The items in square brackets are optional. The meaning of the parameters is as follows:

n	The port number
characters	Number of characters per line (80 or 132)
lines	Number of lines per inch (6 or 8)
PorN	If the value is P, the printer keeps trying to send the data when the 'printer busy' signal is received; if N, this feature is turned off (defaults to N)

The *characters* and *lines* values are effective only on Epson printers and compatibles. The 'P' option is useful if a slow printer continually results in time-out errors but will cause problems if a printer is genuinely not available; in that case you would have to interrupt the loop by pressing Ctrl-Break.

For example, to set the first parallel port to 132 characters per line, the command would be:

```
MODE LPT1:132
```

The commas are only needed if you use the extra parameters. If you omit a parameter in the middle, make sure you include its comma, however.

Serial ports

The format for the command to set up a serial port is:

```
MODE COMn:[baud rate],[parity],[data
bits],[stop bits],[PorN]
```

The parameters determine the communications protocol, as follows:

n	The port number
baud rate	The baud rate, selected from 110, 150, 300, 600, 1200, 2400, 4800, 9600, 19200
parity	The parity error-checking method: N (none), O (odd) or E (even)
data bits	The number of bits used to encode each character that is sent: 7 for ASCII characters up to 127; 8 for the full extended ASCII character set
stop bits	The number of bits used to signal the end of a character (1 or 2)
PorN	If the value is P, the printer keeps trying to send the data when the 'printer busy' signal is received; if N, this feature is turned off (defaults to N)

For example, to set the first serial port to a baud rate of 1200, with 7 data bits and 1 stop bit, the command would be:

```
MODE COM1:1200,,7,1
```

Note the extra comma after the 1200, indicating that the parity is to remain unchanged.

Redirecting output

Finally, you can use MODE to change the standard output port which, by default, is LPT1:. For example, to redirect all output to the first serial port, the command is:

```
MODE LPT1:=COM1:
```

Before issuing this command, the serial protocol must be set up.

The parallel port

Most printers have a parallel port, as do most computers, and this is by far the easiest way of communicating with the printer. There is no protocol to establish and the layout of the port is very simple, since it is the job of the printer to handle the data when it arrives. Data is transferred a byte at a time.

Parallel connector

Most computers have a standard IBM-compatible 25-pin, female, D-type connector. The pin layout of this port is shown in Figure 11.1.

At the other end of the cable is a standard centronics connector. This type of connector is found on some PCs in place of the IBM-compatible 25-pin type.

Although there may be slight variations in the use of these pins, generally there should be no need to make hardware adjustments. The main point to remember is that you should not try to use a parallel cable in excess of about eight feet in length.

Registers

The parallel port makes use of three internal PC registers: 0378h, 0379h and 037Ah.

Register 0378h: data

When data is transmitted, it is stored in the register with address 0378h. The port can only hold one

The parallel printer connector

13 12 11 10 9 8 7 6 5 4 3 2 1

```
0 0 0 0 0 0 0 0 0 0 0 0 0
 0 0 0 0 0 0 0 0 0 0 0 0
```

25 24 23 22 21 20 19 18 17 16 15 14

Pin	Use
1	- (Data strobe)
2 - 9	Data bits 0-7
10	- (Printer acknowledge)
11	Printer busy
12	Paper out
13	Select printer
14	- (Auto feed Select)
15	- (Printer error)
16	- (Reset printer)
17	- (Printer on-line)
18 -25	GND

Figure 11.1

byte at a time. This is a read/write port, so you can use OUT to send a byte to the printer or IN to find out what data is waiting to be collected.

Register 0379h: status

In certain cases, after data has been sent, the printer returns a status code to tell the PC whether the print was successful. This status code is stored in the register at address 0379h, which is a read-only register. The meaning of the individual bits of the byte in that register is given in Figure 11.2.

Certain conditions are indicated by individual bits:

- Printer busy: the device is not yet ready for the next byte of data

- Printer acknowledge: the data was received satisfactorily

Parallel printer status byte

Bit	Meaning if set
7	Printer not busy
6	Printer acknowledge
5	Paper out
4	Printer on-line
3	Printer error
2	Not used
1	Not used
0	Time-out error

Figure 11.2

- Paper out: the printer's paper-out sensor has been activated

- Printer on-line: the printer is on-line

- Printer error: an undefined error has occurred

Note that some of these conditions are indicated by the bit being clear (0 with a value of 0) rather than set to 1, e.g. 'Not Printer Busy'.

Register 037Ah: acknowledgement

Bit 4 of register 037Ah determines the way in which the system will react to an acknowledgement signal from the printer. When bit 4 of this register is set, a 'printer acknowledge' signal in the status port results in the system issuing hardware interrupt 07h.

To start with, this is a dummy interrupt that does nothing but you can replace it with some other machine-code routine. This is usually the task of a device driver (see Chapter 12).

When bit 4 is clear, the 'printer acknowledge' signal has no special effect.

Bit 4 of register 037Ah is sometimes referred to as the 'Enable Interrupt and Acknowledge' flag.

Note that you should not attempt to change other bits of the byte at 037Ah: these are used for other hardware purposes.

BIOS interrupt

You can use BIOS interrupt 17h to send data to the printer. There are usually three steps:

- Initialise the printer

- Send the data

- Check that the status is alright

The initialisation need only be done once.

Initialising the printer

The initialisation is merely to tell the printer that data is on its way and to check that the printer is ready. To initialise the port, use function 01h of the interrupt. (Functions are selected by putting the function number in register AH.)

Interrupt:	17h
Function:	01h
Service:	Initialise parallel port
Entry values:	AH=01h
	DX=port number
Exit values:	AH=status code

The function returns a status code in AH. The meaning of individual bits is shown in Figure 11.3. Note that the layout is slightly different to that of port 0378h. The interrupt also sends bytes with

Parallel print status port (0379h)

Bit	Use
7	Not Printer busy
6	Not Printer acknowledge
5	Paper out
4	Printer on-line
3	Not printer-error
2	Not used
1	Not used
0	Not used

Figure 11.3

values 08h and 0Ch to the printer control register 02FAh.

You should check the status byte before sending data to ensure that the printer is ready for data.

Transmitting data
To transmit data, one byte at a time, use function 00h.

Interrupt:	17h
Function:	00h
Service:	Send character to parallel port
Entry values:	AH=00h
	AL=character
	DX=port number
Exit values:	AH=status code

The data byte is specified in AL and the port number in DX: 0 for LPT1, 1 for LPT2 or 2 for LPT3. The interrupt places the data byte in 0378h, from where it is transmitted automatically. Nothing else can be done until the printer either sends a 'printer acknowledge' signal to indicate successful receipt of the data or sends some other signal to indicate an error condition. If nothing is heard from the printer, a time-out error will eventually be generated by the BIOS and you can recover control of the program.

The function returns a status code in AH, which is identical to that for function 01h.

Checking the port status
At any time, you can check the status of the parallel port with function 02h.

Interrupt:	17h
Function:	02h
Service:	Check parallel port status
Entry values:	AH=02h
	DX=port number
Exit values:	AH=status code

This time, the status code that is returned in Ah is the same as that held in internal register 0379h.

DOS interrupt

DOS interrupt 21h is a general interrupt that performs most activities required by the operating system. As such it has a large number of functions, dedicated to different tasks. For the parallel port, function 05h is equivalent to interrupt 17, function 00h.

Interrupt:	21h
Function:	05h
DOS version:	1
Service:	Send character to parallel port
Entry values:	AH=05h
	DL=character
Exit values:	None

This function sends a single character to the parallel port, as determined by the MODE command. There is no option to choose the port (which is assumed to have been done already), nor is there any status code returned. The interrupt calls its BIOS counterpart but also takes care of the processes of checking that data has been transferred correctly.

The serial port

Whereas the parallel port transmits data one byte at a time, data is transferred from the serial port as a string of individual bits. There are many different ways of sending this data, which leads to a great deal of confusion. In order for the transfer to be successful, the computer and printer must be working to the same system of data transfer, which is referred to as the *protocol*. The protocol determines how quickly the data is sent, how many bits make up each character, how many bits are used to signify the end of a character and whether or not any error-checking is to be used.

The advantage of serial ports is that data can be transferred both ways and transfer is slightly faster than that with the parallel port.

Serial connector

Serial connectors may be either 25-pin or 9-pin. The layout of the 25-pin RS-232C asynchronous serial port is shown in Figure 11.4.

In fact, only two of these pins are used for the actual transfer of data; the remaining lines are either not used or are used for sending signals between the two devices.

The serial connector

```
  1  2  3  4  5  6  7  8  9 10 11 12 13
 ┌─────────────────────────────────────┐
 │ 0  0  0  0  0  0  0  0  0  0  0  0  0 │
  \ 0  0  0  0  0  0  0  0  0  0  0  0  /
   ───────────────────────────────────
  14 15 16 17 18 19 20 21 22 23 24 25
```

Pin	Use
1	Not used
2	TXD (Data output)
3	RXD (Data input)
4	RTS (Request To Send)
5	CTS (Clear To Send)
6	DSR (Data Set Ready)
7	Signal ground
8	DCD (Data Carrier Detect)
9-19	Not used
20	DTR (Data Terminal Ready)
21	Not used
22	RI (Ring Indicator)
23-25	Not used

Figure 11.4

BIOS interrupt

BIOS interrupt 14h is used to communicate with the serial port. As for the parallel port, there are three stages in the communication:

- Initialise the printer and set the protocol

- Send the data

- Check that the status is all right

Serial data transfer byte

Bit	Use
7	)
6	) Baud rate
5	)
4	) Parity
3	)
2	Stop bits (0=1,stop bit,1=2 stop bits)
1	) Data size
0	)

Baud rate codes (bits 7,6,5)

Code	Bit 7	Bit 6	Bit 5	Baud rate
0	0	0	0	110
1	0	0	1	150
2	0	1	0	300
3	0	1	1	600
4	1	0	0	1200
5	1	0	1	2400
6	1	1	0	4800
7	1	1	1	9600

Parity codes (bits 4,3)

Code	Bit 4	Bit 3	Parity
0	0	0	None
1	0	1	Odd
2	1	0	None
3	1	1	Even

Data size (bits 1,0)

Code	Bit 1	Bit 0	Size
0	0	0	Not used
1	0	1	Not used
2	1	0	7-bit
3	1	1	8-bit

Figure 11.5

Initialisation and setting the protocol are performed in a single step, which is carried out once only.

Initialising the printer
Function 00h of interrupt 14h combines the first two tasks.

Interrupt:	14h
Function:	00h
Service:	Initialise serial port
Entry values:	AH=00h
	AL=protocol code
	DX=port number
Exit values:	AH=main status code
	AL=modem status code

The port number is put into register DX while AH holds the protocol code. The way in which AL is split between the baud rate, parity, stop bit and data length is shown in Figure 11.5 above. This figure also gives the possible values that may be taken by the various components which, as you will see, are equivalent to those of the MODE command.

The function returns the status of the serial port in register AH. The meaning of the various codes that are received is shown in Figure 11.6.

Serial port main status codes (AH)

Code (hex)	Meaning
1	Data ready
2	Overrun
4	Parity error
8	Framing error
10	Break detected
20	Holding buffer empty
40	Shift buffer empty
80	Timeout

Figure 11.6

It is also worth noting that this function returns in register AL the *modem status*, which shows errors that relate mainly to communications with a modem. These codes are shown in Figure 11.7 but are of little interest for printer communications.

	Serial port modem status codes (AL)	
	Code (hex)	Meaning
	1	Delta CTS
	2	Delta DSR
	4	Trailing-edge RI
	8	Delta line signal detect
	10	CTS
	20	DSR
	40	RI
	80	Line signal detect

Figure 11.7

Transmitting data

To send the data to the serial port, one character at a time, use function 01h.

Interrupt:	14h
Function:	01h
Service:	Send character to serial port
Entry values:	AH=01h
	AL=character to send
	DX=port number
Exit values:	AH=main status code

The serial port to which the data is to be sent is given in register DX. The status code is again returned in register AH. This gives you the opportunity to check that the data was transferred successfully.

Checking the status code

If you wish to check the status of the serial port at any other time (other than immediately following initialisation or sending the data), you can use function 03h.

Interrupt:	14h
Function:	03h
Service:	Check serial port status
Entry values:	AH=03h
Exit values:	AH=main status code
	AL=modem status code

The status code is the same as that for the other functions.

Receiving data

Interrupt 14h also allows you to retrieve data from the serial port, with function 02h. For completeness, this function is given here.

Interrupt:	14h
Function:	02h
Service:	Get character from serial port
Entry values:	AH=02h
	DX=port number
Exit values:	AH=main status code
	AL=character received

The port is set in register DX. The BIOS checks the port and, if there is a character waiting, its ASCII value is returned in AL. The status code is returned in AH. If no character is waiting and no error has occurred, both registers will be 0.

DOS interrupt

DOS interrupt 21h also has a single function for sending data to the serial port, function 04h.

Interrupt:	21h
Function:	04h
DOS version:	1
Service:	Send character to serial port
Entry values:	AH=04h
	DL=character to send
Exit values:	None

The data is sent to the standard serial port (AUX) as set by the MODE command. By default, the data is sent to the first serial port.

No protocol need be set up, since this is also achieved with the MODE command. It is assumed that the user will have done all this for you before attempting to send the data. Once again, DOS handles all the tricky areas like checking that the data was received successfully, so no status value is returned. If there is any error, then one of the standard DOS messages will appear.

Receiving data

Another DOS function retrieves data from the serial port.

Interrupt:	21h
Function:	03h
DOS version:	1
Service:	Get character from serial port
Entry values:	AH=03h
Exit values:	AL=character

The Print Screen key

Pressing the PrtSc key on a PC-compatible or Print Screen on an AT-compatible usually results in a copy of the current screen being sent to the printer at the parallel port. Pressing this particular key combination results in the hardware issuing an interrupt 05h, which executes the screen dump routine. As a rule, the default interrupt is effective in text modes only; this is one of the ROM BIOS routines.

You can check the current progress of a screen dump by inspecting the contents of memory location 0500h (*not* a register of that address). This returns one of the following values:

00h	The print screen operation has been completed
01h	The operation is still in progress
FFh	A time-out error has occurred

The interrupt can be redirected to some other routine by a memory-resident program. There are many of these in existence, one of the most common of which is GRAPHICS.COM. This is generally supplied with the DOS system and enhances the routine to allow the printing of extended ASCII characters as well as the standard ASCII set. GRAPHICS.COM is only effective with Epsons and compatibles.

Other programs may enhance the screen print facility so that screen dumps of graphics screens can be produced or the contents of the screen display can be stored in a disk file.

For EGA, MCGA and VGA video adaptors, the BIOS provides a routine that allows you to produce a dump of screens that have more than 25 rows of text. This is achieved with sub-function 20h of interrupt 10h, function 12h.

Interrupt:	10h
Function:	12h
Service:	Multi-line print-screen (not CGA)
Entry values:	AH=12h
	BL=20h
Exit values:	None

Time-out errors

When an instruction is given to send some data to one of the parallel or serial ports, the computer attempts to execute the command immediately. Its first action is to check that the device is ready to receive data (by inspecting the RTS line) and, if it is, the data is transmitted.

If there is any reason why the data cannot be sent, a computer waits a short while and then tries again. It keeps on trying until either the line is ready or a certain amount of time has elapsed: this is the *time-out* error.

Time-out errors can occur for a number of reasons. It may be that the printer is not switched on or is not on-line. It may be a slow printer, with a low time-out threshold set, so that it receives and prints some data but, while it is doing this, the computer gives up trying to send the next section of data.

The main problem is that during all this time the computer is tied up with trying to transfer the data. To overcome this problem, you need to adjust the time-out period for each particular printer. This can be quite a tricky task. If you have too long a period, then if there is any fault with the printer you will have to wait a long time before you can get back control of the PC. On the other hand, if you set the time-out period too short, the computer will keep timing out even when the printer is functioning perfectly normally. For example, when you send a form feed to the printer, even though this is only a single byte it will take the printer some considerable time (in computer terms) to actually effect the operation. Therefore, you need to experiment and find a time which is suitable for your particular equipment.

Any program that is written for other users should ideally provide an option whereby they can set their own time-out period to suit their own particular printers.

The time-out registers

The length of the time-out period is determined from the values held in internal registers 0478h to 047Ah for parallel ports 1-3 and in 047Ch and 047Dh for serial ports 1 and 2. The registers hold the number of half-second intervals that the PC should wait before returning a time-out error. For parallel ports, the default value is 20: a time-out of ten seconds. Serial ports default to 1: a half-second wait.

The PRINT command

DOS provides a command that allows you to perform *background printing* for certain files while other operations are carrying on. The PRINT command lets you set up a queue of files, which it then sends to the printer a little at a time. In the meantime, having put the files in the queue, you can carry on with any other tasks on your computer. PRINT uses small slices of computer, in between the times allocated to the main application, to actually transfer the next few bytes of data to the printer. The effect of such background printing is usually to make the response of the computer seem a little slower. In many circumstances this can be well worth while, since it means that the printer is not tied up all the time while waiting for the documents to print.

The disadvantage of the PRINT command is that it will only handle ASCII files. Therefore, to print a word-processed document, you must use the relevant option in that program to produce an ASCII file ready for use with PRINT.

Once the PRINT program is operating, you can add new files to the queue or take files away. Files are added to the queue by typing their names on the command line following the PRINT command. For example, three named files could be added to the queue with the following command:

```
PRINT DOC1.TXT DOC2.TXT DOC3.TXT
```

When you enter the command for the first time, you are asked to give the device to which the data is to be sent. By default, this is the standard parallel port, PRN. Press **Return** to accept the default.

All files included in the queue must be in the current directory. However, once you have started the PRINT program, you can change the current directory and work with another part of the disk.

Files can be removed from the queue by adding a /C parameter. This parameter cancels the file immediately in front of the parameter and any others that follow until a /P parameter is encountered. /P adds files to the queue. It need only be used if /C has been used earlier in the command. As a general rule, it is simpler and safer to use separate commands for cancelling the files and adding files to the queue. /T cancels all printing. Note that a 'cancelled by operator' message is displayed if a file is cancelled while it is actually being printed.

You can enter the PRINT command on its own to display a report of the files that are in the current queue.

Various other parameters were introduced with DOS 3. You can also determine how much of the processing time is allocated to PRINT and how much to the main program. The processing time is divided up into *timeslices*, each of which is measured in terms of the number of clock ticks. The default is that the foreground task is given eight ticks for every two allocated to PRINT. The full set of parameters is as follows:

/P	Add a file to the queue
/C	Cancel a file
/T	Cancel all files
/B:*bytes*	Set the disk buffer size
/D:*device*	Set the printer device name
/N:*number*	Timeslice for print (default 2)
/S:*number*	Timeslice for foreground program (default 8)
/Q:*number*	Maximum number of files allowed in queue (defaults to 10, must not exceed 32)
/U:*number*	Maximum number of ticks that PRINT waits when the printer is busy (default 1)

The maximum values for /N, /S and /U are 255, the minimum is 1 in each case.

The PRINT command can also be used with OS/2 but make sure that the SPOOLON command has been entered first.

12 Device Drivers

All communication between the computer and the peripheral devices – the screen, keyboard, disk drive, printers and other remote devices – is achieved through small programs stored in RAM called *device drivers*.

The purpose of these drivers is to take instructions from an application program and convert them into commands that the peripheral device understands. The system BIOS includes device drivers for a number of standard devices, so unless you have particularly complex requirements these may well be sufficient. The structure of the device drivers is given here.

Types of device driver

There are two main types of device driver:

- The standard device drivers, supplied as part of the BIOS

- The installable device drivers, supplied by an individual application

The standard device drivers are an integral part of the operating system, contained in the hidden files IO.SYS (for MS-DOS) and IBMBIO.COM (for PC-DOS). When the system is started, these device drivers are automatically loaded into memory. You cannot change them (except by changing IO.SYS or IBMBIO.COM) but you can replace them with your own installable drivers.

The standard devices are shown in Figure 12.1. Most of the device names given there should be familiar to you by now. The *null* device (NUL) simply directs output to nowhere. This can be a useful option if you don't want output to appear on the screen; it has little relevance to printers. The *console* (CON) refers to the keyboard for input and the screen for output.

Standard devices

Device	Type	Device Name
Null device	Character	NUL:
Console (keyboard & screen)	Character	CON:
First serial port	Character	COM1: or AUX:
Second serial port	Character	COM2:
First parallel port	Character	LPT1: or PRN:
Second parallel port	Character	LPT2:
Floppy disk drive	Block	Usually A: and B:
Hard disk drive	Block	Usually C: etc.

Figure 12.1

Installable device drivers

Installable device drivers are additional programs which either replace the standard drivers or are provided for devices not otherwise catered for. If they are replacement drivers, they must have the same name as the drivers that they are to replace.

Installable drivers must be loaded into memory when the system is started and this is done by including in the CONFIG.SYS file an instruction in the form:

```
DEVICE = filename
```

The *filename* is the name of the file containing the device driver. The name must include the drive and directory name, if the device driver is not in the root directory. You cannot add device drivers once the operating system has been fully installed.

Device types

Device drivers fall into two different types:

- *Character devices*, which send and receive data one character at a time.

- *Block devices*, which send and receive data in blocks (typically of 512 bytes).

The character devices include the keyboard and screen, serial and parallel ports and the null device

The block devices are usually used for storage devices, such as floppy and hard disks, and are of no particular interest here.

Character devices have *device names*. The device name takes precedence over any filenames given in a DOS command, so once a driver has been installed, you cannot create or use a file with the same name. For instance, you cannot have a file with the name LPT1.

When DOS encounters a name in a command, it first checks its list of device names to see if this includes the name. Only if the name is not a device, does it try to find it as a filename. In this way, DOS treats device names as filenames.

Block devices use drive specifications (A:, B: etc.) rather than names.

Character devices can control just a single device at a time; in contrast, a block device driver may be used for more than one device (for example, two identical floppy disk drives may share the same device driver).

Installation of drivers

The device drivers are loaded into memory in sequence. The first driver is always the null device; this is followed by the installable devices; finally the standard device drivers are loaded.

The drivers form a chain in memory. Each driver has a block of header information ahead of the device driver program itself. Amongst other things, the header points to the start of the next device driver in the chain. When DOS needs to find a particular device, it starts with the null device and works down through the chain until it finds the one it wants. In this way, if an installable device has the same name as a standard device, the installable device will be found, and used, first.

Requests to DOS for the use of a device result in a *request header* being created in memory. DOS uses this part of memory to give information about the function that is required to the device driver and the driver uses the same area to return information about the success or otherwise of the action.

Device driver structure

Each device driver consists of three main sections:

- The *device header* contains information about the device and the driver program.

- The *strategy routine* stores information about the CPU registers when the driver is called.

- The *interrupt routine* is the main program for the driver, which performs the actions requested of it.

The structure of a device driver is shown in Figure 12.2.

Structure of MS-DOS device drivers		
Start Byte (hex)	No. Bytes	Purpose
0	4	Pointer to next device
4	2	Attributes
6	2	Pointer to strategy routine
8	2	Pointer to interrupt routine
0A	8	Device name
12	n1	Strategy routine
12+n1	n2	Interrupt routine

n1 = Length of strategy routine
n2 = Length of interrupt routine

Figure 12.2

Pointer to next device
These two bytes hold the segment and offset address of the location of the next device, pointing to the first byte of the next device driver's header. In the device driver file, the pointer must be stored as -1 (FFFF:FFFF) but this is replaced by the appropriate value when DOS stores the driver in memory. For the last header, the value remains as -1.

Attributes

The *device attributes word* is two bytes of data that contain specific items of information relating to the device, such as the type of device and whether it is able to respond to particular commands. The meaning of these two bytes is shown in Figure 12.3.

Note that two-byte words like this are always stored in reverse order in memory: that is, the byte at the lower address in memory will hold bits 7 to 0, the byte above that in memory will hold bits 15 to 8.

Device attribute word

Bit	Character/Block/Both	Meaning if set (=1)	Meaning if clear (=0)
15	Both	Character device	Block device
14	Both	IOCTL commands supported	IOCTL not supported
13	Block	IBM format	Non-IBM format
12	Character	Output until busy supported	Not supported
11	Both	Device Open/Close and Removable Media commands supported	Not supported
10	Not used		
9	Not used		
8	Not used		
7	Not used		
6	Both	Get/Set Logical Device commands supported	Not supported
5	Not used		
4	Character	Int 29H for fast console I/O implemented	Not implemented
3	Character	Current clock device	Not current clock
2	Character	Null device	Not null device
1	Character	Standard output device	Not std output device
0	Character	Standard input device	Not std input device

Figure 12.3

Pointer to strategy routine

These two bytes hold the offset of the strategy routine from the start of the header. Again, the two bytes are stored in reverse order.

Pointer to interrupt routine
These two bytes store the offset of the interrupt routine from the start of the header, once more in reverse order.

Device name
For character devices, the device name follows the same rules as filenames. It can be up to eight characters long (excluding the colon, which is usually included when the name appears in a DOS command). In the device header, the device name is padded with blanks on the right if it is less than eight characters.

The strategy routine
The only purpose of the *strategy routine* is to store the segment and offset address of the request header, where information is passed between DOS and the driver.

The interrupt routine
The first task of the interrupt routine is to save the CPU registers. It must then determine the particular command that is required by looking at the request header and then call the corresponding procedure. The procedures are contained in the rest of the interrupt routine. There should be a procedure for each of the possible commands that can be received, even if some of these say 'do nothing'.

Each procedure, when it ends, must store a value in the status word in the request header and any parameters to be returned to DOS can be placed in the data area.

Finally, the interrupt routine must restore all the CPU registers before returning to DOS.

It is important to note that interrupt routines are very limited in the instructions they can use. Their purpose is to link two specific hardware devices, so they must communicate directly with the hardware using only the BIOS hardware interrupts, the free RAM and the internal registers. For the most part they must not use other DOS interrupts and functions, since this may result in another device driver being called and a great deal of confusion as a result.

The request header

The request header is a part of memory set aside for passing information from DOS to the driver and back again. The way in which it is laid out is shown in Figure 12.4.

The request header

Offset	Bytes	Meaning	Set by
0	1	Length of header	MS-DOS
1	1	Unit code	MS-DOS
2	1	Command code	MS-DOS
3	2	Status	Driver
5	8	Reserved	
13	n	(Variable)	MS-DOS

Figure 12.4

Length of header

The first byte gives the amount of memory taken up by the header. This is necessary because the data area at the end of the header varies depending on the device that is being used and the command that is being requested. The minimum value is 13 bytes (0Dh).

Unit code

This is the unit to be accessed and relates to block devices only.

Command code

This byte holds the number of the command that is requested. There are only 20 possible commands that can be serviced by a device driver, each one of which has a specific purpose. Those relating to printers are described later.

Status word

These two bytes are used by the device driver to inform DOS of the success or otherwise of the action. The high-order byte indicates whether or not the command was a success; the low-order byte tells DOS the type of error that occurred, if any. The meaning of these two bytes is given in Figure 12.5.

Data area

The data area is used by the driver to return additional parameters to DOS. However, the length of the area is set by DOS itself.

Device status word	
High order byte	
Value	Meaning
80	Error encountered. (Low order byte indicates nature of error)
02	Device is busy. (Response to command 6 only)
01	Processing completed without error.
00	Device driver still processing request.
Low order byte	
Value	Meaning
00	Write-protect violation
01	Unknown unit
02	Device not ready
03	Unknown command
04	CRC error
05	Bad drive request structure length
06	Seek error
07	Unknown media
08	Sector not found
09	Printer out of paper
0A	Write fault
0B	Read fault
0C	General fault
0D	Not used
0E	Not used
0F	Invalid disk change (DOS 3 only)

Figure 12.5

Operation of the device driver

When a request is made to a device, the following procedures are followed:

1 The application program issues a DOS function call.

2 DOS reads through the device headers, checking their names, and locates the required driver.

3 The request header is located by DOS. The register pair ES:EX is set so that it points to the segment and offset address of the request header.

4 The device driver is initialised by a call from DOS to the strategy routine.

5 The strategy routine stores away the segment and offset address of the request header and then returns control to DOS.

6 DOS calls the interrupt routine.

7 The interrupt routine carries out the procedure relating to the command that has been issued and stores the status and data parameters in the request header, then returns control to DOS.

8 DOS acts according to the status that has been returned, then passes control back to the application program. In doing so, it passes its own results to the application.

9 The main application resumes control, and may act according to the parameters passed to it by DOS.

Input/Output Control (IOCTL)

The interrupts described in the previous chapter related to simple output, in which data was sent to the printer a character at a time by being written directly to the ports. DOS 2 introduced a new set of *Input/Output Control* (IOCTL) functions, which provide a more advanced method of data transfer. These functions may be used for all devices, including block devices such as disk drives. If you set up a driver which can use IOCTL functions, bit 14 of the attributes field in the device header must be set. When working with IOCTL functions, a single DOS service performs all communications between a program and the device. This is function 44h of interrupt 21h.

Interrupt:	21h
Function:	44h
DOS version:	2
Service:	IOCTL functions
Entry values:	AH=44h
	(Various others)
	AL=subfunction
Exit values:	(Various)

The values passed to and from this interrupt depend upon the particular sub-function that is requested. Those of the sub-functions relating to printers are listed below. The device information that is returned to some of these sub-functions is shown in the table in Figure 12.6. Those sub-functions relating to block devices, or to data input, are not shown.

Bit	Meaning if set
15	Remote handle (subfunction 0Ah)
14	Device can process control strings
13	Reserved
12	Remote device (subfunction 09h)
11	Reserved
10	Reserved
9	Reserved
8	Reserved
7	Device (0 for disk file)
6	Not end of file
5	Data not processed
4	Special device
3	Clock
2	Null device
1	Screen output
0	Keyboard input

Figure 12.6

Subfunction:	00
Effect:	Get device information
Entry values:	BX=file handle
Exit values:	DX=device information

Subfunction:	01
Effect:	Set device information
Entry values:	BX=file handle
	DL=device information
Exit values:	DH=0

Subfunction:	02
Effect:	Read from character device
Entry values:	BX=file handle
	X=Number of bytes to read
	DS:DX=Number of bytes to read
Exit values:	AX=number of bytes read

Subfunction:	03
Effect:	Write to character device
Entry values:	BX=file handle
	CX=number of bytes
Exit values:	AX=number of bytes written

Subfunction:	06
Effect:	Get input status
Entry values:	BX=file handle
Exit values:	AL= (00h (end of file/device not ready)
	(FFh (not end of file/device ready)

Subfunction:	07
Effect:	Get output status
Entry values:	BX=file handle
Exit values:	AL= (00h (end of file/device not ready)
	(FFh (not end of file/ device ready)

Subfunction:	09
Effect:	Check for networked device (DOS 3 only)
Entry values:	BL=drive number
Exit values:	DX=device information (bit 12=1 if networked)

Subfunction:	0A
Effect:	Check for networked device (DOS 3 only)
Entry values:	BX=file handle
Exit values:	DX=device information (bit 15=1 if networked)

Device commands

As described earlier, each device driver is expected to cater for up to 20 different commands. Many of these refer only to block devices and are not described here in detail. However, all possible commands must be allowed for, even if they are not appropriate for a particular device. Therefore, for those functions that do not relate to printers, there

Device commands

00h	Initialisation
01h	Media check
02h	Build BPB
03h	IOCTL input
04h	Input
05h	Non-destructive read
06h	Input status
07h	Flush input buffer
08h	Output
09h	Output with verify
0Ah	Output status
0Bh	Flush output buffer
0Ch	IOCTL output
0Dh	Device open
0Eh	Device close
0Fh	Removable media
10h	Output until busy
13h	IOCTL function
17h	Get logical device
18h	Set logical device

Figure 12.7

must nevertheless be a procedure, the sole purpose
of which should be to set the status byte in the request header to 10h, indicating that the function
has been completed. The possible commands are
listed in Figure 12.7.

Command 00h (Initialisation)

The Initialisation command is used when the device
driver is first installed (as the operating system is
being loaded). The purpose of this command is to
perform any preliminary operations that are required, such as initialising the printer. This is the
only command that is allowed to use the DOS interrupts, and here it is restricted to interrupt 21h,
functions 01h to 0Ch and function 13h. The other
requirement of the Initialisation routine is to store
the segment and offset address of the end of the

main part of the driver (excluding this initialisation routine) in the data area (bytes 14-17).

Since the Initialisation procedure is used only once, it is usual to place it at the end of the device driver. This means that, once its work is done, the next device driver that is loaded will be written over the top of it.

Command 08h (Output)

This is an IOCTL command. When it is received, the driver must complete the output specified by the IOCTL control stream (see command 0Ch).

Command 09h (Output with Verify)

This is an IOCTL command, which must create the output specified by the IOCTL control string (see command 0Ch). In addition, it must check that the data has been output correctly by reading the data back from the output buffer and comparing it with the original data. Errors are handled by rewriting the data or returning an error code to DOS.

Command 0Ah (Output Status)

The Output Status command is issued by DOS when it needs to know whether or not the buffer of an output device is empty. Bit 9 of the status word in the request header should be set to 1 if the buffer is full or the printer is busy; otherwise the bit should be cleared to 0.

Command 0Bh (Flush Output Buffer)

This command clears the printer buffer. All characters in the buffer should be discarded.

Command 0Ch (IOCTL output)

This command sets up an IOCTL string for output. As with all IOCTL commands, it can only be invoked if bit 14 of the device attributes word is set.

Command 0Dh (Device Open)

The Device Open command, introduced with DOS 3, is effective only if bit 11 of the device attributes word is set.

DOS issues this command whenever the device is opened. The driver can use it, in combination with the Device Close command, in any way: for example, to initialise the printer each time it is opened.

Command 0Eh (Device Close)

This command, which was introduced with DOS 3, is effective only if bit 11 of the device attributes word is set.

DOS issues this command to close activities with a device. It is used in combination with the Device Open command (0Dh).

Command 10h (Output Until Busy)

This command, introduced in DOS 3, is effective only if bit 13 of the device attribute's word is set.

The command has the effect of sending data to the printer until the busy signal is received. It is most frequently used by print spoolers.

the Delete Case command in any way, since
simple to influence this order each time, if so
desired.

D*xxxx* **DPr (Delete Case)**

This command, which was introduced with DBase
II version ..., may work ... of the delete functions
word used.

DOS Basic, this command used to compute both
in Basic. It is used in conjunction with the Do set
Open command (DO).

xxxx **DOr (Rough Editing)**

This command, introduced in DBase II, is effective
only when ... the development programs are in use.
The command has specific keystrokes due to
the added functions, but is seldom seen in the most
most frequently used programming modes.

Emulation Summary

Epson Commands

Page	Command	Meaning
71	BEL	Sound beeper
99	BS	Back space
101	HT	Tab horizontally
107	LF	Line feed
11	VT	Tab vertically
66	FF	Form feed
99	CR	Carriage return
170	SO	Select double-width printing (one line)
169	SI	Select condensed printing
26	DC1	Select printer
169	DC2	Cancel condensed printing
25	DC3	Deselect printer
170	DC4	Cancel double-width printing (one line)
69	CAN	Cancel line
170	ESC SO	Select double-width printing (one line)
169	ESC SI	Select condensed printing
69	ESC EM	Cut sheet feeder control
177	ESC SP	Set inter-character space
179	ESC !	Master select for typestyle and pitch
66	ESC #	Cancel eighth bit control
188	ESC %	Select/deselect RAM based characters for printing
181	ESC &	Define user defined characters
168	ESC (-	Define and apply a style of scoring
204	ESC *	General bit image command
116	ESC +	Set n/360 inch line spacing
166	ESC -	Turn underlining on/off
112	ESC /	Select vertical tab channel
114	ESC 0	Select ⅛ inch line spacing
114	ESC 1	Select $7/72$ inch line spacing
115	ESC 2	Select ⅙ inch line spacing
115	ESC 3	Set n/180 inch line spacing (24-pin printers)
161	ESC 4	Select italic typestyle
162	ESC 5	Cancel italic typestyle
130	ESC 6	Expand the range of printable characters
180	ESC 7	Cancel expanded range of printable characters
70	ESC 8	Disable paper out sensor
71	ESC 9	Enable paper out sensor

187	ESC :	Copy ROM based character set to character RAM
106	ESC <	Uni-directional printing for one line
66	ESC =	Clear eighth bit of incoming data
65	ESC >	Set eighth bit of incoming data
24	ESC @	Initialize the printer
115	ESC A	Set n/60 inch line spacing (24-pin printers)
112	ESC B	Set vertical tab stops
72	ESC C	Set page length in lines
71	ESC C NUL	Set page length in inches
102	ESC D	Set horizontal tab stops
163	ESC E	Select emphasized printing
163	ESC F	Cancel emphasized printing
165	ESC G	Select double-strike printing
165	ESC H	Cancel double-strike printing
189	ESC I	Set/cancel redundant control codes to print as RAM based characters
109	ESC J	Perform n/180 inch line feed (24/28-pin printers)
109	ESC J	Perform n/216 inch line feed (9-pin printers)
204	ESC K	Select 8-bit single-density bit image printing
204	ESC L	Select 8-bit double-density bit image printing
152	ESC M	Select 12-pitch characters
73	ESC N	Set margin for skip-over perforation
74	ESC O	Cancel skip-over perforation
151	ESC P	Select 10-pitch characters
78	ESC Q	Set right margin
127	ESC R	Select international character set
174	ESC S	Select superscript/subscript mode
174	ESC T	Cancel superscript/subscript mode
106	ESC U	Turn uni-directional printing on/off
171	ESC W	Turn double-width printing on/off
204	ESC Y	Select 8-bit double-speed density bit-image printing
204	ESC Z	Select 8-bit quadruple-density bit-image printing
175	ESC a	Select justification mode
112	ESC b	Set vertical tabs in channels
102	ESC e	Set vertical/horizontal tab spacing
100	ESC f	Perform horizontal/vertical skip
152	ESC g	Select 15-pitch characters
72	ESC i	Turn incremental print mode on/off
109	ESC j	Perform n/216 inch line feed (9-pin printers)
139	ESC k	Select font family
78	ESC l	Set left margin
131	ESC m	Select special graphics characters
155	ESC p	Proportional characters on/off
173	ESC q	Select/cancel outline/shadow printing

207	ESC r	Select printing colour
69	ESC s	Turn half speed mode on/off
133	ESC t	Select character table
174	ESC w	Turn double height printing on/off
145	ESC x	Select draft quality or NLQ/LQ fonts
68	DEL	Delete character

IBM Proprinter Commands

Page	Command	Meaning
71	BEL	Beeper
99	BS	Backspace
101	HT	Horizontal tab
107	LF	Line feed
111	VT	Vertical tab
66	FF	Form feed
99	CR	Carriage return
170	SO	Double-width printing by line
169	SI	Condensed printing
26	DC1	Select printer
169	DC2	10-characters-per-inch print
25	DC3	Deselect printer
170	DC4	Cancel double-width printing by line
69	CAN	Cancel data
204	ESC	Select graphic mode (AGM)
166	ESC -	Continuous underscore
114	ESC 0	⅛-inch line spacing
114	ESC 1	$7/72$-inch line spacing
115	ESC 2	Start text line spacing
115	ESC 3	Graphics line spacing
67	ESC 4	Set top of form
74	ESC 5	Automatic line feed
181	ESC 6	Select character set 2
181	ESC 7	Select character set 1
152	ESC :	Select 12 cpi text
140	ESC =	Character font image download
115	ESC A	Set text line spacing
112	ESC B	Set vertical tabs
72	ESC C	Set form length in lines or inches
102	ESC D	Set horizontal tabs
163	ESC E	Emphasized printing
163	ESC F	Cancel emphasized printing
165	ESC G	Double-strike printing
165	ESC H	Cancel double-strike printing
146	ESC I	Select print mode
204	ESC J	Graphics variable line spacing
204	ESC K	Normal-density bit-image graphics

204	ESC L	Dual-density bit-image graphics (half-speed)
73	ESC N	Set automatic perforation skip
74	ESC O	Cancel automatic perforation skip
156	ESC P	Proportional space mode
25	ESC Q	Deselect printer
103	ESC R	Set all tabs to power on settings
174	ESC S	Subscript or superscript printing
174	ESC T	Cancel subscript or superscript
106	ESC U	Print in one direction
171	ESC W	Continuous double-wide printing
79	ESC X	Set horizontal margins
204	ESC Y	Dual-density bit-image graphics (normal speed)
204	ESC Z	High-density bit-image graphics
171	ESC [@	Combined height and width
116	ESC [\	Set vertical tab units
181	ESC \	Print continuously from all characters chart
181	ESC ^	Print single character from all characters chart
169	ESC _	Continuous overscore
25	ESC j	Stop printing
103	ESC d	Move print head right

HP LaserJet Commands

Page	Command	Meaning
99	BS	Backspace
101	HT	Tab horizontally
107	LF	Line feed
66	FF	Form feed
99	CR	Carriage return
140	SO	Select secondary font
140	SI	Select primary font
80	ESC 9	Clear left/right margins
24	ESC E	Reset
59	ESC Y	Display functions mode start
59	ESC Z	Display functions mode end
22	ESC z	Interface self-test
118	ESC & a n C	Move horizontally (by columns)
118	ESC & a n H	Move horizontally (by decipoints)
78	ESC & a n L	Set left margin
80	ESC & a n M	Set right margin
119	ESC & a n R	Move vertically (by lines)
119	ESC & a n V	Move vertically (by decipoints)
167	ESC & d D	Automatic underlining start
167	ESC & d n D	Automatic underlining (general)
167	ESC & d @	Automatic underlining end
120	ESC & f n S	Push/pop position

79	ESC & f n X	Macro control
79	ESC & f n Y	Designate macro ID
74	ESC & k n G	Line termination
178	ESC & k n H	Set HMI
153	ESC & k n S	Set/cancel compressed pitch
117	ESC & l n C	Set VMI
116	ESC & l n D	Set lines per inch
76	ESC & l n E	Set top margin
76	ESC & l n F	Set text length
69	ESC & l n H	Paper input control
74	ESC & l n L	Perforation skip on/off
77	ESC & l n O	Set page orientation
72	ESC & l n P	Set page size (page length)
68	ESC & l n X	Set number of copies
60	ESC & p n X	Transparent print data
74	ESC & s n C	End-of-line wrap
163	ESC (s n B	Set stroke weight - primary font
153	ESC (s n H	Select character pitch - primary font
156	ESC (s n P	Select proportional/fixed space - primary font
162	ESC (s n S	Select character style - primary font
142	ESC (s n T	Select typeface - primary font
154	ESC (s n V	Set character height - primary font
141	ESC (n letter	Select symbol set - primary font
143	ESC (n @	Set primary font defaults
164	ESC) s n B	Set stroke weight - secondary font
153	ESC) s n H	Select character pitch - secondary font
156	ESC) s n P	Select proportional/fixed space - secondary font
162	ESC) s n S	Select character style - secondary font
162	ESC) s n T	Select typeface - secondary font
154	ESC) s n V	Set character height - secondary font
141	ESC) n letter	Select symbol set - secondary font
145	ESC) n X	Designate download font as secondary font
144	ESC (n X	Designate download font as primary font
143	ESC) n @	Set secondary font defaults
144	ESC * c n D	Specify font ID
144	ESC * c n F	Font and character control
119	ESC * p n V	Move vertically (by decipoints)
118	ESC * p n X	Move AP horizontally (by dots)
119	ESC * p n Y	Move AP vertically (by dots)
119	ESC =	Half line feed

Diablo Commands

Page	Command	Meaning
99	BS	Backspace
99	CR	Carriage return
101	HT	Horizontal tab
107	LF	Line feed
111	VT	Vertical tab
66	FF	Form feed
100	ESC BS	Incremental backspace
24	ESC CR P	Remote reset
105	ESC HT	Absolute horizontal tab
110	ESC LF	Reverse line feed
113	ESC VT	Absolute vertical tab
73	ESC FF	Set page length
178	ESC DC1	Set inter-character spacing
70	ESC EM	Paper cassette selection
73	ESC C	Clear top/bottom margin
110	ESC D	Reverse – half-line feed
166	ESC E	Set underlining mode
72	ESC L	Set bottom margin
176	ESC M	Automatic justification mode
164	ESC O	Set bold printing mode
156	ESC P	Set proportional spacing
157	ESC Q	Cancel proportional spacing
166	ESC R	Cancel underlining mode
105	ESC S	Cancel HMI
72	ESC T	Set top margin
109	ESC U	Forward – Half-line feed
164	ESC W	Set shadow printing mode
179	ESC X	Cancel inter-character spacing
136	ESC Y	Special character 2
136	ESC Z	Special character 1
165	ESC &	Cancel bold/shadow printing mode
113	ESC -	Set vertical tab stop
177	ESC =	Automatic centering mode
108	ESC ?	Set automatic carriage return
24	ESC SUB I	Remote reset
113	ESC RS	Set VMI
105	ESC US	Set HMI
108	ESC !	Cancel automatic carriage return
80	ESC 0	Set right margin
104	ESC 1	Set horizontal tab stop
104	ESC 2	Clear all tab stop
120	ESC 3	Select graphics mode
121	ESC 4	Cancel graphics mode

106	ESC 5	Cancel backward printing
106	ESC 6	Set backward printing
132	ESC 7	Print suppression
104	ESC 8	Release horizontal tab stop
79	ESC 9	Set left margin

Index

£ sign 57

A

Accents 134
Active position 117
Adding fonts 138
Addressing modes 202
AGM 110
Alternate Graphics Mode 110
ASCII 36
ASCII character set 126
ASCII files 53
Automatic carriage return 108
Automatic line feed 74

B

Background printing 20
Backspace 99
Backward printing 106
BASIC 76
Batch files 64
Baudot code 36
BCD 35
Beeper 71
Bézier curves 224
Binary 27
Binary Coded Decimal 35
Binary files 58
BIOS interrupts 288
Bit numbers 29
Bit-image graphics 201
Bit-mapped graphics 226
Block devices 310
Bold text 163
Bottom margin 89
Bottom margin 93
Box-drawing characters 135
Buffer boxes 21
Buffer: editing 68
Buffered input 66
Bytes 28

C

Cancel control codes 59
Carriage return 73
Carriage return 99

Centring 175
Channels 111
Character devices 310
Character mode 72
Character printers 67
Character sets 123
Character size 147
Character width 148
Clear tab stops 104
Co-ordinates 223
Colour printing 205
Compatibility 40
Compressed pitch 153
Condensed mode 169
Console (CON) 63
Control codes 38
Control codes: cancel 59
Control codes: disabled 129
Control keys 57
Core instructions 75
CR 73
Cut-sheet feeders 85

D

Data length 65
Databases 79
Decimal-to-hex conversion 30
Decipoints 117
Defaults: restoring 143
Deselect printer 25
Designating macros 79
Device attribute word 313
Device commands 320
Device driver structure 312
Device drivers 309
Diablo commands 49
Diablo emulations 42
Dictionaries 221
DOS interrupts 289
Dot matrix printers 13
Dots 117
Double strike 165
Double-height 171
Double-width 170
Downloading characters 190
Draft mode 145
Drawing boxes 134

Disk Offer

The author has prepared a disk containing a database of information, covering the printers of over fifty manufacturers. The database includes command codes, printer specifications and details of individual printer capabilities. Also included on the disk are a number of sample programs, for all types of printer.

The price of the author's disk is £19.95 inc VAT and P&P.

To obtain your disks, send a cheque with order, stating disk format, to:

Butford Technical Publishing,
Butford Farm,
Bodenham,
HEREFORD
HR1 3LG